The Making Of A CEO

Helping You Deal With The Issues Of Running Your Company

The Making of a CEO
Becoming the Leader Your Company Needs

ISBN-13: 978-1516942534 (CreateSpace-Assigned)
ISBN-10: 1516942531
BISAC: Business & Economics / Leadership
Library of Congress Control Number: 2015919655
CreateSpace Independent Publishing Platform, North Charleston, SC

Printed in the United States of America.

Note: This book is an expanded edition of the book "It's Lonely At The Top"; "A Practical Guideline To Become A Better Leader Of Your Small Company" (iUniverse 2011) with additions and significant changes in its content and a reorientation in its marketing focus.
It also incorporates a number of self-evaluation tools for leaders and business owners.

Also by Oswald R. Viva:

Customizing VLSI IC Update:
A User's Guide to the ASIC Design Center.
Electronic Trends Publications.
ISBN0-914405-16-0

It's Lonely At The Top
A Practical Guide To Becoming A Better Leader Of Your Small Company
iUniverse, Inc.
ISBN-978-1-4620-4653-9; ISBN-978-1-4620-4655-3; ISBN-978-1-4620-4654-6

Fundamentals Of Job Interviewing For Managers
Amazon.com
ISBN-13 978-148022960; ISBN-10 1480222968

Performance Reviews; The Bad, The Ugly, … The Alternative
Amazon.com
ISBN ISBN-13:978-1496144157; ISBN-10:1496144155

Accountability In The Workplace
www.SkillBites.net

You Are The Owner, But Are You The Right CEO?
www.SkillBites.net

Create A Culture Of Empowerment
www.SkillBites.net

Delegate To Succeed
www.SkillBites.net

Exit Strategy And Succession Planning
www.SkillBites.net

A Compilation of My E-Books For The Period 2012 – 2013
Amazon.com

ISBN-13: 978-1497511996; ISBN-10: 1497511992

The Entrepreneurship Game; Can You Win at it?

Amazon.com

ISBN-13: 978-1500520496; ISBN-10: 1500520497

Table of Contents

Dedication:

To my children and grandchildren who give us the joy of their love and their triumphs in life.

To my wonderful and loving wife. She is the engine that drives my motivation and provides the energy to feed my aspirations that made this book possible.

"The only things that stand between a person and what he wants in life are the willing to try it and the faith to believe it is possible"

Richard M. Devos

Preface

As the title of the pre-published book said, it's lonely at the top. As the owner and CEO of a small or midsize business you are alone in the pulpit of the business, with nobody to **really** talk to. You cannot discuss with your staff critical issues such as, the sale of the business, a reorganization plan that would affect those closer to you, soliciting an investment in the business, and all those issues that you prefer to keep confidential.

Loneliness is hard when you are responsible for the wellbeing of all employees, stakeholders and related families, and you must make all difficult decisions by yourself. Having a coach that you can trust and who can understand your vision, your goals and your challenges, can mitigate the isolation and provide the support you so badly need. In these pages I pretend to become your coach and I ask you to deposit that trust in me by reading this book and treat it as our one-on-one coaching session.

The value of a coach is measured by his years of experience in the subject matter and his ability to transmit that experience and knowledge to the people he coaches. I gained the business experience through my long career in Corporate America, my extraordinary involvement with new and embryonic companies, my consulting business, and my ownership of small businesses.

Having participated in eight start-ups either as a Principal or as a consultant in an active executive position, I learned the "what-to-dos", but more importantly, I also learned the "what-not-to-dos" in small companies. This know-how coupled with my work as consultant for businesses worldwide and coaching with many dozens of CEO and executives of small and midsize businesses, gives me an unusually valuable experience to help you in your difficult job as business owner.

After my extensive participation in Corporate America in large (e.g., IBM, Fairchild) and small companies, and my also extensive work as a consultant in world-wide activities, I became engaged with The Alternative Board (TAB). For eleven years I owned a business of Peer Advisory Boards, building one of the most successful franchises in the system. Those years were the most rewarding of my career.

My coaching experience includes over fourteen thousand hours of working with CEO, owners and executives of small and midsize businesses. It is this last facet of my career that I emphasize here because I love small businesses and I love coaching. Marrying these two loves with the knowledge acquired, gives me the opportunity to contribute to you and your venture and be rewarded with the knowledge that in a modest way I am participating in your success.

The recognition of my contributions by those that I have coached, are the gifts I received and I treasure. Testimonials such as the one from Steve Buerkel, CEO of Applied Energy Systems in Malvern, PA are representative of that recognition: *"Oswald was instrumental in helping us grow our company fourfold from 2002 to today. He will be missed in his role in strategic guidance and as a trusted advisor, but perhaps more importantly as the friend he has become."*

Or one from Nissen Isakov, President and CEO of LCR Electronics in Norristown, PA *"Oswald was an integral part of my company's success. Oswald has the unique ability to really understand, not only your business, but you as an individual and your value system in dealing with situations and takes all that in account when offering advice and guidance. Most business owners believe their business to be unique, and many coaches believe all businesses are the same and that a given formula or methodology can work across the board of businesses. Oswald combines the uniqueness of the individuals and business similarities to help guide the CEO in the right direction. I highly recommend Oswald as a business coach to anyone wanting to run a successful business."*

Furthermore, from Nissen Isakov in a letter to me after he sold a significant part of his company: *"Now that the dust has settled and it has hit home that I sold my "baby" it is time to do some inward reflections and I cannot help but think back to the time I met you and how very important you have been to me in helping me reach this goal. I want you to know that you have been a wonderful mentor and to coach to me and were instrumental in helping me grow the business – so this achieved milestone is also your success. I always felt that you had LCR's and my best interest at heart and I truly appreciate your help over these past many years. Oswald, thank you so much for all your guidance and help and more importantly for always having my back. I value you as a friend and a coach."*

And one from Mark DeHarde, President and CEO of Ultraflex Systems in Pottstown, PA. *Throughout a ten year period, Oswald facilitated our advisory board on a monthly basis and provided direct coaching on a one-on-one basis. He proved to be an excellent listener, facilitator and consultant to us, asking the right questions, challenging our assumptions and holding us accountable to the advisory board process and to one another as peers. Oswald challenged us to succeed and helped us achieve aspects of each of our dreams as business owners. He is kind, honest and direct and has become a key mentor, confidant and close friend. This is a testament to his deep experience in understanding human nature and group dynamics and inspiring the very best out of each of us. If you have the opportunity to benefit from Oswald's professional advice, mentorship or friendship, consider yourself a very lucky person.*

Or one from Bob Rigg, President and CEO of Rigg-Darlington Group of Exton, PA. *When I met Oswald I was overwhelmed with my work and had little idea how to balance my home life, work and the rest of the world. Fast forward many years, my business has grown dramatically and we have received several national awards. There is time for personal life and I am a much happier person for my involvement with Oswald. Over the years Oswald has been an excellent mentor, an insightful problem solver and a darn good friend. No matter how you might be thinking of using Oswald's talents I cannot imagine a better man to work with. He also has the ability to put his knowledge and coaching talent in writing, such as in this book and others he authored.*

Or one from Shmuel Yankelewitz, Executive Vice President of LCR Electronics Inc. in Kunshan, China. *Oswald was the facilitator and coach for an advisory board that I joined. In a quiet and measured way Oswald was able to draw out the hard decisions we all know we have to make and are so good at finding the reasons to procrastinate on... In a room full of egos Oswald was always pointing us out of our box so that we don't rest on our laurels or dwell too long in our comfort zone. Oswald always looked for the solid approach, strategic thinking and planning, data driven decisions, financial responsibility, facing reality in all actions, people orientation and timely decision making.*

Accountability and integrity are hallmarks of Oswald's coaching philosophy and he would put them front and center in every meeting and coaching session. I personally have learned and grown from Oswald's experience and wise counsel, Oswald was able to understand the nuances of complex situations and make sound suggestions on how to address them, his calm demeanor and great listening skills made it easy for me to bring out the tough issues.

And one from Paul Barr, President and CEO of Premier Office Solutions of Hatboro, PA. *Over a period of six years, I worked closely with Oswald Viva. During our time together, Oswald has helped me grow as a business person. He has become a good friend and trusted advisor. I value his opinion and look forward to hearing his perspective whenever I am faced with a challenge. Oswald's help has been extremely valuable to helping our company grow and improve our profitability.*

And one more from Joe Gallagher, CEO of Gallagher Fluid Seals of Norristown, PA. *As a coach Oswald has helped me grow as a business person. He is a trusted advisor; I value his opinion and look forward to hearing his perspective whenever I am faced with a challenge. In his writings he applies his coaching value in an easy to follow style that helps readers improve as leaders.*

And many others…...

Why I Decided to Write this Book.

This book is an expanded version of my previous book "Its Lonely at the Top"; "A Practical Guide to Become a Better Leader of Your Small Company". It incorporates two new chapters and a number of self-evaluating tools and adds important information throughout.

There is a world of difference between being the CEO of a large company and your job as the CEO of a small business. I have had the advantage of working for companies as large as IBM and as small as any of the eight start-ups that I participated in at the "C" level, including CEO positions. This gives me some perspective on what the different needs are and what you, as the CEO of your company, must bring to the job.

There are hundreds if not thousands of books on managing business, with the majority of them dedicated to large companies, and most of them don't make a distinction of the differences to account when managing a small business. For example, I always admired many facets of Jack Welch management–as controversial as they are–but his style and his mode-operandi can only work in large organizations and would be detrimental to most small business.

Each subject covered here is deserving of an entire book by itself, but my intent is not to cover them in detail, but to give you a look into the requirements of your job. If I succeed in motivating you to continually work on improving yourself to be the best CEO that you can be, I will consider it an accomplished feat.

This book does not attempt to "upstage" the specialized books in each subject and it is not a "how to" manual to tell you what you should do; rather it is meant as a coaching session with you one-on-one. My job as a coach is not to tell you what to do or to give you the answers, but to ask the right questions or to give you opportunities to think, so that you come up with the answers appropriate for your business and for yourself.

Think of it as a variation of the "Jeopardy" TV show in which they give you the answer and you have to give the questions. I intend to challenge you with questions that are provocative and are intended to make you think and evaluate what's best for you and for your business.

Thus, this book doesn't contain theories or fancy ideas-of-the-week practices. It is based on real-world experience, and practical wisdom learned in real-life situations over many years. I don't intend to teach you to be a CEO, but I want to help you become the best CEO that you can be, for the good of your business and your own happiness.

You have already achieved much more than most people; starting a business and making it successful is a huge accomplishment. You are intent on improving yourself and your business because you want your organization to be solid and well-run, but you also focused on the self-fulfillment of your ambition to be the best. I hope that I can help you achieve both goals.

Working with people like you, capable entrepreneurs who are the engines that drive the US economy, have given me the extremely gratifying opportunity of participating in a large number of small and midsize businesses in many different fields. I like to think that in some modest way I contributed to the growth and success of those businesses, but I also learned much from their owners, and for that I'm grateful to them. Every one of those businesses is led by great business persons, and I have the fortune that many of them have become my friends.

This book is a way to give back from all I learned from those CEO and executives.

Acknowledgments

I am grateful to our wonderful Country for giving me the opportunities to live and work here. I am grateful to God for giving me the health and strength to do all the things that I have done. I am grateful to my parents for giving me the values that I applied in all my activities. And I am grateful to those who gave the training during my initial steps in my career.

I am also indebted to all those who provided me with the opportunities to learn throughout my long career and instilled in me the knowledge acquired in the many phases of my life. I am principally thankful to the many small and midsize business owners, CEO and executives with whom I had the pleasure of working. These relations gave me the reward of witnessing the growth in their businesses and in their personal performance as a result of my coaching.

In addition, these clients also gave me the gift of friendship. It is this gift that I value with the sentiment it deserves, because, while the business relationships were extremely valuable, their friendship made them rewarding and lasting.

I am also thankful to my former colleagues at the various businesses in which I participated for their contributions throughout my association with those organizations. These contributions may not be visible on a daily basis but their cumulative effect is undoubtedly received.

I would be remiss if I didn't give full credit to the most important people in my life. To Elsa, my loving wife, my daughter Diana and my three entrepreneurial sons, Ruben, Alex and William, and their children, for their love and support and to make it meaningful for me to do what I do.

Introduction

The Making of a CEO

In the following pages we will be "talking" about you as well as the job that you chose as a business owner, and the way in which you can become better at it.

You **chose** to hold this position and thus you owe it to yourself, your family, your employees and all stakeholders of the business to become the best you can be at it … or decide what's best for the business and for you.

Perhaps what's best for you and for your company is for you to assume a different role and to have someone else in the role of CEO. In this "coaching session", we will explore this …

Small Businesses

As a small business owner you are in an elite class. According to the US Department of Commerce, small businesses,

- Represent 99.7 percent of all employer firms.
- Employ just over half of all private sector employees.
- Pay forty-four percent of total U.S. private payroll.
- Have generated sixty-four percent of net new jobs over the past fifteen years.
- Create more than half of the nonfarm private gross domestic product (GDP).
- Hire forty percent of high tech workers (such as scientists, engineers, and computer programmers).
- Made up 97.3 percent of all identified exporters and produced 30.2 percent of the known export value in FY 2007.
- Produce thirteen times more patents per employee than large patenting firms; these patents are twice as likely as large firm patents to be among the one percent most cited.

The Small Business Administration (SBA) defines small business as those with fewer than five hundred employees (although for contracting purposes this varies by industry). The SBA claims that in 2009 there were 27.5 million businesses in the US and 99.9 percent of those were classified as small businesses.

You employed approximately fifty percent of all non-farm workers and created sixty-five percent (or 9.8 million) of the fifteen million net new jobs between 1993 and 2009. Seventy percent of new employer firms survive at least two years, half at least five years, a third at least ten years, and a quarter stay in business fifteen years or more.

Unfortunately the data also shows the high mortality of small businesses. Depending on which source you credit the numbers change somewhat, but by any account they are not encouraging. Quoting *from the SBA:*

"Seven out of 10 new employer firms survive at least 2 years, half at least 5 years, a third at least 10 years, and a quarter stay in business 15 years or more". Census data report that 69 percent of new employer establishments born to new firms in 2000 survived at least 2 years, and 51 percent survived 5 or more years.

Survival rates were similar across states and major industries. The data on establishment's age show that 49 percent of establishments survive 5 years or more; 34 percent survive 10 years or more; and 26 percent survive 15 years or more.

In other words, if you start a new business in the US your chances of long-term success are less than 50%, so you must make sure that you have the personality, talent and resources to embark in such an adventure.

Sources for above data: U.S. Bureau of the Census; U.S. Department of Labor, Bureau of Labor Statistics, Current Population Survey; U.S. Department of Commerce, and International Trade Administration, as published in Small Business Development Centers' website; http://www.sba.gov/content/small-business-development-centers-sbdcs (accessed Jan-Mar 2011)

So, as you can see, you are an important member of a select group; a group that is key to the future of America. If your business has survived five, ten or fifteen years you can unquestionably consider yourself successful, and if longer, then you can breathe even easier because it only gets easier after that. Right? If you believe that, then get ready for a huge surprise—because when you are in business, challenges never end. If it seems easier for you now is likely just because you have the experience of going through and overcoming tough times. Nevertheless I'm sure there are things that keep you awake at night ... and it isn't the new baby.

Your Job as CEO

Are you in business to have the lifestyle that you always wanted? Or is it because you have a vision and want to reach that pinnacle? Whatever your reasons you have a huge responsibility because it isn't just you; lots of people depend on you being successful.

Aside from your family, your employees, your suppliers and other stakeholders in the business have at least a part of their life tied to you and your business. It is indispensable then that you do your best in your job and become the best owner/CEO that you can be.

First, you must understand that you not only must assume responsibility for your actions, but also for the action of others, as you are ultimately responsible for everything that happens in your company. The buck stops at your desk.

You must also understand that profits should not be the goal of the company; they should be the reward for managing the core business successfully. While this may sound idealistic, in practice it should be the rule that runs the business if you are to achieve success.

CEOs, particularly those of small companies, have different leadership and management styles driven by different personalities. Their styles are usually the product of their backgrounds and experiences, both in their personal life and in the business world.

Some are aggressive and some are quiet and charismatic, but all are driven to a goal and a Vision.

Style is not important, substance is, and the substance of your job (leadership) can be learned. And like with everything that is learned, practice makes it perfect; Anthony Jay said *"The only real training for leadership is leadership"*.

Successful founders of business typically have at least these seven dominant personality traits:

- Commitment and determination
- Leadership ability
- Opportunity obsession
- Tolerance of risk
- Creativity and self-reliance
- Motivation to succeed
- Visionary qualities

These traits provide founders with a competitive advantage when starting a business, but also frequently hinder their ability to adapt and flex their style with changing organization demands as the company grows. Their strength of personality frequently impacts those around them more powerfully than they might realize.

And then, there is character ...

Abraham Lincoln said: *"Nearly all men can stand adversity, but if you want to see a man's character, give him power"*.

While skills in leadership constitute the efficacy of a leader, character traits determine the quality of the leadership. Your character is important to your job and to your employees as well. I'm sure you are certain that you have good character, but what's important for this subject is to know what traits are expected in a good leader. You can develop the skills to be a good leader but it would be much more difficult for you to develop the character needed for optimum leadership.

Most business owners start a business because they know how to do something well; they are the "technicians" described in the *E-Myth* [1]. Simply becoming business owners does not make them leaders; in fact, the most challenging transition in the complex cycle to become CEO, is moving from the "technician" level to the level where he/she can trust others enough to be able to delegate the work and become the "manager".

One of the most difficult parts of the job is learning "to let go", meaning to have others do what they are used to do themselves (delegating). As we will discuss in these pages, even more difficult is to let go but to hold people accountable for those same activities, in other words, to delegate with accountability.

Letting go is very difficult because nobody else can do the work as well as they can (whether this is true or only your perception), or because they enjoy doing the work and they also feel comfortable doing it. However, the CEO should not be the doer; he or she should be the visionary, the strategist and the leader of the team who will carry out the plan and vision of the company.

A person's success is affected by more than skills and knowledge; it is also affected by how these skills are used and the ability to adapt to varying needs. Improving self-awareness may reveal hidden perceptions that may be hindering the owner's effectiveness.

Developing the CEO in You

As leadership improves, the organization's culture also improves because leadership is the source of the organization's personality. Thus, as the owner grows into a leader, the organization responds by transforming itself into a team that also assumes leadership. As the business grows and the role of the owner grows with it, changing from manager to leader becomes a prerequisite for the success of the business, and of the owner. This change requires more than just the discipline and the desire to do it. It also takes a dose of natural talent and even coaching.

The common saying "leaders are born, not made" is not completely true. Owners can "learn" to become leaders but they must possess the qualifications and talent required; without them and the desire to forgo other duties in order to become the leader, the transition is, at best, uncertain.

Another prerequisite for the success of the business and the happiness of the owner is the synergy between the personal goals of the owner and the goals of the business. It is essential for the owner to understand the demands and rewards, motivators and disappointments, challenges and qualifications pertinent to the CEO job and his/her adaptability to them. CEO performance is about leadership as opposed to management.

The development of CEOs may include two different phases:

- The formation or enhancement of personal traits and understanding of the job.
- The functional, on-the-job performance.

In this book we will cover both phases in a simple coaching style.

Since it is not a novel in which you need to follow a plot in successive pages, you can choose to read parts of this book as separate "coaching sessions". Thus, for example, if you are interested in learning about accountability you can go directly to the chapter on "Accountability".

Enjoy your journey, become the best CEO you can be and remember Jim Collins advice: "Do not reject wisdom just because it comes late".

References:
1. Michael Gerber, *The E-Myth* (Harper, first edition 1999)

Part One – The Formation or Enhancement of Personal Traits

Chapter I – Business Ownership

"Your time is limited, so don't waste it living someone else's life. Don't be trapped by dogma – which is living with the results of other people's thinking. Don't let the noise of other's opinions drown out your own inner voice and most important, have the courage to follow your heart and intuition. They somehow already know what you truly want to become. Everything else is secondary."
- Steve Jobs

This book attempts to guide you to excellence in leadership of your business. As a business owner you face many challenges that can be overwhelming; this coaching guide can help you overcome those challenges so that you can become the CEO that your business needs.

Chances of success are much higher when following the directions and suggestions enumerated here.

Starting a business is a major undertaking that not every person is qualified or ready to attempt. As the owner of a start-up company, you took many risks, and you gave up some of the things that you were accustomed to. It required much sacrifice, perseverance, vision, hard work, and, in many cases, giving up large chunks of income.

As the business grows you will continue to face obstacles or challenges that you must be prepared to survive. These challenges will be in the various aspects of business management that change as the business (and you) go through the many stages of growth.

Business ownership has its rewards; the pride and joy of ownership is a gift reserved for those who elect it. Nevertheless, before deciding that you wanted to join the entrepreneurial ranks, you had to consider the pros compared to the cons. Did you have what it takes? Do you have the talent, traits, resources, risk tolerance, adaptability, and family support necessary to embark in the venture? Were you willing to give up many things and risk many others in search of your dream? Because you are a business owner I assume you answered positively to all these questions.

Toby Thomas uses the analogy of a man riding a lion: "People look at him and think, 'This guy's really got it together! He is brave.' And the man riding the lion is thinking, 'How the hell did I get on a lion, and how do I keep from getting eaten?'"[1]

You were willing to mount the lion of business ownership; are you prepared to survive it?

Entrepreneurship, Definition and Reality

According to *Wikipedia*, "**entrepreneurship** is the process of identifying and starting a new business venture and sourcing and organizing the required resources while taking both the risks and rewards associated with the venture."

From *Merriam-Webster*: "**Entrepreneur**: a person who starts a business and is willing to risk loss in order to make money. One who organizes, manages, and assumes the risks of a business or enterprise."

Starting a business is looked at as glamorous, and its founders are considered heroes and lucky to have that experience, but it is not all cream and roses. Nobody said building a company was easy to do, but it should be clear that it can be psychologically excruciating in some circumstances, with the founders paying a heavy price if things don't go well.

We idolize successful entrepreneurs, such as Michel Dell, Mark Zuckerberg, Bill Gates, and many others, as well as less-known, small-business entrepreneurs who made it big (in varying degrees). What it is not well known is the struggle that many of them had to go through and the toll it may have taken on them before they reached the pinnacle.

In many cases, we do not know the lows of entrepreneurship because business leaders use the fake-it-until-you-make-it approach rather than admit their suffering. Many believe that letting the world know about their struggles would be seen as a weakness, and so they keep it hidden.

The entrepreneur must not be reluctant to ask for help. Medical help if the body suffers—stress is a dangerous weapon against our physical being—even psychological help if he or she is having significant anxiety or depression. It should not exclude the help that friends, colleagues, consultants, and advisors can provide. This type of help can be even more valuable than any health professional's help. (See the appendix on advisory boards).

Most entrepreneurs go through some failures or partial failures before they achieve success. Persistence is one of the required traits for a business owner, and failure cannot be part of his or her vocabulary, but paradoxically, knowing when to cut the losses has to be a key in strategic thinking. Unfortunately it is common to see business owners who lose it all in a faulty pursuit of a solution for an irremediable failure.

> *From my bag: A friend of mine used to say that during a painful startup phase of his now successful business "I was not smart enough to declare bankruptcy". In his case persistence won and he not only saved the business, but made it very successful.*

Thomas Edison said, "Our greatest weakness lies in giving up. The most certain way to succeed is always to try just one more time." As an entrepreneur, this needs to be a rule. There are countless examples of entrepreneurs who failed (some on multiple occasions) but kept on trying until they finally succeeded.

> *From my bag: I always claim that in my many entrepreneurial ventures I learned the "what to do" but more importantly I learned the "what not to do" in business. This experience of setbacks and even failures gives serial entrepreneurs the winning hand when creating new businesses.*

People should be what they want to be and can be. Not everyone can be a doctor, an astronaut, a teacher, or a plumber, and certainly not everyone has what it takes to be a business owner or desire the risk of entrepreneurship. You did it and hopefully you are successful or on the way to be successful.

You decided to become an entrepreneur and you are in a

select group of individuals who contribute to the well-being of the country (and the world). And if your business is successful, you are in an even more select group.

In my coaching career and running peer-advisory boards for many years, I worked with a great variety of business owners, and the self-stated reasons that made them entrepreneurs are as different as their businesses, but there is commonality in their traits and drive. The personalities are very different too, but all of them wouldn't change the hardships of business ownership for anything. When asked if having to do it over again would they, unanimously they would respond with an emphatic yes.

Whether their enterprise is a family business, a solo experience, a partnership, a subset of a large operation, participating in a technical field, a manufacturing or distribution or sales or professional or any other field, they recognize the shortcomings and sacrifices of being business owners, but they relish the experience and congratulate themselves for choosing that route.

> ***From my bag:*** *In my own case, I started businesses at very young age and I also started some later in life. My latest venture was starting a business at 59 and it became perhaps my most enjoyable one. As a CEO Coach I worked with several business owners who became entrepreneurs at an age when other people are thinking of enjoying retirement. Usually, these business impresarios are among the most successful ones.*

What is at risk?

Business ownership is high risk and success is not guaranteed. If the venture fails, the entrepreneur can be without a job, income, and even all the money spent in the venture.

The life of an entrepreneur can be isolated and demanding to the point that the family life suffers. A business owner owes his life to the business. As a business owner, you have the privilege of working an enormous amount of hours, skipping weekends, and giving up sleep. The obvious consequence is that the private life suffers, and with it the family environment.

The risks do not stop there. The stress can take a toll on the health of the entrepreneur, and his or her family life can also suffer. The longer the purgatory of the failed saga, the deeper the damage can be. Trying to separate business from family life—an extremely difficult challenge—can minimize the pain and the damage, but achieving this happens only rarely.

Despite the difficulty, keeping those family ties together is the best medicine for the stress caused by the ups and downs of a new business. I often say that "the business should be a part of your life apart from your life, but it should not be your entire life."

Sadly, as the title of one of my book states, it's lonely at the top, regardless of the size of the organization[9]. That is because, as the top dog, you must make or at least participate in all decisions, and there are some issues that you cannot discuss with others. The buck stops at your desk, and there is a tremendous feeling of isolation as a result.

As a business owner, many times you feel alone and with nobody to go to for help; it's lonely at the top. You feel that nobody understands your problems or help you find answers. You cannot go to your employees because they will see a sign of weakness. You cannot go to your family or your financial institutions because they will be frightened. You want to show strength even though you are scared. You know you must move forward, but you are not sure how.

In some businesses, husband and wife work together as partners. Clearly this helps with the feeling of loneliness because the two support each other and share those issues that cannot be discussed with others, however, unless strict rules are set and applied, this arrangement can be deteriorating to married life.

I have worked with entrepreneurial couples who spend many hours working in the business together. When husband and wife spend that much time together in the business, chances are that they carry the business talk to their house, drastically reducing any other type of communication. The most likely result is damage to the husband-wife relationship.

It is imperative to the couple's marriage to agree on certain restraining practices regarding hours of work, partnership responsibilities, methods of communicating, and, most importantly, relationship outside the business. It is also critical for them to agree on the actual emotional value of the business in relation to the family and to be realistic as to the present and future of the business.

From my bag: I worked with a couple who owned a successful business but that was going through a significant down cycle. As a result both husband and wife worked extremely long hours together and even when they were at home the conversation always centered on the business. Life as a couple practically disappeared and, not surprisingly, they started to grow apart in the marriage while sharing everything as business partners. The thought of a separation or divorce crossed their minds but did not progress because of the uncertainty of what to do with the company if they separated.

My job as their coach was to make them realize that the business was still viable and had enormous potential, and that their work habits were not being helpful to the business (and obviously to the marriage). I convinced them to focus on the long term and not just in the present. More importantly, I assigned specific jobs for each of them, got them to leave the business at reasonable hours and prodded them to go out as a couple at least one night a week and to take at least two weekends off every month.

Although reluctantly, they accepted my advice and changed their work and personal routines and the results became palpable within a short time. Today the business is thriving with several times higher top and bottom lines, and they are a happy couple again.

It is important then to have a support system in place. As a business owner, you have to make many important decisions on an ongoing basis. It can be very helpful to have a business mentor who is experienced, successful, and willing to provide advice and guidance.

I also highly recommend joining a peer-advisory board where you will meet with a group of other business owners to exchange ideas and get support from the group. (See the appendix).

> **From my bag:** *Although somewhat different from the description above, it illustrates the point. My wife was the entrepreneur in this case. She owned a small chain of retail stores and our oldest son was a manager at one of the stores. The conversations at home always revolved around what was happening in the business, particularly at dinner time despite the presence of three other children. One day my son—in a very powerful way—said: what are we doing? This is not a family; this is a business council. My wife and I looked at each other and realized that we were creating a barrier within the family. At that point we decided that business talk was prohibited at dinner time, and we "became a family" once again.*

Is Business Ownership for You?

Owning a business has many advantages, and owners have many privileges, but there is also another side to the ownership coin. On the positive side, there is the pride and personal satisfaction of being the boss and not having to answer to anybody (except to customers, employees, investors, and other stakeholders...not to mention the IRS). Financially too can have significant rewards, assuming the business is successful.

However, as a business owner, you also have the so-called privilege of working half days in which you can choose the half day that you want to work (which twelve-hour period within the twenty-four hours of each day). You are able to *donate* your weekends to the business. You can also have the privilege of deferring your salary so that you can pay your employees or the government.

As a big ego reward, you can give the company your name and give opposing attorneys in a lawsuit the reason to include you personally in collecting the awards from the suit. You will also have the distinct honor of personally guaranteeing any bank loans that the company may need, so if you (or the business) default on the loan, you will not only lose the business assets but also your personal assets.

In his recently published book, *"Hunting in a Farmer's World: Celebrating the Mind of an Entrepreneur"*, my friend and colleague John Dini classifies entrepreneurs as hunters while the rest of the population are farmers.[3]

He explains the differences this way: in business, entrepreneurs hunt for ideas, solutions, new ways of doing things, new markets, and new customers; farmers, on the other hand, are those who do the yearly planning, budgeting, and standardizing and make sure things are organized and people are doing what they are supposed to be doing.

Hunters build companies with vision, creativity, and tenacity; they do not concern themselves (at least at the beginning in start-up mode) with policies and procedures (although they should). They need to be free from routine activities so that they can concentrate on creating, improving, designing, and forming.

Owning your own business can be an exciting and rewarding experience. It can offer numerous advantages, such as being your own boss, setting your own schedule, and making a living doing something you enjoy. But it is not always glamorous (it seldom is) and requires sacrifices, hard work, and a heavy dose of creativity and planning.

Ralph Waldo Emerson said, "Passion is the most powerful engine of success. When you do a thing, do it with all your might. Put your whole soul into it. Stamp it with your own personality. Be active; be energetic and faithful, and you will accomplish your object. Nothing great was ever achieved without passion."[4]

Emerson said, "Stamp it with your own personality," and this is critical because we are all different, and what works for someone may not work for others. Your personality dictates how you must apply your passion to be successful. You need to recognize your passion and nurture it as you implement your dream.

Being a business owner is much like boxing in that it is

hard, lonely, and demands constant and vigilant focus. Regardless of how well you do, you must be ready to get punched again by the demands of the business and its problems. And if you get knocked down, you must get up and face the danger and the excitement again.

Some reasons entrepreneurs succeed:

- have the right personal characteristics and attributes
- got into business for the right reasons
- listen to advice from knowledgeable people
- surround themselves with the right people
- are resilient and never give up
- are good leaders
- are not afraid to admit when they are wrong
- plan, plan, plan, and then plan some more
- execute, execute, execute the plan

My repeated insistence in planning is not exaggerated or capricious. It was said that "running a business without the proper planning is like driving a vehicle looking only at the rear-view mirror; you know where you have been, but you do not know where you are going."

Conversely, do not spend so much time perfecting your product so that, when you are finally ready, the market window has closed. I always say that you can perfect a product to the point of obsolescence. There has to be a judgment call on the difference between market ready and the need to perfect.

From my bag: I consulted for a startup that had a great promising product; an advanced technology in the consumer's marketplace with extraordinary applications. The founders invested a substantial amount of money, hired several engineers, vice presidents of sales, engineering and production, and traveled to the Far East to woo potential investors. All this done with the expectations that investors would flock in attracted by the product.

Unfortunately the technology was not as ready as promoted and it became obvious when demonstrating the prototypes. In addition, the supposedly ready market was not as ready as they thought and there were doubts as to its eventual readiness. After unsuccessfully courting VCs and Angels(individual investors), money ran out and the entrepreneurs were forced to close the business resulting in major losses of money, loss of jobs for everyone hired in the enthusiastic mode, and even some lawsuits for breach of contracts.

If the developers of the technology would have been honest about its status and the hired engineers would have evaluated it consciously, and if the principals would have done a true analysis of the market rather than looking at it with embellished eyes, they could have prevented all this pain and bad experience

The Various Phases of the Life of Business Ownership

From my bag: *One time I was recruiting a lawyer as a potential member for a peer-advisory board I was chairing. He told me: "I don't have a business; I have a law practice." To which I replied, "Oh, I see. Tell me, do you have employees?" And he said he did. I asked, "Do you have HR issues?" And he said, "Boy, do I!" I continued: "Do you do marketing?" He admitted he did to recruit clients. I asked, "Do you deal with banks, profit-and-loss statements, balance sheets, accounts payable, accounts receivable…"*

He interrupted me, saying, "OK, OK. I see where you're going. I have a business don't I?" I said, "Your business is not different than any others; it is just called a different name, but you have the same issues that any other business owner has." He joined the advisory board, and after a few months, he told me: "You were right; my business has the same issues as any of the others." So, yes, lawyers also have their own business.

Your business, regardless of its type, surely goes through growth stages. If you are lucky and your vision drives it, the business will reach maturity, and with it, you will reach success. However, some businesses will get stuck in some of the early stages and some—

many unfortunately—will die there or in some other close stage. I am sure your business has gone or is going through these phases

In its initial phases you start getting stressed out because money flows out, but none is coming in, and your reserves are getting smaller by the day. Nevertheless, you are excited, and you move at a hundred miles per hour. You get a high when you sign your first customer; you get another high when you deliver your first product (or service). The highs follow, with receiving the first payment, hiring the first employee, etc.

A new revelation hits you, and that is that the business may be more than an extension of you—the owner—but you still can't accept the idea of not being completely in charge. Delegation is not in your vocabulary, and decision making is all yours.

You start to realize that you did not know it all, but you are learning and applying what you learn. You make adjustments, and things start improving. You get good feedback from customers; you are happy, and you are working more than ever, but you do it with a smile.

You need to rely on your creativity because business conditions change so rapidly that what you thought was a well-planned business model can quickly become irrelevant without some key changes. Your ability to adjust on the go may save you.

Out of necessity, you realize that one of the keys to success is not having enough resources but being resourceful with what you have. If you do not have what you need, you need to somehow figure out how to get along without it.

Some problems arise; you get worried and redouble your efforts, and family life suffers because you spent too many hours at work or thinking about the business. But it is all part of the game, and you recognize it as such. Those pesky problems are fixed, and you get reenergized.

The business starts to grow nicely. As the business grows, your team grows too, and with it your HR problems—those that you hate so much but you need to deal with. You pay some debts, and that's a nice feeling. You start taking a small salary, and that's an even better feeling. You are on your way to success.

How long did this period take? It depends on a million things, and every business is different. Was it easy? Perhaps and perhaps not, but surely it was stressful, exciting, painful, rewarding, discouraging, motivating, and a few other qualifiers, but looking back from your new perch of success, you would not change it for anything.

Next, you go to phase two. The company grows nicely, but your job doesn't get any easier. It is challenging but with a different twist—one with success in sight but with different issues that pop up daily: people, production, and financing issues. But at least you see payback to your twelve-hours-per-day routine.

In the start-up phase, you, the owner, are everything, but as the company grows, you start adding employees and financial resources. Now is the time to start structuring the operations so that success is not overly dependent on you alone. You need to realize now that the company won't fall apart if you are not there doing everything.

The next phase is totally different once again. Your job has changed. You are no longer the chief cook and bottle washer. You have become or are becoming a CEO. This is new for you, and you need to learn the job; you need to delegate and empower people, even if it is a difficult task for you. And—gosh this is difficult!— you need to hold people accountable.

The path to grow from business infancy (start-up) to adolescence presents some challenges that many owners find difficult to overcome while at the same time relishing the opportunity. It is in this phase that the owner must change to being the CEO (must be a leader from the beginning), and this is where a mentor or a coach can be most useful.

As the CEO and leader, you must create a culture that grows and develops its people. Validate your employees by involving them in management decisions. Allow employees to help develop the objectives and the strategic plan to achieve them. People will support what they helped create, so by involving them, you are helping the company grow.

Tough job, but, hey, this is what you wanted and you enjoy (most of it), and now you are getting the rewards: more money, more recognition, and more opportunities to do what you like, and, hopefully, more time to do them. If you had to do it all over, you would do several things differently, but you learned from the experience, and that makes your value much higher.

This—with variations, depending on the situation, the business, and the individual—is the life of the business owner.

Your Job as CEO of a Small Business

Being a start-up CEO generally is seen as a glamorous job that is also fun. What it is not seen is the downside of the job with all its frustrations, disillusions, and headaches. So don't be blinded by the luminance of the glamour, but be grounded in the reality of the job that you chose.

Your business should be your passion; if you chose this path is because you enjoy the journey, not just the work. Dropbox co-founder Drew Houston said: "The happiest and most successful people I know don't just love what they do; they are obsessed with solving an important problem, something that matters to them". While passion is the key ingredient to entrepreneurship, the ability to execute is its married partner. If you cannot deliver, you do not have a business.

A key question to ask yourself is: am I a visionary? A visionary is a strategic thinker with workable ideas who sees the big picture and is in tune with the market and the industry and the financial environment in which to operate. A visionary entrepreneur is typically good with relationships, solving problems, creating the vision for the business, and having the strength to pursue that vision. Visionaries are creators.

The other side of the visionary coin is that they are not good at details, don't like the boring side of the business (administrative, management, legal, etc.), and they are not good at delegating or holding people accountable. As a business owner you must be the visionary and continue to be it as the business grows, but you also need to be a manager and a leader.

You started a business because you had a vision, a goal, a place you wanted to reach, and a company you wanted to build. You started to implement that vision. You developed a business plan; you studied the market and evaluated your product or service against the needs of the market. You were able to find investors, or you decided to fund it yourself. The base is formed—good job. You completed the visionary stage; now you have to make it happen.

As the owner/founder, you assumed the position of CEO (or whatever title you chose to use), but carrying the title or the position by default does not necessarily mean you are the right person for it. The two main questions you need to answer are: (1) are you qualified, and (2) do you want to be the CEO? These two questions are independent and unrelated to each other, as qualifications and desire are not mutually exclusive. You may be qualified but prefer to do a different job, or conversely, you may want the position but are not able to be the leader the business needs.

Regardless of your title, you are the keeper and driver of the vision. However, the vision is not enough to build the company; you have to take command and actually run it and build it into a real company. Your role has now changed into that of a visionary/leader. As a leader, you must attract the right people, and you must lead and keep them motivated.

The same traits that provide founders with a competitive advantage when starting a business also frequently hinder their ability to adapt and flex their style with changing organization demands as the company grows. Their strength of personality frequently impacts those around them more powerfully than they might realize.

Be eager to learn about everything related to the business. The more you know the better leader you will be and the higher your chances for success. Also, being an expert will get you recognition, as well as recognition for the business. Don't forget that you are the CEO, so your learning should be directed to leading.

Managing Your Business

Cash Management

As a business owner, you are willing (or should be) to invest all your effort, heart, and soul into your company, but you should stop short of investing all your assets. Entrepreneurial focus and dedication are great, but using a retirement account to smooth out uneven cash periods or a home-equity loan during a hard time are actions that you should avoid. Investing and leveraging everything you have to save a business, most of the time, results in failure for the business and pandemonium for the owner.

I am all in favor of avoiding outside investors or partnerships, but destroying your financial security is not a risk worth taking. Before putting extra money into the business, separate an amount that would keep your family safe for a reasonable period until you project recovery of the business.

Not stacking enough cash is probably why the majority of firms go out of business says Bill Klein, president of Consero Global, a financial consulting firm that works with small businesses. Develop close personal relationships with your banker (not just with the bank) from the beginning so you can increase your chances of getting help from the bank when you need it.

> *From my bag:* I have seen too many business owners who do not give money management the importance it deserves. For example, at least two of my clients used the balance in the checking account as the gage to judge the success of the business. They would typically say "I know I'm doing OK because I have a healthy balance in my checking account". Obviously, this is no way to manage a business. Financial management needs to be the primary concern of all business owners.

Most small-business owners fail to think and plan for tomorrow, assuming that the business will cover any emergency.

Retirement plans, college funds, expansion expenses, and other future concerns are not a priority when you are super enthusiastic about your business, but an unexpected quick turn south can find you financially naked and exposed. Be passionate about insulating your family and personal well-being from those risks.

In deciding whether to do something yourself or hire someone to do it, consider your expertise to do it, your preferences, and the costs involved. Are you better off doing this job yourself? Is this what you like to do? Can someone else do it better? Is this the best use of your time? Would you be more efficient doing this or concentrating on your job as the owner?

Coaching suggestion: J. D. Roth in Entrepreneur proposes to use a simple calculation to decide if you should spend your time doing these extra jobs, strictly from a cost-of-your-time point of view.[7] He suggests taking your total income from all sources and dividing it by two thousand, the number of hours in a standard work year based on a forty-hour work week. If this hourly wage is greater than the cost to pay somebody else to do the particular job, pay others to do it; if not, do it yourself.

From my bag: The startup I joined when I left IBM, was not the typical small business startup that I focus on in this book; rather, it was more like a typical VC-backed large-company candidate startup. It was cash-rich thanks to sizeable investments from VCs who believed in the company, and with a large founding team. Nevertheless, it serves to illustrate my points above.

When I reported to work as a founding member and responsible for a good part of the operations, I was told by the chairman and principal founder that I had x amount of dollars to spend to build the piece of the company under my direction. I told him that I did not need that much and that, as a startup, I thought we needed to be frugal and—for example—we could lease the equipment instead of buying it. I was told that the amount had been reserved for that purpose and thus I should go ahead and spend it.

Spending is easy, so I did that. The same

"philosophy" was employed with the rest of the company and, consequently, we drained large amounts of cash. The error of this mandate was experienced when—for a number of reasons that are not relevant here—we exhausted the capital and eventually went into bankruptcy.

Had we been more conscious of expenditures and conserved cash, perhaps we could have avoided the bankruptcy phantom.

Growth

The old saying, "If you don't grow you die," should be considered with its hidden significance. Growth at any cost—meaning bulking the top line—can result exactly in that—a heavy cost, such as financial demise.

Growing without a unique focus on the top line requires more wisdom, humility, and restraint, recognizing the values inherent in the company and the personal values of the owner. Focusing on customer needs and in creating a strong organization would yield benefits long term. Growth in these areas would prepare the company for steady and vigorous advance, securing loyal customers and the technical viability of the company.

A business owner must be continuously asking, "What are the main drivers of my business? Where are we now? Where are we going, and where are we going to be in x quarters or years from now?" Also, "What are we doing right, and where can we improve?" The answers to these questions will provide an ongoing real-time picture of the business and ideas to improve it.

Coaching suggestion: The ability to anticipate problems can be an extremely valuable skill of a business owner. There is a technique used by start-ups and even large companies that the Harvard Business Review has called a pre-mortem.[5] The technique is the hypothetical opposite of a postmortem and it is intended to anticipate failures.

A pre-mortem in a business setting comes at the beginning of a project rather than the end so that the project can be improved rather than analyzed after it fails. Unlike a typical critiquing session in which team members are asked what might *go wrong, the pre-mortem operates on the assumption that the project has failed and so asks what* did *go wrong. The team members' task is to generate plausible reasons for the project's failure.*

Next to money, perhaps the most important personal asset that you must manage is time. That is why managing time is so important, and allocating finite amount of time to the innumerable things on your plate is so critical to the success of your business.

Building the team

Building a team is an essential part of the CEO Job. Having a competitive team is a major component for profitability, cash flow, and the owner's personal satisfaction. In fact, business owners should surround themselves with people smarter and/or more experienced than they are and they should listen to other's ideas and advice. Similarly, when it comes to hiring employees, business owners should avoid the "yes-men" types and look for candidates who can challenge them (in a good way) and contribute with new ideas.

Hiring should strictly follow the need to fill those functions identified as essential in the functional organization chart (discussed later). Make sure you have a definite role to fill and not just a vague position. Define the job with a thorough job description to identify the needs of the business. Exceptions should only be to secure a star employee who will be instrumental later in the growth of the business.

As you build the organization, do not give high titles to people just to be able to convince them to join your company. Giving unjustified titles can create severe problems later on. Creating a vice president role for example, to hire someone who will not be capable to perform at that level as the company grows will severely limit your options later.

From my bag: *A former client and friend hired a very knowledgeable engineer expert in the core business of the company as a key and almost indispensable member of the* *startup. To convince him to take the risk of joining a new venture my friend gave him the title of vice president of engineering. As the company grew and became a successful enterprise it became obvious that the engineer did not act nor had the capability to operate as a high-level executive.*

My friend could not release him because his engineering talents were too valuable to give up, but he faced a conundrum to keep him motivated and also build the organization for the long term. Finally, upon my advice, the VP title was changed to Chief Technical Officer without any managerial responsibilities. He was happy with his new title and my friend was able to continue to build the organization without the wrongly placed person.

The path to growth that any business must follow depends on the creation of the right behaviors in the owner and in the team. Creating a culture of empowerment and accountability within the general culture of the company will drive the business down the right path.[8, 9]

Ask yourself the following:
- If you were competing against your own company, what actions would you take and why?
- Who are your strongest employees and what are you doing to make sure they are happy and motivated?
- Who are your weakest employees and what is your plan for them?

Building the systems

Also pertinent to the growth of the company is the requirement for systems and procedures. Consistency in management and in operations is critical to growing a business and to freeing the entrepreneur/owner to lead. If no aspect of a business is left to chance, the owner's ability to achieve the business and personal goals are greatly enhanced. Also enhanced is the owner's ability to free him or herself from the daily grind of the business. (See Chapter XV Systematizing Your Business).

Follow the mantra from ISO 9000 system: "Say what you do and do what you say".

Crisis Management

As a business owner you must be prepared to deal with crisis because ... crisis will happen and how you deal with them can be the difference from success or failure, smooth riding or chaos. Follow these principles to navigate the rough waters of a crisis:

- Assume the problem is worse than it appears; skip the denial step.
- Assume there are no secrets in the world and that everyone will eventually find out everything. Get ahead of the problem.
- Assume you and your organization handling of the crisis will be portrayed in the worst possible light.
- Assume there will be changes in the process and people; almost no crisis ends without blood on the floor.
- Assume your organization will survive ultimately stronger for what happened.
- Get ahead of the problem.
- Define your position early and often.
- Real crisis do not just fade away.
- You learn something from every crisis that make you smarter and more effective.

Keys to successful management

John D. Rockefeller identified three underlying habits as key to the successful management of a business. The three fundamental barriers to growth that he identified—and the trio of "Rockefeller habits"[10] that he developed to cope with those barriers—haven't changed in their importance since they were first published. They are:

- Leadership: Can the leadership team keep growing in its ability to delegate and predict the course of the business? Can it develop other leaders?

- Systems and Structures: Will the support and operational systems be installed to help drive timely decision making? Will organizational structures be set up to keep clear who is accountable?
- Market Dynamics: Will the organization be prepared to deal with the changing competitive and economic pressures that come with growth? Will the organization recognize when it must shift its economic model?

The reasons businesses fail are as many and as varied as the type of businesses.

- Leadership failure: Dysfunctional leadership will affect the entire company. Lack of leadership can reflect in many ways, from financial management to employee relations. A business without a leader is like a ship without a helmsman.
- Insufficient resources: Whether financial, technical, personnel, or otherwise, not having the required resources can kill a business.
- Lack of adequate planning: Business, sales, marketing, operations, and employment plans can be summarized into a strategic plan, which is the lifeblood of the business.
- Poor financial management: Cash is king, and not managing the financial pieces right means catastrophe.
- Failure to communicate the unique value proposition: If you have a unique value but fail to communicate it, you may as well not have one.
- Bad execution of a plan: Planning is important, but without execution no plan is valid. The plan must include rules for its execution and accountability at all levels.
- Rapid growth and overexpansion: This is a typical mistake many businesses make. Overenthusiastic about the success achieved, they embark on an aggressive expansion that exceeds the resources available.

Execution of the plan is what drives results. A beautiful plan not implemented with equally good execution does nothing for a successful business. This execution gap is a breach between the company's strategy and expectation and its ability to meet the goals and put ideas into action.

> ***From my bag:*** *I coached for years an otherwise brilliant client who "saw opportunities around every corner" and had a tendency to go after all of them. The effect on his business was detrimental because he would constantly take his focus away from the ongoing business to attempt to pursue those shiny opportunities. It took my persistent prodding to get him to refocus on the business at hand and the strategic plan we had developed.*

> *Another former client was an inventor who kept changing his focus and the focus of the business according to his latest invention. The result was a business being run as a hobby shop and not the excellent manufacturing company it was supposed to be. The good news is that we both realized that his happiness was in the inventing part and thus we changed the strategy of the business making it a specialized shop. The business thrived under this new strategy and the owner was very happy.*

Andy Grove, former Intel CEO, said of companies something that can be translated to people: "Bad companies are destroyed by crisis, good companies survive them, and great companies are improved by them." Similarly, an entrepreneur without the right personality can be overwhelmed by obstacles, good entrepreneurs can survive them, but the sign of a successful entrepreneur is one who emerges as a better leader after facing serious obstacles.

You do not know it all; in fact, you do not know what you do not know. So do not make the mistake of trying to do it all alone; get support from others, particularly from someone who has done it before, a coach, or a business support group. An experienced business coach can make the experience a much easier one, but make sure it is someone who you can work with and who understands your vision and personality.

Joining a peer-advisory board will give you the double benefit of a coach and a support group composed of other business owners. This, in fact, acts as your own board to guide you through all the business issues and also deal with some personal issues that may affect the business. (See the appendix.)

You made the decision and started the journey, congratulations; you joined a select group of people who are important contributors to society. Your vision is the goal, and your talent, perseverance, creativity, and hard work are the motivators to lead you to the goal.

But to complete your happiness, remember what I said earlier in this book:

A business should be a part of your life, apart from your life, and should not be your entire life.

This means that your personal and family life must be preserved during the challenging times of starting and running a business. You must sacrifice many things to become a business owner, but to ensure happiness your personal and family life should not be among the things that you sacrifice.

You mounted the lion; can you do what you must do to survive?

References:

1. Jessica Bruder, "The Psychological Price of Entrepreneurship", Inc Magazine, September 2013.
2. Oswald R. Viva, "Its Lonely at the Top"; "A Practical Guide to Become a Better Leader for Your Small Company", iUniverse, 2011
3. John F. Dini, "Hunting in a Farmer's World: Celebrating the Mind of an Entrepreneur", Gardendale Press, 2014.
4. Ralph Waldo Emerson Quotes, Brainy Quotes, www.brainyquote.com.
5. Gary Klein, "Performing a Project Premortem," Harvard Business Review, 2007.
6.

7. J. D. Roth, "Don't Waste Your Time," Entrepreneur magazine, June 2014.
8. Oswald R. Viva. "Create a Culture of Empowerment", e-book, SkillBites.net, 2012.
9. Oswald R. Viva. "Accountability in the Workplace", e-book, SkillBites.net, 2012.
10. Verne Harnish, "Mastering the Rockefeller Habits: What You Must Do to Increase the Value of Your Growing Firm," March 1, 2011.

Chapter II - Are You the "Right" CEO for Your Business?

Evaluate your Qualifications and Desire for the Job

There are hundreds if not thousands of books on leadership and this book does not pretend to be one of them. This piece is intended only as a simple coaching session for small business owners to evaluate themselves as candidates for the CEO chair. I don't pretend to teach you leadership here; only to have you do a self-exam of your qualifications for the job.

What does it mean to be the CEO?

While the following pages may be perceived as written for "CEO-to-be", they are intended also—and mainly—for business owners who are positioned in the CEO chair. Whether you are in that position or plan to be, you need to understand—***really*** understand—all its implications and demands as well as your desires and qualifications. The two main questions you need to answer are: a) are you qualified, and b) do you want to be the CEO. Hopefully, this discussion will help you answer both.

Have you appointed yourself CEO of your company? Did you do it purposely because you believe you are the best person to lead the company? Or are you occupying the CEO role because you started the company and you are "it" by default? Or just because you are the owner you claimed the position without evaluating your capabilities for the job?

Have you thought about what is needed for the job? What qualifications are required? What are the traits that you must have? Have you consider, really consider, what the job calls for? Have you done a job description of the position to see if you qualify? Are you the person to lead the company to the next level and beyond?

You probably started a business because you were good at doing "something", and became what Michael Berger in *"The E-Myth"* calls *the technician*. As the business started to grow you became a manager with whatever title you chose to use. As a manager you most likely did a commendable job and the company continued to grow. As the organization took shape you became the top dog and thus the title of CEO was trusted upon you (likely by yourself).

> *Jack Welch said of leadership for CEOs: "The ideal leader is courageous, strong and persistent, and wise—but what really separates him or her from the pack is passion and vision. It's not enough to be a skilled administrator and world class manager; no, to be a true leader, you need the passion of your dreams and a vision for how to make them real. Passion and vision are transforming forces that will fail unless you fuse them into a powerful source for change". From Welch's website* [1].

So, if we accept what Jack said as a real prerequisite of good leadership, as the CEO of your business you must have or develop that passion and vision. If you started your business and built it to what it is today, I know you have the passion and most likely you also have a vision; a vision for what you want to do with the business and what you want to get from it. Consequently, you have the two things Jack demands; now you need to decide if you have the talent and if you want to be the CEO.

Your Primary Aim

As part of the evaluation you need to do to see if the CEO job is for you, consider your primary aim in life. Your primary aim is the vision necessary to bring your business to life and your life to the business, understanding that the business should not be your entire life. (I say that the business should be a part of your life "apart" from your life).

Your primary aim provides you with a purpose in life and the energy to work on it. It is your greater motivator and the driver of all your business activities. Ask yourself the following:

- What do I value most?

- What kind of life do I want?
- What is that I truly love in my life (other than family of course)?
- How would I like people to think of me?
- What would I like to be doing X years from now?
- What material things are important to me?
- How much money would I need to do the things I wish to do?
- Other than material things, what is important to me?

Don't take these questions lightly; put much thought into them and be honest with yourself. Whatever your answers are, they are OK and you should not feel bad about them. The most important thing is for you to be happy and to do what you like to do and have what you like to have; everything else is secondary, because without your happiness you wouldn't be successful.

Your Development as CEO

Have you thought about the demands and qualifications of the CEO position? Are those demands in line with your goals and what you like to do? Do you feel eminently qualified for the position? A self-analysis is an essential part of the development. You must be candid in answering the following:

What do you have and what does the job entail?

- CEO Job description. Do you *really* understand what the job is? Start by writing the "job description" of your present functions; i.e., what you do every day. Next, write (or get help from your coach to write) the job description of a CEO of your type of business. Compare the two and take action.
- Is the CEO Job what you *really* like to do? Identify areas of personal interest for your happiness. Many business owners prefer one of the main activities of the business (technical, operational, sales) but not the administrative, strategic or visionary demands of the CEO position.

- If you feel obligated to act as the CEO, you will not reach personal happiness and your business will not reach its potential. Both you and the business would benefit if you assume a position of your liking (for example CTO) and another qualified person takes the role of the CEO.

- Analyze your strengths and weaknesses and develop a plan to emphasize the strengths and work on the weaknesses. Take this task seriously. List the three most important or marked weaknesses and work on them. Whenever you (or your coach) consider one of them "solved", add a replacement to the list so that you are always working on three weaknesses. Make this a continuous improvement process.

- Founding CEOs versus second CEOs. Are you capable of taking the business to the next level? Sadly, it is common to find owners that do a commendable job of starting a business and growing it to a certain level, but are incapable of leading it to the next level. In other words, they reach their level of competence in the business development cycle.

- Admitting your limitations and identifying your *critical level of competence* and conceding the CEO Job to somebody more qualified, will drastically improve the chances of success of your business.

- Leading versus managing. Are you a leader? Can you become a leader? As explained above and in the respective section, leadership can be developed (to some extent) assuming that the natural prerequisites are there. Don't let pride fool you as to your qualifications. A coach or your peers, who know you intimately, can help you estimate your chances of becoming the leader that you need to be.

- Do you have some of the traits that define good leaders? Some of the most important ones are as follows:
    - Visionary
    - Honesty/integrity
    - Ability to communicate clearly
    - Ability to inspire self and others
    - Dedication

- Magnanimity/humility
- Creative/innovative
- Assertive/decisive
- Influential

Remember that the primary purpose of a leader is to lead others to a goal.

Management vs. Leadership

Many small business owners realize that it is not easy combining leadership and management, and at the same time motivating others and working *on* the business with all its intricacies. One reason is that they are not sure of, or comfortable with, the differences between leadership and management.

There is a big difference between being a manager and being a leader, and as CEO you *must* be a leader. Owning a business automatically puts you in a leadership position; however, being in that position does not necessarily make you a leader. As a manager, you can direct people in activities and tasks, but it takes the leader in you to enlist their passion in the work they do and in the business you lead. As a leader, you know that having a sense of belonging increases commitment in their job and thus, you want to make your employees "buy into" your vision.

There is also a big difference between being the boss of a budding or very small company and the CEO of a rapidly growing bigger company. The requirements are different, the responsibilities are different and the two must have completely different approaches to the job.

Let's look at the basic differences between management and leadership.

Management is a business skill; leadership is a people's skill. Management is about coping with complexity; leadership is about coping with change. Management is about planning, budgeting, organizing, staffing, controls, problem solving. Leadership is about setting direction, aligning people, motivating, inspiring, adapting and creating change.

In your self-analysis decide if you prefer to be a manager or a leader. This choice is somewhat misleading because as a manager you must have leadership ability too. So, the question really is: are you or do you want to be the operations type or the executive type? You as the owner, have the prerogative to be able to choose your position without affecting your position of privilege.

As we will see later you may prefer to be the COO or the CTO or the Chairman, and leave the headaches of the executive position to someone else. Of course since it is your business you are still the ultimate decision maker and the most affected by whatever decisions are made by others.

Are You Qualified to be the CEO?

Are you ready and qualified to be the CEO that your business needs to move to the next level? As your coach I like to do an evaluation of your qualifications for the job. First let's look at your personal traits:

- Do you have the fortitude, the energy and the ability to be the CEO?
- Are you capable and ready to take the role of the leader as opposed to the management role (as defined above)?
- Have you done a good analysis of your strengths and weaknesses and matched them against the need of the job?
- Have you done a job description for the position and applied for the job?
- And most importantly, do you **really** want to be the CEO?

I'm asking the last question because many business owners prefer certain activities not related to the CEO position and dislike others that are prerequisite for the position. For example, it is typical for engineers to prefer to stay involved in the technical aspects of a company; technology has an attraction that they don't want to give up. However, as a CEO you can stay in touch but not intimately so with the technical side of the business; you have many other things to attend to.

Conversely, they—or many others—may have a pronounced displeasure for administrative functions, which are intimately related to the CEO function. Those people (engineers in this case but could also be from other fields) are better suited to hold other positions that they would enjoy more. For the example of the engineers, being the Chief Technical Officer (CTO) may be a more rewarding position and thus, one that would offer better chances for the company to succeed and for them to be happy.

I have worked with business owners who are excellent managers but are not the visionary type that as CEOs are required to be. My advice to them is to place themselves as COO (Chief Operations Officers) and to leave the CEO Job to more "qualified" people. Unfortunately, in many cases the ego of the owner gets in the way and they can't accept to have others in the position that they believe should be theirs.

I say that there is no shame in being what they like to be and in no doing what they don't like to do. Nobody is going to take the main title away from you—the title of owner—and that your happiness and the success of your company are more important than titles.

From my bag: OP *was the owner of a nice manufacturing company with almost ten million dollars in revenues and thirty-four employees, and growing rapidly. The company dealt in a highly technical field and OP was an engineer by education and by heart. He was so involved in the technical side of the business that the company was not performing as well as it should be and he was not pleased with having to do "all those menial jobs" as he described the administrative tasks.*

I coached him into considering a change of position, and we did some of the evaluations that I suggest in this book. It was not an easy task as he was very reluctant to "take a lower position and have someone else over him" as he saw it, but at the end I was able to convince him. He became the CTO and hired an outside person as the CEO. It was a difficult adaptation period but after some time he admitted that he was happier and the business was doing much better. Today as the company approaches the twenty million dollars in revenues mark, he is appreciative of my advice and the company is doing very well thank you.

The CEO Job

As CEO your leadership activities include the following:

- Defining and implementing the strategy to realize the Vision.
- Defining, developing and leveraging company core competencies, whether technical, human, market, etc.
- Building and nurturing the culture of the organization.
- Developing, utilizing and managing resources—human, capital, facilities, equipment, etc.
- Driving performance based results.
- Leading change and continuous improvement.
- Systematize, i.e., developing and implementing systems so that the company is "run by systems and not by people" (from *The E-Myth*).

And as a "candidate for that position you must ask yourself the following:

- Am I a visionary and think strategically rather than implementing "the idea of the week"?
- Do I have a tactical mind or a strategic one?
- Do I handle stressful situation well without losing focus and directions?
- Am I good under pressure?
- Am I good at building teams and motivating team members?
- Do I accept the responsibility for problems instead of blaming others?
- Do I practice the window and the mirror? (*see definition later*)

- Do I set an example of the type of behavior needed to enforce the culture of the company?

And you also need to consider shortcomings that you may have.

- Do you always strive for excellence? Mediocrity won't get you where you want to go.
- Are you a good delegator? Failing to see delegation as a critical element of leadership.
- Do you have a life outside of the business? Failing to allocate time for yourself and your family and balancing your business and your life.
- Do you assume that because you are good at some skill or trade you are qualified to run a business?

Coaching suggestion: *Write a job description for the CEO position (an example is included). If you are not sure, work with your coach to develop one. Also write a "job description" of what you do now (whatever your present "job" is); compare the two and see where you need to improve. Another worthy exercise is to "apply" for the job as listed in the job description for your company and see if you qualify. You will need an independent and impartial person to evaluate your application; your coach as perhaps the person who knows you best would be the right arbiter.*

Grade yourself as CEO of your company by using the exercise presented at the end of this chapter and also at the end of the next chapter.

Dominant Personality Traits of CEOs

Your personality traits determine if you are entrepreneurial material. What traits or qualities are expected in a good leader? A number of key traits have been identified over the years that are consistently noted and described as being essential for leadership.

The old question, "Are leaders born or made?" can also be adapted to entrepreneurs. Are entrepreneurs born with the distinctive traits required, or do those traits develop over time through experience and teaching? Some innate traits are commonly found in entrepreneurs as the drivers of their entrepreneurial activities, but other traits are developed from the experiences lived.

Passion is a key trait that drives the entrepreneurial voyage of not only starting a business but also growing it and making it successful. Achieving success requires passion for what you do and the dedication to learn and practice management fundamentals. While passion is important, without a healthy dose of business fundamentals, passion has as much value as a dream. Passion alone won't help you.

Your vision drives you, but other traits are required to complete the disposition of entrepreneurs. Vision is required to take an idea and make it a reality by building a business for it—a vision to see things and consider the possibilities before they exist, even if the world is saying, "It won't work."

As the CEO of your company you are its leader and the leader of the organization; as such you must have the personality traits that distinguish good leaders. Check yourself against the list below and see if you have them or need to improve on them.

- As the leader you must lead people towards a goal; the goal is the vision you created of where you want to take your organization.
- Commitment to the vision and the determination to be successful.
- Creativity and the self-confidence to apply that creativity.
- Ability to inspire followers to embrace the vision. As a leader you must "sell" the vision so that it becomes everybody's vision and everyone works to reach it.
- Strategic thinking to recognize your and your organization's strengths and weaknesses, along with the external opportunities and threats, quite clearly.
- In parallel with your strategic side, you must have a tactical side as bottom-line oriented and be obsessed with execution.

- Ability to seek opportunities to pursue and to recognize opportunities in every challenge.
- Awareness to be a risk taker but recognizing "safe risk".
- Focus on the job on hand and in the long range issues to guide your company.
- Motivation to succeed and to motivate others through persuasion rather than intimidation.
- Emotional intelligence and interpersonal skills.
- Ability to make quick decisions, even with incomplete data.
- Strong values to guide your actions.
- Empathy for others, their needs and wants, and also the desire to develop others.
- Ability to communicate clearly and to deal with conflict management.

Coaching suggestion: In "Good to Great" [2] *Jim Collins proposes for managers to use "the mirror and the window" concept in dealing with employees. It means as follows: when something goes wrong in the business, look in the mirror and place the blame on yourself because, after all, you are ultimately responsible for everything that happens in your company. On the other hand, when celebrating success, look out the window and praise your employees. The payoff will be a lot of respect for you and much self-satisfaction for them, which in turn will translate into stronger loyalty and motivation.*

What about Character?

Our character and values communicate what we are. If leadership skills constitute the efficacy of a leader, the character traits of the leader determine the quality of the leadership. But it is one thing to develop a skill, even a leadership skill; it is something else altogether to develop character traits. The character that you exhibit as CEO is important to you and your employees.

When it comes down to becoming a real leader in your business it is helpful to remember the primary purpose of a leader:

to lead others. Knowing first and foremost where you are going with your business is absolutely essential for being a leader. All the rest becomes a matter of accrued experience.

We don't always recognize the strengths that we have and some of the traits that can make us good leaders. Referring back to the owner in the *"From my bag"* above, when we started to work together he did not recognize the strengths he had, but to me they were evident, and he became the leader he needed to be, because of those strengths. He simply wouldn't have assumed he was ready to lead at that level.

He believed me and invested himself in getting better, day by day, step by step. As he got better success fed his own confidence and satisfaction, and his willingness to keep pushing himself. The truth is we can achieve excellent in almost anything we practice with sufficient focus and intention.

To be a leader you must have followers, and followers are not assigned or imposed by an organization chart, they are recruited and retained by the ability of the leader. Your ability— that includes personality and talent—will determine the loyalty of your followers.

As *Antony Jay* once said, "The only real training for leadership is leadership."

And another: "You can judge a leader by the size of the problem he tackles. Other people can cope with the waves; it's his job to watch the tide."

You need resilience to overcome obstacles and, yes, even failures, because, chances are, there will be failures. Ability to get things done because is not enough to have the vision; business owners also need to have the ability to get the job done—in other words, to make goals become reality. Vision without action is a dream without end.

As a business grows and the organization grows with it, people management becomes a large part of the job. This can be demoralizing because people problems are the most frustrating and painful of the headaches that businesses can offer the owner. The owner must learn to delegate effectively; as explained in the appropriate chapter, this is an essential aspect of company management and one that is difficult for many to learn.

Do what you love and love what you do. Focus on what you can do and ignore what you cannot do.

People should be what they want to be and can be. Not everyone can be a doctor, an astronaut, a teacher, or a plumber, and certainly not everyone has what it takes to be a business owner or desire the risk of entrepreneurship. You did it and hopefully you are successful or on the way to be successful.

You decided to become an entrepreneur and you are in a select group of individuals who contribute to the well-being of the country (and the world). And if your business is successful, you are in an even more select group.

In my coaching career and running peer-advisory boards for many years, I worked with a great variety of business owners, and the self-stated reasons that made them entrepreneurs are as different as their businesses, but there is commonality in their traits and drive. The personalities are very different too, but all of them wouldn't change the hardships of business ownership for anything. When asked if having to do it over again would they, unanimously they would respond with an emphatic yes.

Whether their enterprise is a family business, a solo experience, a partnership, a subset of a large operation, participating in a technical field, a manufacturing or distribution or sales or professional or any other field, they recognize the shortcomings and sacrifices of being business owners, but they relish the experience and congratulate themselves for choosing that route.

Catering to the Needs of Individuals

Leadership is person specific; to be effective you need to use different styles to deal with different people. Just as children tend to be all different and the challenge as a parent is to adapt our parenthood tactics to the personality of each child so is the need of a leader to adapt to each individual being led.

Good leaders understand that how they make people feel, day in and day out, has a profound influence on how people perform. Everyone has a range of core needs—physical, emotional, mental and spiritual, it is a sign of a good leader to focus on helping employees meet each of these needs, recognizing that it helps them to perform better and more sustainably.

As a leader you must seek to understand and meet your people's needs and make this a focus of your activities. As individuals, we have a need for self-expression; one of the most demoralizing experiences for employees is to feel micromanaged. Employees can develop a feeling of ineptitude and loss of self-confidence.

The job of leaders is not to do the work of those they lead, but to serve as motivators to bring the best of each employee to work every day. Good leaders invest the effort to clearly define what success looks like, and then empower and trust employees to figure out the best way to achieve it.

Perhaps an even more serious offense in the eyes of employees is the perception of being ignored by the boss. This happens when you don't make them participant of plans or decisions that affect them and/or the company. Your ability as a leader includes the knack to make employees feel important and that you trust their input and value their contributions.

Coaching suggestion: Develop the aptitude not only to include employees in plans and decisions, but to show that you value their contributions. When discussing ideas you don't have to accept theirs if you believe that your ideas are better, but you can "sell" your ideas in such a way that they appear as coming from them. This will significantly increase their motivation and their admiration for you as their leader. This "talent" may require some practice for you to become good at it, but it is worth the effort because it is a sign of good leadership.

It is the responsibility of the leader to define the expected results in the form of concrete deliverables, not to micromanage. Once that is done, and you have defined what needs to be done, and how, get out of the way. Trust your employees to figure out for themselves the best way to get their work done. They may take wrong turns and make mistakes, but they will learn and grow stronger along the way.

All of us struggle, whether we're aware of it or not, with our self-worth. We tend to believe that we are not good enough for some things and in certain occasions. If you make employees feel valued, in spite of their imperfections, the less effort they will spend asserting, defending and restoring their value, and the more energy they will have to create value for the business.

> ***Coaching suggestion:*** *Meet privately with each employee to learn their needs and wants and make it a priority to do what you can to satisfy those needs and wants. It may help you to keep a file on this indicating the actions you are taking to do it, and what their reaction is. You should do it for your direct reports and teach them to do it for their people. Repeat this practice at least once a year.*

Conclusion

There is no guaranteed path to becoming a good leader or CEO. It is a process requiring a lifelong commitment to personal development so that you will be prepared to confront the enormous complexities leaders face and to fulfill your responsibilities honorably and successfully. The challenges are great but the satisfaction of knowing you made a positive difference in the lives of others is even greater.

References:
1. "The Welch Way". http://www.welchway.com/ (accessed Jan-Mar 2011)
2. Jim Collins, *Good to Great; Why Some Companies Make The Leap … And Others Don't* (HarperBusiness; 1st edition October 16, 2001)

Grade Yourself As The Leader Of Your Company

1. **Establishes and accomplishes company goals and vision by**
   - taking educated risks
   - conducting annual strategic planning
   - developing annual budget & financial review
   - conducting business planning
   - recommending strategies to staff and advisors
   - initiating programs & processes
   - meeting financial obligations
   - evaluating and reporting results

2. **Organizes the business by**
   - selecting and developing key personnel and successors
   - assigning accountabilities
   - setting objectives & key priorities
   - integrating business efforts
   - monitoring and evaluating results
   - providing resources
   - developing strategic partnerships/alliances

3. **Serves customers, employees and vendors/suppliers by**
   - creating depth of management team
   - compensation for greater performance
   - maintaining legal compliance with state & federal HR laws
   - establishing critical service, operations, and productivity criteria
   - maintaining state-of-the-art technology
   - exploiting market channels
   - leading commitment to quality service
   - evaluating service results
   - representing the company to major customers/suppliers/vendors

4. **Creates understanding and positive image of the company by**
   - building relationships with, and providing information to, the financial community, media, government, and the public
   - building credibility with investors

- building employee commitment to the company and community.

5. **Maintains company stability and reputation by**
   - establishing and communicating a company value system; enforcing ethical business practices; complying with, or influencing the development of policy, procedures and systems

6. **Maintains professional knowledge by**
   - participating in professional associations
   - attending educational workshops
   - reviewing professional publications
   - establishing professional networks
   - benchmarking state-of-the-art practices

7. **Contributes to business growth by**
   - researching opportunities
   - implementing a succession plan
   - creating a compelling company vision
   - developing a meaningful mission statement
   - creating the company's unique selling proposition
   - ensuring alignment to strategic objectives at every level
   - developing an annual marketing plan & campaign
   - developing an annual IT plan

Chapter III – Founding CEOs versus Second CEOs.

Are you capable of taking the business to the next level?

The Business Growth Cycle

It all starts with your business and personal vision. It drives everything you do. It's where your energy and passion resides. You move into the second stage which brings new challenges, new plans, new goals and a new you. The cycle continues until you reach your exit strategy.

For many, the transition from first stage—the founders stage—to the second stage—the stage of growth—is the most difficult one. I know that some of you—perhaps many of you—are already at the second level in the growth of your business, but perhaps it will be useful to review what you need to do and who you need to be, to succeed in this stage and beyond.

If your transition from the initial stages as a founder to the second stage was successful, I commend you, but I urge you to reinforce your present position and get ready for the next level. Remember the saying "What got you here won't get you there".

Transition from First Stage

It is common to find owners that do a commendable job of starting a business and growing it to a certain level, but are incapable of leading it to the next level. In other words, they reach their level of competence in the business development cycle.

Admitting their limitations and identifying their critical level of competence and conceding the CEO Job to somebody more qualified, will drastically improve the chances of success of their business.

From my bag: I worked for years with an owner, founder and CEO of a CA semiconductor company. He did a very good job of building the company from a dream into a $10 million company, where it reached a plateau. After much work I convinced him that to move the company from "neutral" to the next level he needed to add a management team strong enough to lead the company and supplement his own deficiencies as leader.

Despite his reluctance, with time he added a qualified team. As a result and with steady performance the company grew to approximately twenty million dollars where it found itself in another plateau. At this point he was successful in selling the company to an investment group that brought in additional management. Under this new team the company quickly grew to forty million dollars and continued on a positive growth trend.

In the *from my bag* example above, my client was a very capable entrepreneur who was able to guide the venture through its initial stages; however, he was not the right man to take the company to "the next level" and beyond. Was he unique? Absolutely not! This is not an uncommon situation. Not all—or many—entrepreneurs are the "second stage CEOs" type, capable of driving a business through the various stages of growth.

From my bag: Another of my clients is the perfect image of the entrepreneur who thrives in the first stage but has difficulty moving to the second stage. He is a professional with a successful practice and is also the founder of four companies in completely different fields. Three of the four drift along without real growth because the owner doesn't "function" as he would have to if he really wanted them to grow. He is happy being involved in all the details, making all the decisions and being the only voice in their management.

In other words, he doesn't want to or is not capable of moving the businesses to the second stage. By contrast the fourth company is extremely successful and it is growing by leaps and bounds. What is the difference? In this company he has two partners that are the drivers; they not only drive the company to success, but they also drive my client to be their equal. This is a good example of traits of first and second stage CEOs.

There are different definitions as to what constitutes an entrepreneurial or a second-stage business. The term 'entrepreneur' refers to small businesses, but entrepreneurship usually includes small-business entrepreneurs and growth-oriented entrepreneurs. For example, there are individuals referred to as entrepreneurs but in reality are "only" self-employed because they are in business by themselves but creating jobs isn't a priority for them; they prefer to stay small.

Some define second-stage businesses as those with ten to ninety-nine employees and annual revenue ranging between one million dollars and fifty million dollars. Others peg the size at twenty to forty employees and consider a business "grown" by the time it reaches one hundred, and yet others define them in other terms. However, the key measure is that they are past the initial period of formation and into the growth period.

Of course these numbers are industry dependent; for example, a manufacturing company will need a larger number of employees to reach a certain sales number, while a (strictly) sales company can reach the same amount of revenues with fewer employees.

According to *YourEconomy.org* between 1993 and 2008, second-stage companies only represented 10.9 percent of U.S. businesses but represented 35.7 percent of jobs and 24.8 percent of positive job growth. Second stage includes companies with potential for high growth and those with steady and less dramatic growth but still impressive.

In his book *"No Man's Land"*[2] Doug Tatum calls this the adolescence phase in companies' lifecycles where they are "too big to be small but too small to be big". Second stage is a critical time for growth entrepreneurs because they face an entirely new set of challenges. "What got you here won't get you there", means that your enthusiasm and drive by themselves—the forces that made you successful as an entrepreneur—won't make you successful in second stage.

During your business' early years the business was your whole life and you had to give up everything, including sleep. (Yes, I know for many of you it still is like that, but I'm generalizing). But as a CEO of a second-stage company you have a different role; i.e., a leadership role, leading an organization. With the new role come other responsibilities and the need for expanded talents.

Founding Owners vs. Second-Stage CEOs

Webster defines entrepreneur as "one who organizes a business undertaking, assuming the risk for the sake of the profit." An entrepreneur usually takes on all the roles within a company until profits and/or investors allow for hiring employees. He/she enjoys the experience and usually thrives in it. I'm calling them the owner-founder of the business.

An executive is defined as "one who administers or manages matters of business of a corporation." He/she oversees the structure and the day-to-day operations, and gets pleasure in growing the company and the organization. As a second stage CEO you become an executive with these duties.

Founding CEOs and second or long-term CEOs have unique characteristics. Most notably, a second-stage CEO needs to have a vision that goes beyond the initial years of a company. He/she must also have the qualifications and experience to build the organization that can take the business into successive levels, and the systems and procedures to guarantee the successful voyage.

Assuming that the founder(s) of the company continue to be the main shareholders (owners) but not the CEO, the second-stage CEO, who is really a successor to the founder(s) must have the ability to achieve the goals of the owners. The goals may include that the company remain private, or possibly that a buyout is pursued as an exit strategy, or that growth be achieved via acquisitions or that the company will remain small but be a technological leader, etc. The vision of the founder likely will remain intact, but it is the CEO's responsibility to make it happen.

What can the first-stage and second-stage CEOs learn from each other? The entrepreneur must understand that for the company to grow, the business should be able to run without him … or at least without his total involvement. The executive or second-stage CEO needs to keep "the fire in the belly" that made the entrepreneur so driven.

Can founders also be the leaders for the second stage of the business? Yes, of course, provided that he/she has the basic talent and personality required and that he/she strives to grow his/her leadership ability as the business grows. And here lies the key to success; i.e., having the ability and self-understanding to recognize strengths and weaknesses and possession or absence of necessary traits.

In large companies there are many examples of founders becoming excellent late stage CEOs; names such as Steve Jobs, Andy Grove, Bill Gates and Michel Dell come to mind. It is more typical though that once a company goes public, the original founders must be ousted. This is the result of the myth that says that entrepreneurs are great for getting a company started, but fail when the company reaches a certain level and is under constant scrutiny by the public, the media, and most importantly, the investors.

Sadly, it is also true that many founders are ousted as soon as outside investors get in the act. Differences in personalities, perceived differences in what is required to lead the budding company, or simply out of a desire of the investors to be dictatorial, are some of the reasons. It follows then, that the only founders who can assure their ability to continue as CEOs past the initial stages, are those who don't bring outside investors.

So, the point is not that founders cannot be second or later stage leaders, but that they must have what it takes in order to succeed. Founders are passionate about an idea and a vision, but not necessarily disciplined in a business sense. The discipline comes with the experience of "doing it" and learning as they go.

During the initial stages of a company there are few—if any—employees, so while the owner has a myriad of things to worry about, HR issues are minimum. On the other hand, personnel issues in the second stage grow as the organization grows. It's easier to attract employees because the financial position of the company is better (or at least it has more credibility and financial wherewithal), but HR issues are directly proportional to the number of employees.

One of the critical issues for the second stage CEO is the development of the organization; how many employees are needed to match the growth, what kind of personnel is needed, what support positions are needed, what specialties should have priority, and many other questions must be answered in this stage.

I favor the development of procedures and systems in general to be done when the company is small and to grow them as the company grows; however, in most cases, the owner doesn't have the time, the energy or the concentration to "think about details" when day-to-day survival is on the schedule. Consequently, it is in the second stage when there is even a hint of systemization.

One of the challenges for owners transitioning into stage-two business is to learn to delegate effectively and to motivate the staff while gaining and giving trust. This is a change in the role of the entrepreneur, and one in which many are not comfortable or don't know how to play it.

A common mistake of stage-two CEOs is their belief that to be successful in this stage they need to continue with the same attitude that made them successful in the initial phase. Love for the dream, passion and the ability to wear all hats doesn't do it after the initial phase; leadership and vision are the key traits needed.

Dave Haviland, Founder and CEO, Phimation Strategy Group, says that there are five tools that a Second Stage leader should use to create a productive organization. Most leaders are good at two or three of them, but that's not good enough, they need to become proficient at the others too. They are:

- Tool #1: People. People are not the main asset of a business; the right people are. You must get the right people for the right jobs.
- Tool #2: Process. As the business reaches the second stage it becomes more complicated, and you need to

have the right processes. Systemizing becomes very important. *(See chapter on Systemizing)*

- Tool #3: Structure. While in stage one you and your employees (if you have them) can wear many hats, good organizational structure is a requirement for any growing company; in stage two you must define all roles and make sure the right players are in the right positions. *(See chapter on Organization).*
- Tool #4: Measurements. Stage one measurements are easy; they may be reduced to "what comes in and what goes out", but in stage two you need to know how that all sections of the business are performing, and for that you need to apply the right controls. *See chapter on Performance Management).*
- Tool #5: Compensation. This is one of the tools that are usually not used properly by businesses, even in stage two. You need to be fair and consistent, and not to be swayed by favoritisms or the "just because we need him" syndrome.

Successful CEOs blend the high traits of the entrepreneur and the requirements of the new position; they have a sense of passion for what they do while balancing it with systems, and they integrate a structure that allows the business to operate without their one hundred percent involvement in all details.

> ***From my bag:*** *Several years ago I started to work with the owner/CEO of an electronic component manufacturer that at that time had approximately four million dollars in revenues. He confided then that he did not see himself qualified to lead the company to the ten million dollars level in revenues and beyond. I told him that I did not agree and that I believed he had what it takes but only needed the opportunity to do it, and coaching.*
>
> *We have been working together for about ten years (I as his coach) and today the company is at eighteen million dollars in revenues and growing rapidly with a very acceptable profit margin. He is not only very confident in his position at this level but now believes he is the right person to take the company to the next level. What is the secret to his success?*

He always had the talent required and with continuous coaching he developed into the excellent CEO the business needed.

Wolfgang Amadeus Mozart once said, "Neither a lofty degree of intelligence nor imagination nor both together go to the making of genius. Love, love, love, that is the soul of genius." Of course, in business love alone won't do it, but love for what you do is an irreplaceable ingredient for success.

Knowing When to Give Up Control

For entrepreneurs giving up control is difficult; it is an emotionally huge step. However, you don't have to give up control; you can still be the big guy (or gal), control as much of the ownership stock as you want (or can), and be the ultimate decision maker. But what you need is to bring specialized help that will complement you and/or assist you in leading the company. Find out what your strengths and weaknesses are and bring people in with the strengths that you are missing. *(See questionnaire in this section)*

Work on reaching the point in the growth of the company (and your personal growth) when you can step back and focus on the company's direction, rather than on micromanaging every account. In other words, strive to be working **ON** the business rather than **IN** the business all the time.

***Coaching suggestion:** You need to make time to working ON the business despite having to fight fires almost 24/7. One way of doing it is to go to the office an hour earlier than you normally do, close the door to your office and put a "do not disturb sign on the door", send all incoming calls to the voice mailbox and instruct all employees not to disturb you during that time. Clear your mind of the fires around you (easy to say, right?) and think about what you can do to improve the company and yourself.*

Once you come up with a list, write it down, develop plans to implement the actions, and set deadlines to make them happen (and hold yourself accountable to do it). You notice I didn't suggest doing this at home, and that's because I want you to separate business from family, but if you believe you have better chances of a quiet time at home, then by all means do it at home. Wherever you do it you must have the discipline to concentrate only in actions to improve the company and yourself.

As a second-stage CEO you need to not only assume but to embrace new roles; you need to change from being the doer to being the manager or the coach. For this you need to start delegating, and as we see in the *Delegation* section of this book, delegation is not easy to learn, to do it right.

The entrepreneur is used to doing many jobs and wearing many hats, but as he/she goes into stage two that needs to change. Rather than having a list of things to do, as many entrepreneurs do, they need to put together a list of things to stop doing and work on this faithfully. The health of the business and the health and happiness of the CEO are at stake.

As an entrepreneur and lone or nearly lone employee you didn't have to communicate with a lot of people, but in your new role things are different, you have external and internal audiences listening to your "wise words" and directions. Your vision is not just your vision anymore, it is the vision of the company and you must continually communicate it throughout the organization.

Too Big to be Small and Too Small to be Big

Second-stage companies are those that have grown past the startup stage but have not grown to maturity. They have enough employees to represent a challenge to the owner/CEO and started to add professional managers, but they do not yet have a full-scale management team. They are in what Doug Tatum calls "*No Mans Land*".

Typically, the complexity of a business is driven by the number of employees that it has. Another telling fact is when the efforts of the entrepreneur are not enough to get the business to perform, or when the entrepreneur struggles with issues and decisions that he/she has never faced before. The feeling that they are losing control of their business is a horrible one and must be eradicated as soon as possible.

But, who says you have to have a large business in order to be successful? It is important for business owners to understand that is OK to be small. What's important is your happiness and if you are happy owning a successful small company, then it's OK to stay small.

Bo Burlingham in *"Small Giants"; "Companies That Chose to be Great Instead of Big"* [3] praises those companies that are successful while remaining small. There is a popular saying that contends that "if you don't grow you die", but growth can be achieved in different forms; a business can grow in profits, in technical competence, in market recognition, and in other ways without necessarily growing in size.

If you reach your vision and can have fun doing it, you can consider yourself successful regardless of the number of employees you have or the total revenues you obtain. Nevertheless, you need to know that even staying small, to be successful you will need to have at least some of the tools mentioned above.

Characteristics of Founding CEOs vs. Second CEOs

So far we looked at founding owners reaching the second stage and how they adapt to it. Now let's look at how they compare with CEOs that are not the founders of the company, but came in when the company had already reached the second stage.

Founders have the passion for the business that a successor cannot have; it is natural that when you create an entity you will have a passion for it that nobody else can have. As a comparison, it's the difference between your love for your own children and how you love other people's children. Both founders and successors can be equal in the energy devoted to the business, but how that energy is applied is different.

Founders own the dream and their focus is in reaching the vision they created and—most likely—in creating personal wealth. Successors have a longer term focus and possibly focusing on a successful exit strategy and providing shareholders value (that may also include personal wealth). A founder has his fingers in every part of the business with a desire to build his "baby", but his successor will want to develop the organization to obtain both growth and profitability.

A founder has the opportunity to establish a culture from scratch, while the successor has a need to nurture it and ensure it does not degrade. As he builds the culture, the owner also starts building the organization, and the second CEO has the responsibility to use it most effectively while continuing to build it.

The owner entrepreneur by his nature is willing to take risks that the second CEO cannot take, but he, the second CEO, is chartered with taking the business to the next level with discipline and systems, and to validate the vision of the owner.

In the revised edition of *"Growing Pains: Transitioning From An Entrepreneurship To A Professionally Managed Firm"*[4], Eric G. Flamholtz and Yvonne Randle provide advice on how to survive and thrive through the "rigorous organizational demands of rapid growth."

They describe seven predictable stages of growth from start-up to mature corporation:

- New venture; the entrepreneur has an idea or decides that he can do something better than others and make money at it, so he starts a business.
- Expansion; the business is successful and starts to grow nicely.
- Professionalization; as the growth continues the organization starts to grow too and department managers are now carrying most of the load.
- And consolidation, diversification, integration, and decline and revitalization.

The first three are the stages that we deal in this book; the rest of them apply to large companies and are not relevant for us.

Regardless of what stage your business is at, you need to know the important steps to be taken at each successive stage so that you can build the best possible foundation for long-term success.

References:
1. YourEconomy.org (http://www.youreconomy.org/) accessed February 18, 2011.
2. Doug Tatum, *No Man's Land: A Survival Manual for Growing Midsize Companies,* Portfolio Trade; Reprint edition (December 30, 2008).
3. Bo Burlingham *Small Giants; Companies That Chose to be Great Instead of Big,* Kindle Edition, (Mar 27, 2007).
4. Eric G. Flamholtz and Yvonne Randle, *"Growing Pains: Transitioning From An Entrepreneurship To A Professionally Managed Firm",* Jossey-Bass; 3 edition (April 13, 2000).

Your Strengths and Weaknesses as CEO

While it is critically important to identify one's weaknesses and work to eliminate them, it is equally important to recognize one's strengths and emphasize them in the performance of the CEO Job.

Please list your strengths and weaknesses as you perceive them, in the following areas;

Leadership

Management

Vision

Strategic Thinking and Planning

Team Development and Motivating

Resource Management

Delegation and Accountability

And The Four "Es" of Jack Welch:

Energy Level – *dedicated to the business*

Energize Others – *ability to motivate*

Edge – *ability to make tough decisions*

Execution – *the ability to deliver on commitments*

Chapter IV - Leadership

Leadership is the ability to influence, inspire and motivate others to accomplish a specific objective.

Ken Blanchard and Drea Zigarmi in *"Leadership and the One Minute Manager: Increasing Effectiveness Through Situational Leadership"* [1] wrote:

"You may think of the words "manager" and "leader" as two concepts representing opposite ends of a continuum. The term manager typifies the more structured, controlled, analytical, orderly and rule-oriented end of the continuum. The leader end of the continuum connotes a more experimental, visionary, unstructured, flexible, and impassioned side. Managers and leaders are not the same. They think differently internally, and behave differently externally.

In truth, leaders and managers tend to see different aspects of work and organizational life as important, and therefore, worthy of their time. They tend to treat people differently and they spontaneously react to others differently. They tend to allow their people to have different focuses and to limit their people in different ways. You can understand why these differences result in varied organizational cultures and, finally, why different reactions result from those who are being led."

"A leader is one who knows the way, goes the way, and shows the way", John Maxwell.

"A leader is best when people barely know he exists, when his work is done, his aim fulfilled, they will say: we did it ourselves"; Lao Tsu.

"Great leaders are almost always great simplifiers who can cut through argument, debate, and doubt, to offer solution everybody can understand"; General Colin Powell.

"Progress occurs when courageous, skillful leaders seize the opportunity to change things for the better"; Harry Truman.

"No institution can possibly survive if it needs geniuses or supermen to manage it. It must be organized in such a way as to be able to get along under a leadership composed of average human beings"; Peter Drucker.

For a business to succeed it needs leadership. The quality of its leadership drives the ability of the business to meet its own goals and needs, as well as the needs of its stakeholders. It is important to realize that just because someone is in a leadership position, doesn't necessarily mean they should be.

You are the owner but this title does not guarantee leadership, and the business needs a leader if it is going to succeed. You probably consider yourself a good manager, but that's not enough; your transition from entrepreneur to CEO requires you to become a leader. Management is a business skill; leadership is a people's skill. A leader realizes that success depends on the people that surround him and the play of the entire team.

As the owner and CEO, you are by definition, its leader. As such you are supposed to continue to grow both in your job and in your personal life moving toward where you want to be and you want your company to be.

Accepting the position of CEO is a great responsibility; it can be both invigorating and terrifying at the same time. This job is your choice and to succeed at it you must forget the terrifying part that may hold you back. You must reinforce the invigorating part and set yourself fully on becoming the best you can be at it.

A leader has the vision for the company and communicates it well and continuously. He is the dream, his dream of the company and transmits it to all others. He is not an omnipotent personality but only a member of the team; he is the MVP of the team, but still only a member of it. "My way or the highway" leadership styles are not what a business needs; this style would result in a fractured culture and in a non-productive organization.

Over thirty-three thousand studies conducted to analyze the qualities of business leaders, identified vision as their most common trait. Leaders prefer to think about where they are going rather than analyzing the past. They also showed that only about ten percent of the general population has this ability to focus on the future. Because of the job you chose, you need to be among this group. Self-confidence in your ability to focus on the future gives you the ability to strategize.

Alpine skier Kjetil André said "Excellence is obtained by those who care more than others think is wise, who risk more than others think is safe, and dream more than others think is practical". You must aim for excellence if you are to reach success for yourself and your company.

So, the real work for you, the business owner, is rising to the challenge of becoming the best leader that you can be, because if you don't develop those skills your business will stagnate. Fortunately, even stagnant business can be revived with effective leadership.

- Do not be the boss; be the leader.
- Authority does not create commitment.
- Authority does not create change
- Authority will not inspire contribution.

Are Leaders Born or Made?

The common saying "leaders are born, not made" is not completely true. Owners can "learn" to become leaders but they must possess the qualifications and talent required; without them and the desire to forgo other duties in order to become the leader, the transition is, at best, uncertain.

Leadership is a combination of skills that can be learned, practiced, and perfected by anyone willing to put in the time and effort. But success in leadership requires more than just the discipline and the desire to do it. It also takes a dose of natural talent and even coaching.

Coaching suggestion: If you are not sure of your leadership talents use one of the many self-assessments available to determine where you are in that respect, and then develop a plan to improve what you can.

True leadership is what changes entrepreneurship into a real business and thus, it is imperative for you to develop effective leadership skills. Steven Covey said: "Management is efficiency in climbing the ladder of success; leadership determines whether the ladder is leaning against the right wall" [2].

To be a leader you must have followers, and followers are not given; you can't assign followers, you must earn them. Just as beauty is in the eye of the beholder, leadership is in the eye of the led and the perception of you as a leader must be earned and respected.

Developing leadership skills is a process that may take time, but you must understand that if you apply yourself in your daily functions to becoming the best leader that you can be, you will succeed.

Coaching suggestion: keep notes of what you identify as strengths and weaknesses in your leadership skills, and how you perceive the progress you make. Use those notes to motivate you to improve in them.

For you as an entrepreneur one of the challenges is to gain the strength and insight to not just manage but to lead. Leadership is about making other people better and consequently sometimes you must put your personal goals aside in favor of other people's success. Making other people a priority is a challenge, but I am confident that when you limit your own needs and fears in favor of your people's benefits, you will discover a new level of energy and meaning channeled to leadership.

Be aware too of your need to project a certain image as this can be distracting and rob you of energy to pursue what's really important. Any needs to be seen as superior, intelligent, likable, friendly or decisive can lead you to suppress critical feedback loops. In other words, you must choose between the image that you would like to portray and what a real leader should look like or act like.

The Main Functions of a Leader

An old and well known proverb states that leadership is "doing the right thing", while management is "doing things right". From this we can also deduct that management is about tactical skills and leadership is more about strategic skills. Another differentiation extracted from this is that management usually refers to operational levels of the organization, and leadership to the executive levels.

In a small company the differences become less marked and the two disciplines many times overlap. In the management ranks leadership is a trait needed by all, albeit in different degrees.

What are the main functions of a business leader and the things that you must excel at to be a good leader?

- Defining, developing and leveraging company core competencies.
- Defining and implementing strategy and vision; defining the critical success factors.
- Building the culture of the organization; a culture based on values.
- Team building as part of the culture; getting the right people and placing them in the right places.
- Developing and allocating resources; human, financial, physical and all other resources.
- Driving performance-based results.

The ability to think, inspire, motivate and empower are essential components of leadership. As a business owner you get caught up in the daily grind of getting the job done and you probably fail to set time aside to think and reflect on the proactive work that can lead to innovating, creating a vision and choosing a strategic position. This is an essential part of leadership as it is the part that focuses on the future.

To inspire is the most visible component of leadership. To be effective as a leader you must inspire, motivate and energize, but you must also set the example. You must "sell" the vision but also confront reality. You must ask the right questions and give hope for a bright future but you must be realistic about your ability and the business' capabilities.

To motivate others is to mobilize people to perform a task. To move a task to completion you must be able to build coalitions, set targets and encourage networks. You must engage with and influence key players and their contributions.

Empowering people is an essential part of delegating to get things done through others, so execution depends on managing authority and delegating power. Part of this task involves allocating resources, deploying assets and even disempowering those who misuse the authority. Keep in mind that if you are the only one making decisions, you are not much of a leader.

You must operate well on all four of the above dimensions to get a passport to great leadership. Good leaders seek to create an environment where people understand the strategy, have loyalty to the company and are empowered to spot strategic opportunities. You must be able to and feel comfortable with getting out of the way and letting people to function independently. Obviously to do this you must have the right people, the right organization and the right culture.

The key to success is creating a structure that aligns the organization's goals, culture and people.

An effective leader is only as good as the people surrounding him and the culture that demands dignity and respect and a commitment to the vision and goals of the company. Employees won't start respecting you until you start respecting them, and they will not trust you as a leader until you start trusting them as the valuable team members they are.

As the leader you must create new roads and must show that road to others by being the example as a member of the team. You must be committed to your dream and transmit that dream to the team. You must be secure in your position but caring to others and accountable for your actions.

You must communicate well and serve the cause that you are committed to, as well as serving the organization and stakeholders. Communication must be a two-way street; communicate with words but listen with your heart considering what's important to others.

Peter Drucker, as cited in *www.ForbesASAP.com* [3], sees the following as true leadership traits:

- Leaders start projects by asking, "What has to be done?" instead of "What do I need?"
- Leaders next ask, "What do I have to do to make a real contribution?" The answer best suits the leader's strengths and the needs of the project.
- Leaders continually ask, "What are my organization's purposes and objectives?" and "What qualifies as acceptable performance and adds to the bottom line?"
- Leaders don't want clones of themselves as employees. They never ask, "Do I like or dislike this employee?" But they won't tolerate poor performance.
- Leaders aren't threatened by others who have strengths they lack.

Good leaders don't manage people, they manage goals.

Your Leadership Capabilities

I'm sure you got to where you are because you "get stuff done"; you are the go-to person and key to everything, so leadership skills were not part of the job description before, but now they should be. Make learning leadership skills an item of priority. If at all possible work with a good coach in honing your leadership.

You probably think that you are a good leader, and probably it is so but, nevertheless, there is always room for improvement. There is much to be learned in the subject of leadership and the more you learn the better you will feel and the more respect you will pull towards you from others.

Let's do an analysis of your leadership capabilities; better yet you do a self-analysis responding to the following questions and be totally honest with yourself:

- Am I a visionary and think strategically rather than implementing the "idea of the week"?
- Do I have the ability to formulate ideas for the business; to identify opportunities and the need for change; to visualize what the business will look like in the future?
- Can I think strategically and not just tactically?
- Do I have the ability to see the big picture and decide what actions I need to take to get the business to where I want it to get; can I create the policies to govern the business?
- Is my company as successful as it should be (or could be)?
- Do I hold people responsible and accountable without micromanaging?
- Do I handle stressful situations well without losing focus and direction? Can I function well in a crisis?
- Am I good at building teams and motivating team members?
- Do I set as a priority to think about what other people in the organization need to be successful?
- Do I have a core group of people who help me make important decisions? Do I allow them to make them?
- Do I accept the responsibility for problems instead of blaming others? Do I accept the fact that I'm ultimately responsible for everything that happens in the business; do I give credit where credit is due?
- Do I help people achieve mutually agreed on goals?
- Do I make the difficult choices that sometimes have to be made, in a calm and confident manner?
- Do I show calm when the waters get rough? Am I good under pressure?
- Do I set an example of the type of behavior needed to enforce the culture of the company?
- Do I hold myself accountable for all actions I commit to take as an individual and as the leader?

- Do I encourage and lead change initiatives and promote continuous improvement?
- Do I drive change and not just cope with it? Do I promote change as a key element of success?
- Am I a good communicator? Do I possess the skill of communicating the Vision and strategy; do I instill in the organization the enthusiasm and dedication that I have for the business?

Coaching suggestion: If any of these questions call for a "no" answer start developing a plan to change from a negative to a positive answer. Be honest with yourself and be as candid as you can possibly be, and make the plan a commitment that you must hold yourself accountable for.

Some specific suggestions to increase your leadership effectiveness:

- Get feedback on your present level of effectiveness from your peers and coworkers that you respect.
- Pick the most important behaviors for change; those you believe will enhance your effectiveness as a leader. Work on these and when you see enough improvement, pick one or tow others and repeat the process.
- Seek continuous feedback from others as to your leadership performance. Listen to their ideas and make the changes that you believe are more critical.
- Listen to your employees too; they will amaze you with what you don't know.
- Give yourself 30 to 60 minutes a day to collect data, practice and plan the next move (to improve).

Coaching suggestion: Joining a Peer Advisory Board will benefit in several ways, but most importantly it would help you develop as a CEO and to manage the day-to-day issues of your company. (See "Advisory Boards and Coaching" in the Appendices).

Level 5 Leaders

Jim Collins in the well-known book *"Good to Great"*[4] defines the "Level 5 Hierarchy" as follows:

> Level 1 – Highly capable individual; makes contributions through talent, knowledge, skills and good work habits.
>
> Level 2 – Contributing team member; contributes to the achievement of group objectives.
>
> Level 3 – Competent manager; organizes people and resources toward he pursuit of predetermined objectives.
>
> Level 4 – Effective leader; Catalyses commitment to a clear and compelling vision.
>
> Level 5 – Executive; Builds enduring greatness through personal humility and professional will.

Jim Collins says that Level 5 leaders:

- Create superb results. Are clear catalysts in the transition from good to great. Demonstrate and unwavering resolve to do what must be done to produce the best long term results, no matter how difficult.
- Set the standard of building and enduring a great company and will settle for nothing less.
- Look out the window, not in the mirror. Meaning that they give credit to those who contribute in a success, rather than taking credit because "they are the boss". However, they look into the mirror when something does not give the results expected.

Can you identify yourself with the above statements from Collins? Think about it carefully and reflect on what you are missing to get to the steps up to Level 5 leadership.

I prefer to use a different version developed by my colleague John Dini, included at the end of this section. Do an honest evaluation of yourself and see where you are in the progression to "The Strategist". In practice though, as the owner of a small business I don't expect you to be one hundred percent in

Level VII. More likely you will be spread over multiple levels.

> **Coaching suggestion:** *Complete the chart and visit it periodically to see if you are making progress towards achieving a higher level in the leadership development process. Work with your coach to see what you need to do to get there.*

Realistically, there are times when you need to "work *in* the business" rather than "working *on* the business". Case in point: in a downturn when you need to "wear many hats" and contribute in the trenches, you can be forced to postpone your efforts to advance in the process. My advice however, is to go back to your plan to advance as soon as possible.

For most entrepreneurs and business owners working on their leadership skills most often goes to the bottom of the list of things to do; however, it is imperative for you to learn how you can take yourself to the next level. As with everything else, to be good at leadership requires practice. Start today a conscientious practice of applying the above requirements and keep judging yourself on each of them.

Evaluating the leadership qualities of the management team should be an essential part of developing the organization. One way to do this is to use what is commonly called a 360 degree survey in which all members of the team evaluate each other. Two examples are included at the end of this chapter.

"Continuous improvement is better than delayed perfection"; Mark Twain.

From *"Good to Great"*:
- Do not confuse celebrity with leadership, and
- Start your journey now; do not reject wisdom just because it comes late.

References:
1. Ken Blanchard and Drea Zigarmi, *Leadership and the One Minute Manager: Increasing Effectiveness Through Situational Leadership*, (William Morrow; 1st edition, October 20, 1999).
2. Brainy Quote, Stephen R. Covey quotes, http://www.brainyquote.com/quotes/authors/s/stephen_covey.html.
3. Peter Drucker, http://www.forbes.com/asap/, Fall 2002.
4. Jim Collins, *Good to Great,* (Harper Business; 1st edition, October 16, 2001).

What's Your Level?

We say it all the time: "I want my business to get to the next level." Consultants, business books and seminars all promise it. "This will take your company to the next level." What is the next level? Do you know what level your business is on now? Do you know where you are taking your company? Do you know how you are going to get there?

Level I: The Producer

You are responsible for the daily production of the company. Revenue flows directly from your personal efforts. You may have assistance, but all employees perform tasks that you assign. Frequently, strategy and tactics are luxuries that you put aside until after hours or when you have some free time.

Level II: The Entrepreneur

You have employees who handle routine production under your supervision. They make the product or deliver the service as you direct. You may have a few employees who make sales calls, but you still have direct responsibility for major customers.

Level III: The Manager

You have a layer of supervision between you and at least some of your employees. You do not directly hire or terminate everyone in the company, but you probably still approve all employment decisions. Your focus is on administrative tasks, including budgeting, cash management and productivity. You have defined some structures and guidelines, which allow others to make decisions that are in line with your wishes.

Level IV: The Specialist

You have defined your role in the company according to what you prefer or what you feel it is that you do best. You focus on a single functional area of the business (e.g. sales, design or production). Managers have both authority and responsibility for other functional aspects of the business. They manage according to systems you have developed or approved.

Level V: The Executive

You are not involved in day to day activities of the business. Your time is spent interacting with other executives, networking, and raising the company's community presence. You manage largely by report. You allocate resources to management, and determine organizational priorities. Systems are developed and implemented without your direct input.

Level VI: The Strategist

You decide the direction and the vision of the organization, and others figure out how to make it happen. You are responsible for anticipating trends, identifying market opportunities and creating alliances. You manage by financial statements, with little input as to how the organization is managed, as long as it complements the culture you have selected for the company.

Leadership Activities

Review the list of leadership activities under each of the 5 Key Leadership Activities headings. Identify what you consider are the 3 most important leadership activities over the next 2 years, in each of the 5 Key Leadership Activities.

Defining and Implementing Strategy

- Our Company's Strategy is clearly defined
- The Strategy is communicated and reinforced on a regular basis
- Strategic planning framework goes at least 3 years into the future
- Strategic planning process is understood by managers
- Information connections with customers and the marketplace provide early indications of dynamics that might require a review of strategy
- Goal setting at all levels is linked to the strategy
- Managers participate in developing the strategy
- Business decision making processes are regularly evaluated and changed as needed

Defining, Developing and Leveraging Company Core Competencies

- Standards for defining a core competency are clearly understood
- Company core competencies are well-defined
- Strategy optimizes core competencies for competitive advantage
- Market data, customer information and other trends are assessed and evaluated on a regular basis
- Search for new/additional company core competencies is on-going
- Information connections with customers, markets and the competition provides early indication of needs or opportunities that could affect core competencies

Developing and Utilizing Human Resource Assets

- All positions have well-defined job descriptions and candidate qualifications
- Employees understand their roles, responsibilities and parameters of authority
- Interviewing and selection skills and processes are effective
- Recruitment and retention plans are in place
- Budgets for compensation and training and development are, within the economic realities of the business, fair and rewarding of performance.

- A process for identifying and implementing training and development needs exists and is utilized
- Training and development objectives are part of company, individual departments and individual employees performance objectives
- The development of people is a management and company metric
- Employee knowledge and abilities are well-utilized
- Decision making and problem solving authority are appropriately delegated
- All employees understand the desired behaviors and core values
- Coaches and mentors are available to people
- Succession planning processes are organized and robust
- People are viewed as an organizational asset, not the property of any one department

Driving Performance Based Results

- Measures exist for short, mid and long-term objectives of the company, departments and individuals
- Performance measures address:
  - Financial performance
  - Customer satisfaction and loyalty
  - Continuous improvement
  - Developing people

- Measurement and performance objectives between departments are linked wherever necessary
- Employees understand the key business measures and desired results
- Performance plans and reviews systems exist for all employees
- Employees understand how their performance affects company results and how it is measured
- Behavioral performance is an integral part of rewards and performance appraisal
- Progress against the objectives (company, departments, teams and individuals) is monitored and evaluated at regular and appropriate intervals
- Changes in strategy are reflected in appropriate changes in performance measures
- Shortfalls and successes in performance drive learning and improvement actions
- Rewards are directly related to measured results against objectives
- Evaluation of measurements needed and the ability to accurately measure is an on-going effort

Leading Change and Continuous Improvement

- Organizational change requirements have been identified
- A process for implementing change is in place and used
- A process is used to monitor external changes (e.g., markets, products, competition, customer preferences) and determine if an organizational response is needed
- Continuous improvement is viewed as a proactive organizational effort, not just the role of the quality department
- There is a culture of internal customer-supplier relationships
- Best practices in key systems and processes have been identified and implemented

- Baseline information on key systems and processes has been collected and is used to drive continuous improvement
- Customer feedback processes are used to drive continuous improvement
- Change is, wherever possible, proactive rather than reactive
- Creating and sustaining organizational culture and core values is a core leadership process

Leadership Alignment

Effective leadership includes the creation of the culture that supports the Vision of the company. Leadership behavior is directly connected with the culture and by influencing the behavior of others it can have a marked effect on the culture throughout the organization. Your leadership behavior must develop an effective work environment that supports the strategic objectives of the company.

Grade yourself in each of the following questions and determine your score in your leadership behavior. Use a scale of 100 where the maximum score represents full compliance with the subject.

1. Have I clearly established the direction, creating the vision, values and strategies needed to achieve my goals? Are they formalized?

2. Are my Vision, Mission and purpose clear to me AND my team members?

3. Have I crystallized my thinking so that I know where I stand now and where I want to go?

4. Has the leadership team clearly identified the desired culture and the supporting business case?

5. Have I clearly and frequently communicated the vision and strategies to insure people understand and know what part they must play in achieving the goals?

6. Do I delegate responsibility and authority, involve people in some of the decisions, motivate and energize them to be resourceful and overcome typical bureaucratic barriers?

7. Do I help to create change by supporting the free flow of ideas and implementing processes and resources that are consistent with the culture?

8. Is there full buy-in by the organization on the target culture and strategic goals?

9. Do I find ways to satisfy the basic needs for achieving, belonging, recognition, self-esteem, a sense of control over one's life, feedback and role modeling?

10. Have the leaders and managers analyzed how they need to change their behaviors? Do I know what behaviors need to change throughout the organization? Are there visible role models?

11. Is the organization prepared to provide any necessary training and coaching and hold people accountable for those behaviors?

12. Do the leaders establish good working relationships with many people in the organization to create a collaborative, participatory environment where there are shared vision and goals?

13. Do I have a detailed, written plan to achieve each important personal and organizational goal, and have I set a deadline for attainment?

14. Are my personal goals balanced with the need to help my organization achieve?

15. Do my personal goals represent a balance among the six areas of life (family, financial, mental, physical, social and spiritual)?

16. Do I have a burning desire to achieve the goals I have set for myself?

17. Have I developed within my team members and myself a passion for achieving the success we've envisioned?

18. Do I have supreme confidence in our ability to reach our goal?

19. Have I accepted personal responsibility for the success of my team, and for the achievement of my own personal goals?

20. Do I possess the iron-willed determination to follow through regardless of circumstances or what others say, think or do?

Your Score in Leadership Alignment

1 to 40: You are not the CEO that the company needs to achieve its Vision. Work with a coach to start developing your behavior as soon as possible if you want to achieve the Vision (do you have a Vision for the business?)

41 to 80: You probably have the capabilities to develop your behavior in favor of the right organizational culture, but you are consumed by the urgent issues and don't work on the important issues. You need to start working on the culture today.

81 to 120: You are doing a good job but can improve it by identifying your shortcomings and applying the actions to correct them. You must establish clear objectives and getting senior team buy-in. Identify and communicate examples of behavioral alignment.

121 to 160: You have a fairly good handle on the leadership alignment of your company. Competent leadership is emerging and most strategic goals are being achieved. Make sure that you do what's necessary to maintain it and to continue to improve it.

161 to 200: The direction of the organization and identification of the efforts to achieve the strategies are clearly established, communicated and supported throughout the organization. Leadership and culture are aligned and support each other. You must continue to dedicate the effort to maintain these conditions.

Identify what actions need to be taken to support the culture and direction of the organization.

Chapter V - Setting Goals

The road to "someday" leads to the town of nowhere. Procrastination is the silent killer

—Anthony Robbins

Delete "someday" from your vocabulary; set firm dates for your goals.

Insanity is doing the same thing and expecting different results.

—Albert Einstein

Invite and drive change in your organization; without change your company will not grow.

If you don't set goals you can't regret not reaching them.

—Yogi Berra

Get in the habit of setting goals and putting in the effort to meeting or exciting them.

If you set your goals low enough you will inevitably meet them.

—O. R. Viva

Make your goals ambitious but realistic; you will feel a sense of accomplishment when you reach them.

Your Personal and Business Goals

The discussion that follows is intended to apply both to personal goals and to business goals; i.e., the goals that you set for yourself, to become the best CEO that you can be, and the goals that you set for the business to succeed. The business goals should (must?) be developed by the entire team, not just by you. This discussion also applies to goals set for the team and for individuals within it.

Successful goal setting isn't as simple as wanting something. To have a goal is more than just wishful thinking; it's a process that has to be followed. Setting goals is more than deciding what you want to do. It involves figuring out what you need to do to get where you want to go and how long it will take you to get there.

Goals are set to meet defined objectives and the way in which you set them will affect how effective you will be in making them happen. Goals should be straightforward and emphasize what you want to accomplish.

Focus on Your Strengths. Search out the opportunities in the areas that you or your company are comfortable or familiar in already. If goals involve a new technology, process or market where you don't have experience, focus on your strengths to go after those goals and get the help you need to reach them. Successful goal setting means continually utilizing your strengths to get you ahead while keeping a secondary eye on the weaker parts of your game.

- The first step to success is to know where you want to go. The second step is to have a plan to get there. Your goals are your road map. Follow them and you'll be well on your way.

- Start with your long-term objectives. Next, establish short-term goals. These include monthly, weekly and even daily targets that will move you toward your long-term objectives.

Evaluate. Constantly strive to see what is working, and what is not. Don't restrain yourself from tweaking things that aren't working as well as you would like, and expand where you are doing things well.

Coaching suggestion: Set a weekly or monthly reminder to go over your progress and readjust where necessary. Sometimes the difference between successful goal setting and failing is a simple tweak or two.

Be careful not to push yourself or your team to hard or two fast and be careful not to set yourself or your team up for failure. You have to stretch your talents and your company's resources to grow, but it's important to set reasonable goals.

Ensure the goals you set are very specific, clear and easy. For example, instead of setting a goal to increase revenues set a specific goal to increase revenues by ten percent by year end and another ten percent for the following six months. Business goals must be in line with the strategic plan, and personal goals must be in line with the personal roadmap (see appropriate section).

Always use the S.M.A.R.T. model for setting goals.
- Specific
- Measurable
- Attainable
- Realistic & Responsible
- Timeline

Specific

Goals should be straightforward and emphasize what you want to happen. Specifics help you to focus your efforts and clearly define what you are going to do.

Specific is the What, Why, and How of the SMART model.
- What are you going to do? Use action words such as direct, organize, coordinate, lead, develop, plan, build etc.
- Why is this important to do at this time? What do you want to ultimately accomplish?
- How are you going to do it? (By...)

Measurable

If you can't measure it, you can't manage it. In the broadest sense, the whole goal statement is a measure for the project; if the goal is accomplished, there is success. Short-term or small measurements should be built into the goal in order to monitor progress or make adjustments.

Choose a goal with measurable progress, so you can see the change occur. Establish concrete criteria for measuring progress toward the attainment of each goal you set. When you measure your progress, you stay on track, reach your target dates, and experience the exhilaration of achievement that spurs you on to continued effort required to reach your goals.

Attainable

When you identify goals that are very important to you or to your business, you dedicate the effort to make them come true. You develop the attitudes, abilities, skills, and financial capacity to reach them. On the other hand, you probably won't commit to doing goals that are too far into the future or presently out of your reach. You may have the best of intentions, but knowing that it's a stretch for you, subconsciously you will stop giving it your best effort.

The feeling of success that you get by seeing progress in attaining a goal helps you to remain motivated.

Realistic

This is not a synonym for "easy." Realistic, in this case, means doable. It means that the learning curve is not too steep; that you have the skills needed to do the work and that the project fits with the overall strategy and goals of the organization. A realistic project should push the skills and knowledge of the people working on it but it shouldn't break them.

Be sure to set goals that you can attain with some effort. If a goal is too difficult you may be setting yourself for failure, but if it's too easy it may send a message that you aren't very capable. Set the bar high enough for a satisfying achievement.

Timely

Set a timeframe for the goal. Putting an end point on your goal gives you a clear target to work towards. If you don't set a time, the commitment is too vague. It tends not to happen because you put it off in favor of "urgent" or perceivably more important things. Without a time limit, there's no urgency to start taking action.

Time too must be measurable, attainable and realistic.

Goal Setting as Motivator

Goal setting encourages participants to put in greater effort as they are driven to meeting them, and because managers are compelled to follow them, there is little chance of inadequate effort going unnoticed. Employees who participate in the process of developing the goals—either for them or for the business—tend to set higher goals than if the goals were set for them.

Goals focus attention towards goal-relevant activities and away from goal-irrelevant activities. They act as motivators; higher goals will induce greater effort while low goals induce lesser effort. However, if people are limited by constraints with regard to resources their work pace will suffer.

Inspiring Your Employees

Getting people to accomplish something is much easier if they have the inspiration to do so. For employees to be inspired you need to be passionate about the business. If you as the leader project great enthusiasm for the business, you will generate a trickle-down effect in the organization. If you do not communicate excitement, how can you expect your people to get excited about it?

Your primary responsibility is to develop people and enable them to reach their full potential. Your people may come from diverse backgrounds, but they all have goals they want to accomplish. Create a "people environment" where they truly can be all they can be.

You will create that environment by having employees involved in the decision making process. If they are, they will participate much more enthusiastically than if you just give them orders. When given specific goals, employees tend to perform at a higher level. Telling them to do their best or giving no guidance increases ambiguity about what is expected and results in inferior performance. Employees need a set goal or model in order to perform at their best.

Don't make goals too easy or unimportant; increasing your employees' goal difficulty increases their challenges and enhances the amount of effort expended to achieve them. However, goals must be realistic. The more difficult goals lead to increased performance if they seem feasible, but if they seem too high, employees will give up when they fail to achieve them.

Listen to your employees and tell them you value their opinions, but you need to be sincere, not just give lip service. Prove it by incorporating their ideas when it makes sense to do so. Providing feedback enhances the effects of goal setting. Performance feedback keeps their behavior directed on the right target and encourages them to work harder to achieve the goal.

> *Coaching suggestion: I favor a "Management by Objectives" culture and in MBO employees are judged and graded by their accomplishment of goals. See the section on "Employee Reviews" in Chapter VI dealing with this issue.*

The enhancement of performance through goals requires feedback. Goal-setting may have little effect if individuals cannot check where the state of their performance is in relation to their goal. Let them know clearly and often how they are performing and how their performance affects (either positively or negatively) the performance of the company.

> *Coaching suggestion: do not wait to check on the progress of a project or task until a goal's target date is upon you because it will be too late to make corrections or to nudge the employee to improve progress. Instead, set firm periodic review dates when setting the goal and check on progress made and quality of the performance. This rule applies to all supervisors managing goals, from you, the CEO, to the lower line supervisor.*

Limitations

You must realize that goal-setting may have some limitations. In an organization, a goal of an employee may not align with the goals of the organization as a whole and they may even come into direct conflict with the goals of the company. It is critical then to assure that individual goals match the company's goals. Without aligning goals between the organization and the individual, performance may suffer.

Moreover, for complex tasks, goal-setting may actual impair performance. If an individual becomes more preoccupied with meeting the goals, rather than performing tasks, performance may suffer. These limitations are prevented by making sure that the goals follow the SMART definition.

Setting Goals Effectively

In summary, answer the following questions when you are working on a strategic plan:

- Am I thinking the goals through and all aspects of them?
- What skills do I (the company) need to achieve them?
- What information & knowledge do I (the company) need?
- What help, assistance or collaboration do I (the company) need?
- What resources do I (the company) need?
- What can block progress?
- Am I (my team) making valid assumptions?
- Is there a better way of doing it?

Coaching suggestion: Train your employees to set and manage goals. Regardless of their title or position they should be knowledgeable in the subject and should use goals on a regular basis. You may want to consider contracting a consultant to do the teaching.

Yearly Goals And Objectives

To ensure continued growth and profitability for your businesses, to practice continuous improvement, to maintain or improve your personal health and family life, and to give us the accountability that everyone needs, you must set goals based on the strategies defined for your businesses.

I encourage you to set personal and business-related goals that you commit to achieve over the next period (typically a year). Committing involves devising ways to accomplish them. These can be simple decisions or they can be comprehensive plans that include mayor changes and/or actions, depending on the goals to be achieved.

The following template can help you set those goals. It only includes simple measurements that you can use to monitor the progress of your company and your progress as an entrepreneur and company leader. It also includes a personal scorecard to ensure the correct balance of business and personal life.

Your goals should be SMART, that is specific, measurable, action-oriented, realistic and time-constrained, as well as have the potential to result in significant impact to your business. You may want to discuss these goals with your partner or key members of your staff.

1. In the calendar year 20XX our revenues were/will be $_____, For 20YY, our Goal is $_____, an increase (decrease) of _____%.

2. The ONE THING that will most affect our ability to achieve the above goal is:

    _____

    (hint: it should be related to your areas of excellence as determined by your strategic driving force)

3. Our profit margin (gross or net - whichever you use more to manage the business) will go from _____% in 20XX to _____% in 20YY

4. We will maintain/achieve revenues per employee of:
   $ _____

5. We will maintain/achieve profits per employee of:
   $ _____

6. We will maintain/achieve expenses per employee equal to or less than: $ _____

7. The single most important improvement we can make in my company in the coming twelve months is:

   _____

8. By the end of calendar year 20YY, my personal role in the company will have changed in the following manner (moving to the Next Level as CEO):

   _____

9. The ONE THING that needs to be accomplished in order to realize the goal stated in number 8, above is (be specific: e.g. if you need to delegate, what duties must be delegated?)

   _____

10. In 20YY, the ability of my business to provide the quality of life I am seeking will be indicated by my ability to meet my goal on the following "Personal Score Card."

    _____

    (e.g.: # of nights each week I'm home for dinner, rounds of golf per month, # of total weeks of vacation;, MUST BE MEASURABLE!)

11. In 200Y I will improve my health by doing the following:

    _____

12. In 20YY I will improve my business by implementing, improving, or replacing:
(Indicate by writing the action to be done next to the issue)

Documentation/Systems _____
Training Programs _____
Marketing Program _____
Quality Program _____
Market Research _____
Strategic Planning _____
Bidding process _____
Organizational Structure _____
Policies and Procedures _____
Distinctive Competencies _____
Computer Software _____
Turnaround times _____
Staff Members _____
Cost of Goods Sold _____
Middle Management _____
Customer Satisfaction _____
Competitive Differentiation _____
Purchasing or Cost Controls _____
Value Added Services _____
Accounting Systems _____

Some may not apply to you, but think hard before you disregard them.

To help you get started, ask yourself the following:
What part of your business needs the most improvement?
What could you do to have the most positive impact on your business?
What action would give you the best ROI?
What major effort will take the year (or close to it) to accomplish?
Which project must be done first in order to accomplish the others?

Make sure that you complete all eleven statements and the list in # 12.

Part Two - Your Functional Development

Chapter VI - Planning

"If you are failing to plan you are planning to fail"

And there is another saying that goes like this:

"Managing a company without a plan is like driving a car looking only at the rear view mirror; you know where you have been but you don't know where you are going".

Planning is a vital component of managing a business and thus an essential part of your duties as the CEO.

What plans do you need to have?
- Business
- Marketing
- Sales
- Operations
- Investment
- Organization
- Others pertinent to your business

Or one all-inclusive that incorporates all of the above and is called:
- Strategic plan.

You shouldn't ignore also the following pieces:
- Succession planning (for all key positions in the company)
- Exit strategy for yourself

Strategic Plan

In real life strategy is straight forward; you pick a general direction and you implement like hell. In business you must follow a plan or at least a thinking process. First come up with a big aha! for your business; a smart, realistic, relatively fast way to obtain competitive advantage. Put the right people in the right jobs to drive the big aha! forward. Relentlessly seek out the best practices to achieve the big aha!, whether inside or out; adapt them and continuously improve them.

Strategy is simply finding the big differentiator for your company and setting a direction applying the right resources behind it and them executing with an unyielding emphasis on continuous improvement. For this you need to formulate a plan; a strategic plan.

Formal strategic planning became popular first with big companies in the 1960s. Traditional strategic planning was probably appropriate in that environment of slow changing, stable companies. It was usually very long process dictated by management and generated by those at the top of an organization or department. It was mostly carried out by specially trained, highly analytical people.

Someone once said: "Strategic planning is organizational masturbation. It makes the guy in charge feel good, but it doesn't do much for anyone else." That type of strategic planning process that was once such a great idea, has outlived its usefulness.

From my bag: Early in my career during my employment in one of the largest multinational companies, we did strategic planning every three years. We worked on it for a long time and ended with a document several inches think that we put on a shelf and didn't touch again until it was time to do the "exercise" again. What good was that for the company? Did it have any value other than forcing people to think and plan but with no chance of making it happen? How much did the "exercise" cost the company?

That form of traditional strategic planning may cost companies more than it contributes. More importantly, they often get in the way of real work—especially in small to midsize businesses, where quick adaptation is the key to survival.

That type of strategic planning may be dead, but strategy has never been more important, regardless of company size. What is needed now is a new version of strategy, one that reflects the realities of today's business environment with hypercompetitive markets, dizzying product life cycles, and increased globalization.

I dare to say that strategic planning is more important now than ever before. Strategic planning is much more than the projection of a string of financial data for some future time period. The true value is in creating aggressive but realist projections and in the foundation of those projections.

What really is strategic planning? It is *THINKING*; like that, with capital letters. Thinking about where you are and where you want to go. What you have and what you would like to have. What your business is what you would like it to be. What resources you have and what resources you need, and, most importantly, how you are going to get where you want to go and how you are going to get what you want or need to have.

Let's assume your company has long-range goals, either stated or implied, that include some measure of profitable growth. I believe it is also fair to assume that most of your competitors have similar goals. What actions will your business take to support achievement of your goals? What are your key strategies to beat your competition? How will you coordinate key programs involving decisions and actions on personnel, capital investment, R&D, new processes and production techniques, new products, new markets, or new prices?

A good strategic plan is not a static document that collects dust on a shelf (as the one in the *From my bag* example). It's a dynamic process that involves all key employees in all functions of a business. It starts with a shared vision (aside from your personal Vision) and ends with strategies and the corresponding execution, and demands a lot of collaborative thinking about goals and measurements.

A good plan leads to effectiveness in daily as well as longer-term decisions and actions. I'm of the opinion that because we live in a changing world and business environments change too, a good strategic plan is not a static plan, but one that can accept modifications as situations change; however, the strategic direction should not be altered without a major rethinking of the plan.

There are various techniques and programs promoted to do strategic planning. All claim to be the most practical, effective and low cost and most of them have some merit and validity depending on the type of business, size of company and status of the business.

For small and midsize businesses some of those plans being promoted include The One Page Business Plan [1], The Rockefeller Habits [2] (which curiously claims to result in a one-page plan), and others from different organizations, such as The Alternative Board's (TAB) Strategic Business Leadership [3]. Nevertheless, while the methods may differ, the steps to be completed and the results that must be obtained for the plan to be successful are the same or at least similar.

In the strategic planning process we must answer the following:

- Where are you? Capabilities Assessment; a thorough analysis of your company including business model, organization, resources and financial status.
- Where do you want to go? The owners' Vision for the company (not the personal vision); where do you see your company going and how.
- How do you get there? Develop the plan working with your team.
  - Develop Mission Statement to define or update the role of business.
  - Develop specific objectives to support strategic Mission.
  - Develop goals to be achieved.
  - Develop strategies to achieve the goals.
  - Develop an action plan to achieve each strategy. Action plans must be detailed and include person or persons responsible, schedule, resources needed and periodic review targets. Without an action plan objectives are merely a wish list
- How much does it cost? Resources needed for the entire plan, including people, facilities, equipment and money.
- When do you arrive? Compounded schedule to achieve the entire plan. Determine priorities and resources.

- Is it working? Review progress periodically and make the necessary adjustments to schedules, resources and results expected.
- Who is responsible? For the plan to work there must be accountability for each assignment. Each team member must be accountable to management and to the team because lack of progress in any action plan can have repercussions in the total schedule and/or cost or results.

Making Strategy Real

The first step of making strategy real is figuring out the big aha to gain sustainable competitive advantage. To do this you need to answer five sets of questions as a way to test the strategy. Assuming that you have a strategy either written or in your head. Having a strategy doesn't mean it is working.

1. What has the competition been up to?
   - What has each competitor done in the past year to change the playing fi9eld?
   - Has anyone introduced game-changing new products, new technologies or new distribution channels?
   - Are there any new entrants and what have they been up to in the past year?
2. What have you been up to?
   - What have you done in the past year to change the competitive playing field?
   - Have you bought a company, introduced a new product, stolen a competitor's sales person, or licensed a new technology?
   - Have you lost any competitive advantages that you once had, a great salesperson, a special product, a proprietary technology?
3. What the playing field looks like
   - Who are the competitors in this business, large and small, new and old?

- Who has what share, globally and in each market? Where do we fit in?
- What are the characteristics of this business? Is it commodity or high value or somewhere in between? Is it long cycle or short? Where is it on the growth curve? What are the drivers of profitability?
- What are the strengths and weaknesses of each competitor? How good are their products? How much does each of them spend on R&D? How big is each sales force? How performance driven is each culture?
- Who are their businesses main customers and how do they buy?

4. What's around the corner?
   - What scares you most in the years ahead?
   - What 1 or 2 things can a competitor do to nail you?
   - What new products or technologies could your competitors launch that may change the game?
   - What M&A deals could knock you off your feet?

5. What's your winning move?
   - What can you do to change the playing field? Is it an acquisition, a new product, globalization?
   - What can you do to make your customers stick to you more than ever before and more than to anyone else?

What You Need To Do

1. Relentless upgrade your team using every encounter as an opportunity to evaluate, coach and build self-confidence.
2. Make sure people not only see the Vision but they leave and breathe it.
3. Get into everyone's skin, exuding positive energy and optimism.
4. Establish trust with candor, transparence and credit.
5. Have the confidence to make unpopular decisions and tough calls.

6. Probe and push with a curiosity that borders on skepticism, making sure people's questions are answered with action.
7. Inspire risk taking and learning by setting the example.
8. Celebrate.

A strategic plan must predict the future for the business and the organization, keeping past performance as a reference, and remembering that today is yesterday's future.

The process includes the following steps:
- Gather information
- Assess capabilities
- Make assumptions
- Make strategic assessments
- Formulate strategies
- Establish goals and objectives
- Formulate tentative plans
- Finalize action plans

Vision

Personal Vision

A strategic plan for small and midsize businesses starts with the Vision for the company and the Vision for the owner. The Vision for the company is a critical statement that becomes the guiding light of the business; it must be known and **embraced** by all employees and constantly reinforced by the owner/CEO.

The Vision for the owner on the other hand is a private piece that resides only with the owner. What do you **really** want to get from the business? Is it a financial reward and if so, what is it? Is it fame and/or recognition from peers and the business world? Is it a technical challenge that you must conquer? Is it "a way of life" that provides the standard of living that you desire?

When answering these questions be as candid with yourself as possible; i.e., don't just "feel good" by stating some altruistic sentiment that is not your primary reason for being in business. Whatever the reason(s) they must be clear and honest because accomplishing your personal Vision will be a key component of your happiness and success of the business.

Your personal vision defines what you want to achieve in your life, both at a personal level and at a business level; what lifestyle you want and how the business would make it possible. For you to realize your Vision it must be accounted for in the company's Vision.

As the owner, you have the power to determine what your role in the business is and how much time you want to spend doing it. Your job description should focus primarily on activities that will help greatly in achieving your dreams and can make a major positive impact upon your company. I encourage you to include time away from your business as time important for reducing stress and for enjoying your personal life.

Is the business "your life" or do you have other interests outside of it? How many hours or days per week do you want to dedicate to the business? Is vacation time a must? I claim that the business should be a part of your life *apart* from your personal life, and that it should not be your entire life. Finding a good balance of business and family or personal life is a prerequisite for a happy life and a successful business.

Coaching suggestion: Limit your hours and days to reasonable amounts and take time off periodically. Working too many hours or days becomes non-productive and causes stress. What is reasonable time off? You can only determine that, but it should be sufficient to "give you a break" and let you reinvigorate your dynamism and desire for the business.

Consider your strengths and activities at which you excel and enjoy (engineering, research, sales, etc.), but also consider activities that you don't enjoy or prefer not to do (administrative, sales, HR, etc.) and you prefer to delegate.

Coaching suggestion: do a SWOT analysis for you to identify personal strengths and weaknesses but also add desires and wants. Make a list of the weaknesses, keep it near you (at your desk, in your pocket, or anywhere you can look at it all the time) and develop a plan to work on them. Make a commitment to yourself to improve on each of them within a fixed time frame.

Financial rewards are obvious benefits that you can expect, and your personal Vision should include a dollar amount to provide the life style you desire. Other rewards that are important to you, such as recognition by peers and industry should also be included.

Don't neglect to consider non-business activities or achievements that can bring you contentment, whether they are sports, family, hobbies, humanitarian, political, or any other. And of course you must consider how long you want to work and what your exit strategy would be. If possible include what actions you expect to execute to maximize the value of the business at exit.

Since the personal Vision is just that, personal, you define it and keep it to yourself. The company Vision on the other hand should be a shared concept and as such your team should participate in its definition.

Coaching suggestion: In the strategic planning process, after the personal Vision is defined by the owner, the entire management team must participate. The owner should be just one member of the team and not the preponderate voice in the discussions. A facilitator in these processes should not allow the rest of the team to just be echoes of the owner.

Company Vision

What is your Vision for the company? Do you want it to grow to be included in an elite group within your industry? Do you want it to be the best in quality in your field? Do you want to revolutionize the world with outstanding inventions? Do you want to be an ideal "green" company to help the environment? Whatever your Vision, it must be realistic and achievable and it must satisfy your personal desires.

You not only need to be capable of developing a Vision for the company, but you must be able to develop the Vision necessary for the company to succeed. Furthermore, you must communicate and "sell" the Vision to your employees and all stakeholders. You must get everyone in the organization seeing the same clear image of where the business is going and how is going to get there. This sounds easier than it is.

Your Company Vision describes what you would like your business to look like in the future. It comes from your company's purpose and visionary goals while reflecting your core values. Everyone's work effort should support and be aligned with the Company Vision. To accomplish this you must make sure that all employees buy into the Vision and it becomes their vision for the company too.

The Company Vision should include why the business exists (other than to make money), products and markets served, methods of distribution, how all stakeholders benefit from the company, and how society would benefit too. It is not the same as the Mission. The Vision is your mental picture of what you what to achieve; the Mission is ongoing. It is not the same as the strategic plan either; you develop the strategic plan after you figure where you want to end up.

Your core values, beliefs and principles are important to you and therefore should be reflected in the company values and thus in its Vision. Values also drive the culture of the company and thus the culture must be defined in the Vision.

Values

You cannot effectively lead if you do not know your values. Understanding your values gives you insight about others. Values-based activity is the basis for commitment— yours and others.

Because leadership starts with your values, your core values must be reflected in the company Vision. In fact, your core values are the most important thing that you have and can implement in your company. Therefore your values must become your company's values and be imbedded in the organization.

Establishing your core values you are saying "this is our culture" and "this is how we do business", and when you implement this as an integral part of the company it becomes the law and the driving force of all your actions and the actions of the organization. When you establish clear values to follow decisions become easier. However, having a set of values isn't enough; having the courage to act on them is what it takes to exercise good judgment and to be a good leader.

> *Coaching suggestion: define yourself and your values clearly and make sure everyone knows them. If you don't define yourself others will, and you may not like how they define you.*

SWOT Analysis

The next step in strategic planning is to do a comprehensive evaluation of where your business is. A SWOT (Strengths, Weaknesses, Opportunities and Threats) analysis will accomplish it. SWOT analysis must first start with defining a desired end state or objective.

The aim of any SWOT analysis is to identify the key internal and external factors that are important to achieving the objective. These come from within the company's unique value chain. SWOT analysis groups key pieces of information into two main categories:

- Internal factors – The *strengths* and *weaknesses* internal to the organization.
- External factors – The *opportunities* and *threats* presented by the external environment to the organization.

The internal factors may be viewed as strengths or weaknesses depending upon their impact on the organization's objectives. What may represent strengths with respect to one objective may be weaknesses for another objective. The external factors may include macroeconomic matters, technological change, legislation, and socio-cultural changes, as well as changes in the marketplace or competitive position.

- **S**trengths: characteristics of the business or team that give it an advantage over others in the industry.
- **W**eaknesses: are characteristics that place the firm at a disadvantage relative to others.
- **O**pportunities: *external* chances to make greater sales or profits in the environment.
- **T**hreats: *external* elements in the environment that could cause trouble for the business.

Identification of SWOTs is essential because subsequent steps in the process of planning for achievement of the selected objective may be derived from the SWOTs.

Start with the strengths because as you consider strengths you will also identify weaknesses. Identify the things in your business at which it excels and consider each of the strengths as something that can be leveraged by your company into additional business success. In this process identify those strengths that can set your business apart and have big potential.

Consider the management team and employee strengths related to experience, technical knowledge, loyalty, leadership ability, etc. What are the internal strengths that your company has, whether in operations, marketing, sales, products, processes, and any other operational type? Don't neglect too, key relationships that can be leveraged financially or strategically.

Do you have any market strengths such as cost leadership, brand awareness, universal coverage or distribution? What about location, product certification and approvals, facilities, physical assets, inventions or trade secrets? Do you consider your culture a strength? Don't discard anything even if you think are not important.

Coaching suggestion: when you think of strengths also think of weaknesses and list them as detailed as possible because your next step will be to develop action items to eliminate or minimize all weaknesses.

Following are examples of SWOTs; these are only short lists as examples but I'm sure you can identify many more, particularly those specific to your business.

Examples of Strengths:

- Competitive advantages (product, price, distribution, geography).
- Unique selling points.
- Resources (assets, people, facilities).
- Experience and knowledge.
- Financial (reserves, cash flow, balance sheet).
- Marketing (brand recognition market awareness).
- Accreditations/qualifications (patents, copyrights, ISO9000).
- Technology (processes, systems, IT).
- Organizational (management, expertise, succession).
- Cultural (attitude, values, change driven).

Examples of Weaknesses:

- Gaps in capabilities (technological, operational, organizational)
- Competitive posture (products, prices, quality)
- Financial (cash flow, over-extended, lack of funds for expansion)
- Cultural (people turn-over, lack of loyalty, lack of team work)
- Organizational (poorly staffed, lack of accountability, gaps in management)
- Technological (poor engineering, no innovation, obsolete technology)
- Sales (poor revenues, weak coverage, training)
- Any item listed as a possible strength can also be considered a weakness.

Example of Opportunities:

- Vulnerability of competition.
- Industry trends.
- Technology development and availability.
- Markets (new, growing, vertical).
- Sales (global markets, new applications).
- Technology (new products, inventions).
- Business relations (strategic partnerships, acquisitions).
- Seasonal (weather, fashion).

Example of Threats:

- Competition (number and size of competitors, market positioning).
- Political (new regulations, restrictions, market avoidance).
- Environmental (weather, seasonal demands).
- Economy (downturn, domestic, global).
- Technology (obsolesce of technology, slow developments).
- Market (changes, difficulty of penetration).
- Capabilities (low production, lack of subcontractors).
- Organizational (difficulty in finding qualified personnel, loss of key staff).

The next step is to develop plans to eliminate or at least minimize the weaknesses identified. Assign specific responsibilities with target dates and action items. Hold people accountable to those actions and dates.

Critical Success Factors

Critical Success Factors (CSF) are those strategies identified as critical in the success of the company and the strategic plan. From these, you must develop/identify those that are most important and label them the Driving Critical Success Factors.

Examples of CSF:

- New product or process development to gain market share.
- Expansion of geographical or applications markets.

- Expansion of capacity to serve new markets or products.
- Development or adoption of new technologies.
- Expansion of engineering capabilities.
- Sales force development.
- Change or upgrade of distribution methods.
- New building to house expanded facilities.
- Sustainable acquisitions strategy to grow.
- Achieve annual operating budget.
- Improve communications and accountability throughout the organization.
- Continue to promote engineered solutions and value added services to differentiate company from competitors.
- Succession planning for all critical positions.

Goals

Creating Company Goals. *(See Chapter V, Setting Goals)*

Now you need to identify Goals that will satisfy the Critical Success Factor. The Goals, like all goals, must be S.M.A.R.T., that is:

- *Specific.* In order to work, objectives need to be concrete (not as abstract as your long-term aims) and highly detailed.
- *Measurable.* Put a figure or value, such as a dollar amount or percentage, to the objective.
- *Action-oriented.* Lay out which actions need to be taken by which people, and when.
- *Realistic.* Make goals challenging, but consider your resources so that you can actually achieve them reasonably.
- *Time specific.* Set a deadline to keep things on track.

Coaching suggestion: Make each Goal measurable and achievable within three years. The measurements must be of a type that can be easily tracked by Key Performance

Indicators that you can review on a regularly scheduled basis. Limit goals to no more than six or as many as can be realistically achieved. Accountability is key to ensure accomplishing the goals. (See Chapter XIII, Performance Management).

Your most important goals are those associated with your Driving Critical Success Factor (DCSF). Your DCSF Goals need to have company-wide buy-in, commitment and focus. Your written Company DCSF Plan Goals should become a well-memorized mantra known and supported by all your management and employees. They should keep it at the forefront of their day-to-day thinking and in focus for everything that they do.

Example of Goals:

- Achieve acquisitions to expand to market regions. One new acquisition for each of next three years.
- Improve accountability throughout the organization, measured by meeting target dates established.
- Improve internal communications by adopting a firm schedule of weekly operations meetings. All schedules to start in March of 201X.
- Secure alternate source of products both domestic (by 6/30/201X) and foreign (by 12/31/201X).
- Develop executable succession plan for all key positions; in place by 10/31/201X.
- Expand product offerings to medical and alternative power applications. Sales plan ready by 9/30/201X.
- Achieve error free operations. Ninety-nine percent error free by 10/31/201X.
- Accelerate vertical integration (can be part of acquisition strategy). Plan ready by 6/30/201X.
- Develop one new product within ten months, two within twenty-four months, and another two within thirty-six months for a total of five more products.
- Maintain gross margins at a minimum of twenty-three percent after first year.
- Hire and train a new COO to assume a minimum twenty-five percent of my current operational responsibility within one hundred and eighty days.

- Increase sales of current products in current markets by ten percent by end of year.

Strategies

Example of Strategies:

For Goal #1:
- Peter to develop a plan that includes identifying potential targets and time line for contacting them.

For Goal #3:
- Institute daily/weekly huddles that include all employees, by departments.
- Monthly Team reviews of strategic plan.
- Quarterly state of the company meetings.
- Implement Progressive Discipline policy.
- Monthly Team review of accountability of Team members.

For Goal #4: Sales and Engineering will develop by 6/31/201X a strategy that includes:
- Definition of needs.
- Identify potential sources (working with World Trade Center).
- Report probability of success with each.
- Target completion of relationship.
- Timing for introduction of products.

For Goal #5:
- Each manager to identify successor or alternate (already in place).
- Peter (CEO) to formulate plan for his succession or alternate.
- Ensure training of each successor or alternate.

For Goal #6:
- Identify market TAM and SAM for each specialty.

- Develop plan to penetrate each market.
- Identify product sources for each.

For Goal #7:
- Identify key areas to improve.
- Analyze source of errors.
- Team to develop plan to progressively achieve ninety-nine percent or better error-free operations.

For Goal #8:
- Team to decide how it is to be pursued.

And so on for the rest of the Goals.

Making it Happen *(See Chapter XI, Execution)*

Action plans must be put in place to execute the strategies. It is in these plans that we develop and enforce the accountability; without accountability the entire plan is in jeopardy and most likely it won't happen.

Final Comments

There are plenty of books and publications written on the subject of strategic planning, and there is much more that can be covered, but it is not my intent to give a detailed lesson on strategic planning.

To summarize this chapter I permit myself to use a statement by my colleague Doug Roof who said it very well: "Predicting the future is difficult. But strategic planning is not so much about accurate predictions as it is about being prepared for and helping to shape the future. It's not so much about financial data as it is about the journey to achieve financial objectives. In a world of constant and rapid change, that journey involves establishing competitive advantage again and again. I can't imagine doing that without a plan. Can you?"

Another very important plan is the exit strategy for you, the CEO/owner; it is covered in its pertinent chapter.

References:

1. Jim Horan and Tom Peters, *One Page Business Plan,* (The One Page Business Plan Company, March 10, 2004).
2. Verne Harnish, *Mastering the Rockefeller Habits: What You Must Do to Increase the Value of Your Fast-Growth Firm,* (Gazelles, Inc., March 1, 2011).
3. The Alternative Board, *www.thealternativeboard.com.*

Chapter VII - Organization

People are the bridges you must cross to get to where you want to go.

This statement summarizes the importance of building a great organization and fomenting team culture. Jim Collins in *"Good to Great"* teaches us that you must "have the right people in the bus", but the big question is: who are the right people for you and for your business? There is also a saying claiming that "people are your most important asset", but I contend that it should read "the right people are your most important asset".

As the leader, you must guide your team on the key priorities, set the goals to be achieved, develop the strategies, formulate the action plans, assign duties and responsibilities, and hold people—and yourself—accountable. Developing a strategic plan is a key item on your agenda as the leader. A strategic plan should be the guideline to run the company through the right phases.

Build your team with the best possible members. Do not hesitate to hire people who are smarter than you or know more than you do. The better your team, the better are your chances of winning the race to success. Great ideas are important but even more critical is to have the right people in the correct positions to execute them. The more talent on your team, the easier it will be for you to lead.

To build a team that will play as a team—as opposed to a group of individual players—use the terms "we" and "our" when referring to the business. This practice will multiply the talents in the game and lead to a better company. Conversely, selfish owners who only think of "my" company and "my" glory are far less likely to form a real team, and thus, they limit the potential of the company.

As noted by Jack Welch, "Your success as a leader will come not from what you do every day but from the reflected glory of your team's performance." Another quote from Jack Welch very applicable to our subject is "before you are a leader success is all about growing yourself; when you become a leader success is growing others".

You must understand that, while your team may be motivated, no one will have the same drive as you have as the visionary. You will feed their motivation by leading the team to execute the strategic plan and demonstrating that it is the right plan to achieve the vision. Vision was the reason your company was born, but leadership will be the reason it becomes great.

Surrounding yourself with great people is a sign of good leadership. You can't build a great company by yourself; you need the right people in the right places to help you do it. But to hire top talent you must have value to offer; values such as good leadership and a sound business model that includes the right products for the right market. Consider too that assembling a team of strong individuals is not the same as molding a team. Molding a team means to have a team that works together.

Top talent at any level are attracted not just by a good salary and benefits but more so by a good environment (read culture), good prospects for advancement and promises of stability for the company. They are also attracted by participative management styles, recognition to those who deserve it, and leadership from the top. Another attraction is the opportunity to learn, develop as managers/leaders, and advance, thus a management development program must be implemented in the company. A strategic management development program will result in multiple advantages, including:

- Ability to attract and retain talent.
- Ability to adapt to change (which is imperative in modern organizations),
- Controlled growth of the organization

Management development—and people development in general—must be a leadership priority and become part of the culture of the company. You must embrace the belief that everyone, including your top performers, can improve; in fact, you should focus your development efforts on your best people rather than on the problem employees. They in turn will contribute to the development of others.

The program should not be a "one size fits all" type, but rather it should be tailored to the needs and personality of each individual and each individual must take responsibility for their own development. You should not force the plan upon individuals; get buy-in from each and lead them into the process. Share the plan with everyone and get support from all and keep it visible such that they can see improvements. And, like in the case of accountability, include yourself in the plan to set an example for all.

Developing a second-in-command

As the company grows and your job becomes bigger, you must prepare the company for continued growth which should include an expansion of the leadership and a backup of your position. This is a critical step in organizational development and as such it must be made with careful thought and vision. When done properly the development of a number two executive can provide a host of benefits to you, the owner, and to the whole organization. It can help propel the business to a new level of growth with a stronger management team. The process can also create potential problems and thus you must consider all the possible pitfalls.

Naming a second in command represents the appointment of a successor to your position and will be looked by the rest of the employees either as an additional leader and resource or as an unwanted filter between them and you. How that person is accepted will depend on how much thought you put into its selection.

- Will you promote from within or hire from outside for that position?
- Did you consider internal candidates before looking outside?
- Did you develop a job description for the position, including expectations and rewards and penalties?
- What will the new executive provide that current management team doesn't?

- How will this change affect the rest of the team?
- Will the new person be accepted by all (this is particularly important in family business if nepotism is suspected).
- How will your role and interaction with others change?

If you promote from within you must select someone who is a recognized leader by the rest of the employees; one who is respected and liked as a team member. If you bring someone from outside you must consider how well he/she will fit in the culture of the company. Unless the new person has an undisputable pedigree that will command respect from the onset, you must bring him/her up slowly until he/she is fully accepted by all.

If this person is the expected replacement for your position you must include him in the succession plan for the business. Moreover, you must ensure the preparation of this person to take over in the eventuality of an emergency succession; i.e., if you become unable to fulfill your role as CEO. As a designated successor of the CEO the candidate must participate in a well formulated development plan designed specifically for the position.

Organization alignment

We also need to talk too about organization alignment. Alignment is more than a simple interchange between two entities or departments; it's the alignment of resources, forces and goals within the organization aimed at producing maximum output with minimum consumption. Implicit in an internally aligned organization is a state where clarity of mission, vision, and values prevail. Internal alignment creates energy and inspirits. Shaping and managing the culture so it supports this alignment becomes crucial for the success of the company.

Knowing when to hire people is a challenge for most small business owners; hiring too late and hiring too soon are both maladies that can seriously affect a company. For small businesses there is a delicate balance in building the organization to match the growth and needs of the company, without adding unnecessary payroll expenses.

I have worked with both ends of the spectrum when it comes to hiring timing; some owners that hired much earlier that they needed to, and owners that lost excellent business opportunities for not having enough (or the right people) onboard.

> **From my bag:** *A client of mine suffered from "optimisms"; an illness that affects the thought process of a smart and cautious small business owner. He had the "ability" to see opportunities much before they were apparent, and convinced that they were coming his way he had the habit of building the organization to levels that he thought the "opportunity" would demand.*
>
> *Unfortunately, many times those opportunities didn't materialized and he had to release the extra manpower not needed for the real level of business. This clearly had an impact on his finances, but the most damaging impact was in the morale of the organization that heard great promises of growth that never materialized, and saw people getting let go because of the owner/CEO's lack of realistic planning.*
>
> *I had the opportunity to work with another owner who had the opposite disease; the one I call "exaggerated conservatism". This disease prevented him from hiring people ahead of the needs of increased demand for the business. As a result, many times he got into a panic mode of hiring because the performance of the business was suffering.*
>
> *Hiring in a panic invariably results in mistakes (hiring wrong) and the organization as a whole suffers. Thus, his mode-operating had a double negative effect of poor performance (late deliveries, poor quality) and loss of opportunities (mot being ready for them). The teaching of these examples is to be aware of opportunities but to use caution to build the organization on an as needed basis and not too soon, or waiting too long and lose opportunities.*

Owners delay hiring for various reasons that in reality are nothing more than excuses. Owners have told me "I know I need to hire but I don't have time to do it right now", or "yes I know I need them now but if business slows down soon I don't want to let them go soon after they are hired", or "I can hire some people now but I don't have time to train them", or "we are swamped but I can't afford the expense at this time".

But the worst excuse people have given me is "I don't want to hire anybody because nobody can do what I do, so I'll just handle everything myself". This is a perfect formula for failure.

There is a saying that goes "small business owners are too quick to hire and too slow to fire". How true this is! I hope I don't appear heartless by making this statement, but it is a fact that we tend to "carry dead wood" far too long. Why do we do it? The answer is as simple as it is wrong. When we need somebody we need them *now* and we tend to rush the process to cover the pressing need. However, when we know we need to fire someone we tend to delay the action because "we don't have anybody else to do that job", or because we feel sorry for the person getting fired.

Are we doing the business good by these actions? Of course not; small businesses cannot afford the luxury of keeping someone just because they don't have anybody else to do the job, or to be magnanimous by keeping a less-than-efficient employee because we feel sorry for that person.

It is also unfair to the employee because most likely, he or she is in the wrong job and at a dead-en in the company as a low performer. Releasing the person would give him/her an opportunity to get into a better situation and have a better future.

> ***Coaching suggestion:*** *When remorse stops or delays you from doing what you must do—releasing someone—think about it this way: your responsibility is not just to that person, but to all the other employees and their families (as well as yours) and other stakeholders of the business. Keeping an employee that is causing damage to the company hurts the present and the future of all those people. Releasing him/her, on the other hand, sends a message that the health of the business and the wellbeing of all employees and stakeholders are more important than feeling sorry for one.*

Of course, not all mistakes need to be permanent. Some people take longer to develop into a job but they can be very valuable once they reach the level of competence required. In these cases, it is the manager's responsibility to train and develop new (and all) employees and to give them the opportunity to reach the target level.

To hire the right people is extremely important to all small companies. Large companies can afford to hire employees that are not the best (not that it is recommended for them), because one or even a few weak links among dozens, hundreds or even thousands of employees won't be noticed, but you as the owner/CEO of a small company cannot afford to hire even one "loser" because it can have a great negative effect in the organization and in the business.

Imagine for example, that you hire the wrong salesman in a sales force of one; this person can poison the image of the company while losing a tremendous amount of time and possibly market share. The same can be said for all key positions within the company.

> ***From my bag:*** *I'm an admirer of Jack Welch and his teachings from the experience he gained as CEO of one of the largest companies of the Country. However, we must remember that not all his experiences apply to small or midsize businesses. Case in point: In "Winning", while writing about hiring and selecting the right people, he admits to having picked the right people only fifty percent of the time as a young manager, later improving to eighty percent. While this "batting average" may be good for large corporations, it would be disastrous for small businesses.*
>
> *Furthermore, he preaches "don't beat yourself up if you are hiring wrong some of the time". I beg to differ with him on this too. Hiring "wrong" can be a killer for a small business, so you must make people selection a high priority talent to be developed. And when you make a mistake in hiring, you must not only correct it as soon as it is detected as a mistake, but you must learn your lesson, decide where you went wrong and take the necessary measures to prevent the mistake from happening again.*

One more point. In answer to the question "how long does it take to know if you've hired right?" he says that one should know "usually within a year, and certainly within two". Again, this may work for GE but in a small business you cannot "carry a mistake" for a year or two. Performance in some jobs are more difficult to define than in others, and some people are more difficult to evaluate than others, so setting an arbitrary time to detect and correct mistakes is not realistic. Nevertheless, "mistakes" should not be carried one more day after they are detected, and this time must be as short as possible.

Coaching suggestion: *My advice to CEOs and managers: don't wait for a year before you review new employees; do a review within thirty and sixty days. By identifying and discussing weaknesses early, you have a better chance of correcting them before they become large negatives. I also suggest having a newly hired manager or executive write a report—thirty or sixty days into the job on how they see the company, its management, its systems and its outlook. By doing this you will get two benefits: a) you get a fresh perspective into the company, and b) you learn how the new person thinks and acts.*

We already said that successful leaders are successful because they surround themselves with great people. Are you surrounded by great people? Be truly honest with yourself and analyze your staff; do they share your core values? Are they loyal to you, to the company and to the business model you have implemented? Are they the best you can find for the jobs they do?

You also need to look at your organization structure. In "Second Part-Your Functional Development" under the subtitle "Your Route to Being a Better CEO" in *Coaching suggestion*, I recommend to do a functional organization chart and hire only to cover holes in the various functions.

"Most companies organize around personalities rather than around functions; that is, around people rather than accountabilities or responsibilities. The result is almost always chaos." Michael Gerber, *"The E-Myth Revisited"*[2].

A functional organizational chart depicts all of the ingredients necessary for the continuing operations and growth of your company. Its purpose is to identify and assign all of the functions and sub functions necessary to meet your operating and growth objectives. It is intended to eliminate duplicated authority, identify any unattended responsibilities and begin to build accountability.

When you hire according to a plan based on the functions to be filled, is strategic hiring as opposed to opportunistic hiring. Should there ever be opportunistic hiring? Yes, when the right candidate is available ahead of the need to fill a hole, or if you have the opportunity to hire a superstar that would help you grow the company, and that person may not be available if you bypass it now, by all means take advantage of the opportunity. But if you do, make sure he or she will fit a definite role and will occupy the right place in the organization. Failure to do this can be cause for problems later.

Coaching suggestion: In addition to doing a functional organization chart to define all functions in the company, do an "upside-down" chart depicting the customer at the top, followed by the various levels in the organization, then by your management team, and with you, the CEO, at the bottom. The purpose of this is to send a message that the organization exists to support the customers. It also suggests that you are the base of the organization and your job is to support it.

Building Your Organization

The formula to have the right people in the bus is composed of three elements: selection/hiring, managing, and retention. If you fail at any of the three you will not have the top talents that you need to have. Let's discuss each of the three.

Selection/Hiring

Start by defining the job to be filled and writing a comprehensive job description *(see Job Descriptions below)*. Look inside first; are there any employees qualified and with the desired to fill the vacancy? Use behavioral personality assessments at least for the three or four final candidates, as well as a work environment assessment (for example DISC instruments).

Conduct realistic job interviews and allow key staff members to participate in the interview process. *(See "Interviewing" later in this section)* Above all make sure that the candidate that you chose will fit the culture of your company.

Research studies have shown that behavioral assessments are a critical element of selection. The probability of a successful hire by using "gut-feel" alone is one in five; the resume should only be a "door-opener" (or closer) since it will only say what the candidate wants it to say, and the interview is valuable but incomplete in what it can discover.

The big mistake is that many organizations don't validate if the candidate will fit into the organization's culture. You can have the best sales manager prospect in the world, but if he or she does not meet your ethical standards, you have a poor hire; behavioral assessment can help you with this.

If you want to improve your effectiveness in recruiting high quality people, you and your people must have a good working knowledge of the position and be able to communicate it—many organizations are woefully poor here—because without it you are not going to get good candidates.

If we use a scale of one-to-ten to judge people for performance, where ten is representative of top performance, fourteen percent of the population falls between eight and ten. Of course these are the candidates that you want, but be conscious that managing tens requires outstanding leadership and managerial skills and you and your team must be up to the task.

Yes, these are the people that you want but you need to understand that the candidates that you want—top performers—most likely are not sitting at home waiting for your call; they are working and if you want them you may have to consider poaching (this may not be above-board but it is practiced all the time).

Food for thought: if you already have top talent but you're not winning, it may be time for a little self-assessment and a managerial audit.

> ***Coaching suggestion:*** *The references listed in a resume or presentation letter are the references that the candidate wants you to consider. It is obvious that the candidate will not include references that would not speak well of him/her; therefore, those references may not be of much value to you, except to reinforce a positive outlook that the candidate wants to portray. My suggestion is to contact previous employers, or better yet, leaders of companies where the candidate worked before but he did not include as references.*

I recommend reading *"How Small Businesses Capture Talent; 164 Strategies for Recruiting and Hiring Winners"*[3].

Managing

Regardless of position, training is imperative; make sure that you have a training plan ready when the new employee joins the company. Part of the orientation should be to confirm to the new employee the following:

- Where we are going as a company.
- How we are going to get there.
- How you are expected to contribute.

To build the winning team, you not only need to show people what direction the company is headed in, but you need to get them to "buy into" this direction. Otherwise, you can't expect people to support the organization if they don't agree with where it's headed or, worse, don't even know where it's headed.

I strongly recommend having the new employee sign the "contract" represented by the job description that also includes expectations of performance and rewards or consequences for it. This document will eliminate any disputes later on what the job should be, what the responsibilities and duties are, and what the rewards or penalties are. Furthermore, agree on a development plan with career objectives and goals to be achieved.

Published statistics show a staggering twenty-two percent of staff turnover in the first forty-five days of employment, and in most cases it is for a mismatch of what they expected and what they found. Being honest and open during the interview, and comprehensive mentoring and coaching after the hire, can prevent this.

Coaching suggestion: As part of organizational development and aligning is a good idea to do 360 degrees reviews of all employees, but particularly for the management team and/or key employees. There are multiple benefits to be gained by this including each employee knowing what others think of them or how they are perceived by peers. Based on the results of the evaluation you can formulate customized plans for individual development, or better yet ask them to develop each individual plan themselves.

There is an inherent risk in this practice though, and that is that some may take offense to what is said about them by peers. To prevent or minimize this risk all evaluations must be anonymous. The first time is the most difficult one; after that it becomes easier for people to understand the intent of the comments. There are simple and economic software programs to handle all the mechanics of doing it and reporting it.

Ongoing management is covered throughout this book in its various chapters.

Retention

People don't leave companies; they leave their boss.

This is demonstrated in large part by a survey of American workers done by Harris Interactive that revealed the following:

- Seventy-seven percent are not satisfied with the strategy and vision of the company and its leadership.

- Forty-eight percent are not satisfied with the relationship they have with their boss.
- Sixty-six percent are not satisfied with their compensation.
- Seventy-six percent are not satisfied with future career growth opportunities at their company.

These data suggests that if you want to retain your employees you must address four key areas:

- Culture
- Compensation
- Career growth path
- Alignment with the business model.

Coaching suggestion: *In just about every survey ever done in organizations of any size, communications was identified as the number one complaint. This included both the lack or incomplete communication from management to employees, and the level or tone of communication; i.e., "talking down" to employees, not being truthful, or misguiding employees.*

I suggest having a minimum of quarterly "state of the company" meetings with the entire organization where you explain truthfully about business, position of the company, and opportunities and possible threats. Having these meetings should not be a reason not to have departmental, staff, reporting, or any other operational meetings.

Another vital element in employee retention is for you to know what your employees want and need. You are not going to bow down to them or give them everything they want, but you need to understand what their wants and needs are because if you don't understand them, they are going to find another employer that will.

In his book *"The Seven Hidden Reasons Employees Leave"* [4] Leigh Branham says that employees leave when one or more of four fundamental human needs are not being met, and he calls it the ROBS syndrome:

- The need to be **recognized**, to feel a sense of worth. Employees feel confident that if they work hard, do their best, demonstrate commitment and make meaningful contributions, they will be recognized and rewarded accordingly.
- The need for **opportunity**, to have hope. Employees believe they will be able to grow, develop their skills and have the opportunity for advancement or career progress.
- The need for **belonging** and trust. Expecting the company and manager to deliver on promises, to be honest and open in all communication with employees, to invest in employees, to treat employees fairly, and to compensate employees in a fair and timely manner.
- The need for **security** and the need to feel competent. Employees expect they will be matched to a job that aligns with their talents and their desire for challenge.

Analyses of employee's surveys conducted have shown that the single greatest reason employees quit is because they felt unappreciated. Money was very low on the list. People quit bosses, not companies.

A *Towers Perrin* [5] study suggests that only one-fifth of employees are truly engaged in their work and would work extra hard for their employer; of the rest, thirty-eight percent are disengaged and forty-one percent felt indifferent about their work and their employer. While the study may have been done for large companies, there is probably some relation with employees of small businesses too.

Coaching suggestion: It is good to use some sort of employee perception survey. You will probably get more credibility if it is done externally by a third party, though you could do it internally, but keep in mind you need to know what your employees perceive about their jobs, their co-workers, and their working environment with you. I also suggest the use of a mentor program for an initial period; it is well worth the cost and effort.

Reward and recognition are the two most common methods for motivating and engaging employees, but there other ways to do it as well. Recognition can take the form of public acknowledgment of achievements, inviting employees to attend conferences or meetings, having them participate in some visibly important group, inviting the employee to lunch with the CEO, and any number of non-financial perks. And don't discount a personal note to say thank you; this can go a long way in the appreciation of the employee.

> ***Coaching suggestion:*** *If an employee has invested an "above expectations" effort to the benefit of the company, as for example working significant amount of extra hours, a personal note to the spouse—not to the employee—can have a huge impact. Particularly when the employee is a male and the wife is at home with children, a nice note from the boss thanking her for the time he took away from her to dedicate to the company, will have a more positive effect than even a monetary reward. For extra effect accompany the note with a gift certificate (for example, for a nice dinner for two).*

You made a significant investment in the new hires and thus you must do what you can to conserve that investment.

Job Descriptions (As explained by my colleague Wayne Berry of Aquarius International, of Jefferson City, MO).

A good job description is more than what the name says; it is a narrative of what the job calls for but it is also a contract between the management and the employee. It includes positioning, responsibilities and expected performance and its consequences.

Seven Elements of a Complete Job Description

The **basic function** is to define in one to two sentences maximum, the reason the job exits. Example: "The basic function of the sales manager of XYZ Company is to achieve the sales and gross margin objectives of the company while maintaining high levels of customer service." It is very, very broad; if you can't write the basic reason for having the position, chances are the job should not exist.

Reporting Relationships. There are three elements of reporting: upward reporting; "The Sales Manager of XYZ Company reports directly to the President, to whom he/she is accountable for his/her performance." The other two are many times ignored. There is downward reporting. "The following positions report directly to the Sales Manager". And there is sideways (or functional) reporting. "The Sales Manager maintains a functional (but not supervisory) reporting relationship with the following other function heads of XYZ Company". (A, B, C, D etc.).

Authority is power, this is where the decision making authority comes in to play; it comes from you (the owner or CEO), you assign it or not assign it or give limited authority. It is the power to take an action or to make a decision without additional permission. There are only certain possible authorities: hiring & firing authority, pricing authority, product line authority, check signing authority, and so on. The best way to determine an authority is to complete the sentence *"Has the authority to ......"*

Responsibility is the charge to make things happen. Not necessarily to do them (those are duties), but to ensure something is accomplished or in place. *"Is responsible for regulatory compliance"*. The best way to determine a responsibility is to complete the sentence *"Is responsible for ....."*

Duties are what they actually do. Duties cannot be delegated. Duties always start with a present tense action verb. Examples are: designs, performs, supervises, reports, approves, authorizes, investigates, and countless more actions. The catch twenty-two is always the last principal duty: *"performs various other assignments and duties from time to time which may be requested by the immediate supervisor"*, which means in case we forgot anything it will be covered here.

The most important of all the components is the **standards of measurements of performance**, the communication of the expectations. This is where you build accountability. If we do not communicate expectations to our people we are not going to get the performance we want.

So how are job descriptions used? They should be used in recruiting, in interviewing, training, and for performance reviews. I suggest that unless you really have a tightly focused job description so there is a mutual understanding of what that job is all about, you will not be effective in hiring, developing and retaining high performing people.

> **Coaching suggestion:** *When agency investigators or class-action-minded attorneys come to look at your company, the first stop is the job description. The fed's favorite job description checkpoints are ADA, FLSA, and discrimination. From the ADA standpoint, in accommodating employees with disabilities, they must be able to accomplish the essential functions of the job with or without reasonable accommodation. Inability to perform nonessential functions does not disqualify the individual.*
>
> *A function may be essential in one setting, but nonessential in another. It's not the time a person spends on the task that makes it essential; each work situation has to be taken into account as well. Describe an essential function more as an outcome than a method, and do it now, not after the fact. Clearly define "Essential".*
>
> *In addition to making your essential/nonessential determination, it's helpful to pin duties down with a clear description of requirements and conditions. You might mention: Supervision, physical requirements, mental requirements, performance requirements, environmental factors, tools and equipment, other requirements. While it is important to be detailed and precise, be sure that all the elements you list are true. If things listed are not true, it will make everything that you claim suspect.*

Building Your Team

Effective management requires that you know what you want your team members to do, make sure they know what you want them to do, train them on how to do it, and motivate them to want to do it. Building the winning team requires more than just hiring a bunch of talented people; it means hiring people who will work well together and will have positive, formal and informal interactions between group members.

It also means developing a shared vision and commitment and instilling a "winning" attitude throughout the organization. You must be alert for team-building problems such as jealousy, cynicism, and defensive behavior, and be ready to quickly reverse them.

Perhaps the most difficult part of building a winning team is encouraging positive, informal interaction between team members when you are not present. To help solve this problem do the following:

- Have team members participate in the hiring process of new employees.
- Assign specific projects for groups to work together.
- Create an incentive-pay plan based on common goals such as profitability.
- Have a specific part of the performance review dependent upon "interaction with others."
- Take your team off-site for formal meetings as well as casual get-togethers to build a sense of bonding.
- Find reasons to celebrate; even small triumphs can give you the opportunity to recognize good work.

Coaching suggestion: *Make it your project to find reasons to celebrate, but don't diminish the value by using markedly unimportant reasons. Always celebrate as a group, never leave out even small contributors. Be sure you emphasize the company's positive achievements to the group as a whole.*

Liz Wiseman in *"Multipliers: How the Best Leaders Make Everyone Smarter"* [6] describes a study of leaders who use their intelligence to enhance the smarts and capabilities of their people. She classifies leaders into "Multipliers" and "Diminishers". Multipliers are described as leaders inspiring employees to surpass expectations. Diminishers are described as executives who promote their own plans or results, ignoring the ability and resourcefulness of employees. Her research shows that Multipliers got two times better results from their people.

The organizational development that you may envision can be altered by the following:

- Resistance to change. To some people making a change or even considering it, it's threatening. Thus, unless there's a good reason for changing, people resist change. Since I said that change is a necessary effect of a business to succeed, your program must include actions to take to overcome resistance to change.
- Poor management skills. Some people fear their management skills are inadequate. They may feel capable of maintaining the status quo but cannot see themselves exercising the kind of leadership that's required to bring about changes in position.
- Poor time management. People at all levels of the organization are hesitant to commit themselves to a goals program if they're having trouble managing time. They cannot see how they can find the time to change anything.
- Inadequate communication. If communication is perceived as an issue, the goals of the organizational program break down. If you fail to tell people what's expected of them and fail to give or seek feedback about the process and about the operation of the program, they will not feel confident about it.
- Lack of personal goals. When key people in the organization don't have meaningful personal goals, they have no reason for wanting to be a part of the organizational goals. Without the motivation of personal goals, people are not motivated to make an effort to improve their work habits.

I recommend doing a "team evaluation" periodically to check the health of team work as you promote it and want it. I have found that a good way to do this is to use Patrick Lenzione's *"The Five Dysfunctions Of A Team"*[7]. He defines them as:

- Absence of trust. This can be among team members and/or team members to management.
- Fear of conflict. Again, this can be related to conflicts between members or between team members and management.
- Lack of commitment. Commitment to the team, to the project, to the company, or to the vision of the company.
- Avoidance of accountability. Lack of accountability of some member(s) can lead to non-performance by the team.
- Inattention to results. No concern for results obtained by the team, or more concerned about individual results than team results.

In my experience Avoidance of Accountability is the most prevalent dysfunction. If you, as the CEO, do not create a culture of accountability, there will never be effective team work. I cover this extensively in the "Accountability" chapter.

To determine the performance of your team start with a look at its foundation; does it incorporate the essential elements of a high functioning team as described? Too often we tend to consider only the effect on the bottom line and no other important factors such as overriding performance of individual members clouding the overall team performance. Your team should have sustainable performance, be able to adapt to changes and occasional turnover, and insulated against corporate raiding.

As we discussed in "Leadership", you are the boss but as the boss of a small business you are also an active team member, and not only a team member but the team leader. As such you are in charge of molding the team dynamic. There is a difference between forming a team and molding a team; you form a team by naming the players, but to mold a team takes work (and practice).

Think of a sport team; the manager, the coach or the club name a group of players to represent the club, but it only becomes a team after a lot of work by the coach. In the work environment is the same, you put together a group of very capable individuals and then you work with it to form a team.

As in the sports analogy, the higher the proficiency of the players, the more challenging the job of the coach to mold the different personalities (and egos) will be. While a group of very capable individuals can be great contributors, the contributions are greatly enhanced when they work as a team.

As the leader you have other organizational responsibilities:

- In an impasse or when you don't agree with a conclusion by the team, don't hesitate to make the final call, but don't dictate it and work with the members to reach what you consider the right call.
- Stand up to those who are not valid team players. Team work is the requirement of all members and those who don't practice it cannot be on the team. If necessary, act swiftly to remove non-players.
- When you must say no, do it without creating hostility because if you don't you will never recover the true team spirit.
- Make sure your business doesn't outgrow your team. As the business grows the team needs to grow too, not necessarily in numbers, but in proficiency related to the business of the company. Development of the team is a key function of its leader.

And since we are talking about development of the team, let me ask: do you have a "bench"? Who is on the bench and who is ready to move up? What are you doing to add players to the "bench"? What are you doing to develop the bench and the "bench warmers"?

When you promote employees be extra careful not to promote people to "their level of incompetence". What do I mean by this? An employee may be very good at a certain job and you reward him/her with a promotion to a higher position (usually a management or supervisory position); however, is he/her qualified for that new position? I have seen countless of examples of people being rewarded like this and then being fired for incompetence in their new position. This is extremely damaging to the individual but also to the team and to the business.

Again, let's use the sports analogy. At the end of their playing careers some great players often become coaches ... and they proceed to fail miserably. Being a great player doesn't necessarily transmit into being a great—or even a good—coach. Being a coach requires talents different than those of a player.

Similarly in business the requirements of an individual contributor and those of management are very different and require very different personalities and talents. Be aware of these differences when you are considering promotions.

> ***Coaching suggestion:*** *to have your bench ready and to know who is supervisory or managerial material, be proactive and have evaluations of each employee done as a practical rule. Evaluations should include behavioral assessments to determine managerial capabilities and responsiveness to the demands of future jobs.*

> ***Coaching suggestion:*** *A huge mistake made by many small business owners is to "give" a high-level title to someone in order to entice the candidate to join the company. I have seen countless of examples of owners hiring at executive levels, when the candidate is not really high-level material. For example, giving the title of VP of Engineering to a candidate needed for his/her technical knowledge, but realizing later that the employee does not have the qualities to be a manager and much less an executive. Avoid this practice at all cost.*

Employee Performance Reviews

Traditionally, business managers are required to do—or elect to do—formal performance "reviews" of employees on a fixed schedule (usually yearly). But why? Does this practice make better employees? Does it make better managers? Does it guarantee excellence in performance? Do they really work? ... No, they don't really work and I argue that they are mostly a waste of time and effort.

I favor a different approach and a different method to determine employee performance. In a well-run organization employees (of any level) are being reviewed daily by continuous interaction with management or supervisors. These interactions give both sides the opportunity to review activities and results.

For the formal reviews I propose "Management By Objectives (MBO)" and a Review by Objectives (RBO) method for measuring (as opposed to "judging") performance. My book "Performance Reviews, The Bad, The Ugly, …The Alternative [10] explains this technique.

Obviously the MBO is not a new system or management fad; to the contrary, it has been around forever (it seems). It was first outlined by Peter Drucker in 1954 in his book *"The Practice of Management"* [8]. The system many times it isn't well understood or used.

A prerequisite of this system is that the objectives have to be in line with the company's objectives. The system aims to improve performance by matching the goals of the company with the individual and departmental objectives of the entire organization.

> **From my bag:** *A recent article whose author I don't remember, discussed the MBO system and related theories of Peter Drucker and Paul Deming. The article included supporters as well as detractors of MBO. I found it interesting that most of the detractors were executives or employees of large companies. In fact, Deming also disagreed with Drucker but later in life Drucker claimed that if MBO fails it would be because it was not implemented correctly. I can understand the difficulties of integrating in a large company all the different hierarchical levels into common objectives, but this should not be a problem in small or midsize companies.*

What is the difference between RBO and the standard review method? RBO eliminates the objectivity of performance judgment; i.e., it does not depend on the difficult impartiality of a manager over multiple employees. With the RBO method—when used properly—there is no subjectivity, no favoritisms or personal dislikes; results are clear, the goals were met or they were not, there is no ambiguity.

In a RBO process a manager still meets "formally" with the employee but they meet to review progress achieved on the goals previously set. Judgment then is easy; were the goals met? Were they met on time? How many did not reach completion and why? Did performance exceed the goals set? Did the employee achieve extra merits?

The same meeting is also used to develop and set new goals for the new period. These goals must be jointly developed and agreed to—rather than being dictated by the manager—to ensure buy-in of the employee and to prevent future discrepancies. The frequency of these meetings depends on the length of the goals, but always ensuring that there are periodic ongoing progress reviews. Managers must not wait until the target date for completion to see if the goals will be met or not.

I've heard people claim that the RBO process cannot be used for production line workers or other low level employees because it is not practical to set goals for them. This is a fallacy as goals can be easily developed, monitored and measured for employees of any level.

Another benefit of the RBO process is that, contrary to the traditional method, all parties benefit from it. The employee learns and improves because the manager guides him/her through the goals set and, hopefully, teaches the employee to accomplish them. Also, the employee knows exactly how he/she is being measured and what is required of him/her.

The manager benefits because he/she has employees that respond to the guidance and become more productive and efficient, and the company benefits from the increased productivity generated by happier employees and managers.

Coaching suggestion: Another erroneous practice is to tie-in performance reviews with salary increases. Creating this practice aggravates all the negatives of the traditional reviews and also of the RBO program because employees feel inevitably entitled to an increase at "review time". I much favor a disengagement of the two, associating increases only to the achievement of goals as jointly developed.

I favor scrapping the traditional employee performance reviews and adopting a Management by Objectives (MBO) and Review By Objectives (RBO) process that ensures value of the process, fairness in performance judgment (measurement), and eliminates all the negative consequences of the traditional process. Of course this is a suggestion and you must use the system that appeals to you the most. If you prefer a "standard" process I include an example of a form to use at the end of this chapter

Also included at the end of this chapter are two suggested forms to do team reviews using the 360 degrees method by which all team members review each other.

Interviewing

Interviewing and hiring are critical elements of organization development and thus, of the performance of a business. I define them as "the science of hiring and the art of interviewing". We already discussed the importance of hiring right; let's talk about the interview process.

Firstly, before you start interviewing, think about the following: do you really need to hire someone? Is the need immediate or are you hiring based on opportunities that may be coming your way? Can this hiring wait without jeopardizing an opportunity or the performance of the organization?

Consider the effects of hiring or not hiring another employee:

Costs of no hiring:
- Lost productivity
- Cost of overtime needed because of insufficient labor
- Cost of temporary help (agencies and salaries)
- Lost sales or opportunities

- Effect on the morale of the organization because of extra hours
- Lower performance of the company.

And the cost of hiring:
- Advertising, search firms, referral fees
- Relocation and travel
- Additional overhead (salary, benefits, tools, supplies, etc.)
- Possible additional management or supervisory cost

Considering all of the above, decide on the need to hire additional manpower and the timing for the hiring.

And if you decide that you need the extra person(s), do you have anybody in the organization that can do the job or take the position? Is this the right opportunity to reward a good employee by offering him/her this position? If in doubt, interview your best employees and see if they represent a better pool of candidates than what you can find outside.

Above all, make up your mind not to compromise your expectations and not "to settle for what is available". Decide exactly what you want in a new employee and do not deviate from that.

Develop a hiring plan considering our discussion above; i.e., the timing and requirements of hiring. The plan should include:

- A budget that includes all expenses of recruiting, hiring and the expenses of extra overhead.
- A valid job criterion that defines the requirements for the candidates to meet.
- A comprehensive job description for the position(s) to be filled. (See recommended process above.)
- Any changes to the organization as a consequence of bringing in additional people.
- Pipeline management; using the "continuous hiring" concept.
- Profiling and assessments of candidates and of the job(s) to ensure good matching of the two.

Before you start the process consider the following potential mistakes to avoid:

- Hiring too quickly. As explained above, there is a critical balance between hiring too soon and hiring too late.
- Trusting your "gut" feeling. As explained below, is OK to trust your "gut" but don't make the final decision based only on this measurement.
- Hiring on references. The candidates will give you only those references that he/she is confident will speak well of him/her.
- Accepting recommendations. While recommendations give you a certain degree of confidence, keep in mind that those making the recommendations may not know your culture and other issues peculiar to your company.
- Approving the candidate because he/she did great in the interview. Depending on the level of the position(s) to be filled and in the level of the candidates, there are organizations dedicated to train candidates in the interview process. Candidates come prepared and their performance in the interview may not necessarily give you a true picture of him/her.
- Choosing candidates because of impressive resumes. As with the interview, there are plenty of consultants dedicated to embellish resumes.

The job criteria must include skills and talent you want in the candidate(s), as well as the valued and not valued personality traits to look for. Define if and how the candidates will fit in the culture of your company; this is perhaps more important than whatever skills the candidate(s) has.

From my bag: A client in the insurance industry asked me to interview a candidate for a Vice President position. When I met the candidate, his first question to me was "how much you know about the insurance business?" My reply was "nothing, and that's my competitive advantage". What did I mean by this? Since I am not knowledgeable of the particular industry, my perspective was not influenced by it's peculiarities and I could judge the candidate only by his talents and qualifications as a leader, not as an insurance expert; that part of the interview was reserved for my client the CEO. The moral of the story is that you must decide what the purpose of the interview is and limit your questions to the appropriate level.

Complete a Work Environment profile that defines exact expectations of how the job is to be done and match the behavioral style of the candidate to the job. Use the concept of "if the job could talk what characteristics would it ask for"? Applying this concept by using behavioral assessments you increase the probabilities of getting the right match of employees to job and positively affecting performance and longevity of new employees.

Before the interview review the resume, cover letter and application. Look for patterns, inconsistencies or gaps. Identify what questions you and your staff will ask the applicant. Make sure the questions are open ended and don't have a "built-in answer" in them. Avoid "light" questions that don't tell you anything of value but you use to fill-in time.

It is a fact that most business owners (and even their key people) are very poor interviewers. They have never learned the basic principles of interviewing. Interviewing is an art; learn the process and practice to become good at it. A good practice is to do the behavioral assessments before the interview, because the assessment's report gives you questions to be asked or at a minimum they give you the basis for questions.

Use behavioral interviewing and be sure you understand what they enjoy and don't enjoy doing. Use personality and cultural fit interview and ask about preferred working environment. Make sure their desires match the work environment profile assessment conducted.

When you interview you should speak only about twenty-five percent of the time and let the candidate use the other seventy-five percent. Use the silence treatment to entice the candidate into speaking more or give you extended answers that contain more valuable information for you. "He who speaks first loses" can be a valuable technique.

The candidate will sell him/herself to you and you should sell the company to the candidate, but be careful not to over sell; if you do it can be cause for unhappiness later and in extreme case, even for legal action by the employee because of false promises or misleading information. Remember that past performance is the best predictor of future behavior.

Use multiple interviews; the higher the position the larger the number of interviews to the top candidate(s). Have your staff interview the candidates too. Depending on the structure of the organization, the manager-to-be of the candidate should be the first to interview, but also peers-to-be should participate either in group interviews or on on-on-one sessions.

> ***Coaching suggestion:*** *Ask a peer to take the candidate to lunch; candidates tend to open up more in a non-threatening environment and with someone other than the boss. It is also a good idea for the "boss" to take the candidate to an informal meal; this will make the candidate more appreciated and willing to share information. Depending on the level of the opening to be filled, this outing may be a dinner in a "better" restaurant. If the spouse of the candidate is available, it can be very effective to include her/him in the dinner. Avoid treating this outing as an interview; keep it on a casual level and you can still learn a lot about the candidate.*

Be very aware of the legal requirements for the interview; what questions can be asked and what subjects are illegal to ask. Any question related to age or any of the other subjects considered discriminating taboo are of course to be avoided. Also, for example, questions regarding plans to get married or to have babies are out of bounds. A good practice is: if it can be suspected of legality, avoid it.

After the interviews are completed have a meeting with all who participated in the process and discuss everyone's assessment of the candidate. Depending on the position, on the feedback and on your own wishes, you may use a weighted consideration of the input from the staff, but don't be dictatorial or you may face difficult situations later.

Learn to identify basic types of personalities, as follows:
- Technical: enjoys details, analysis and implementing processes.
- Managerial: good at managing and organizing teams.
- Entrepreneurial: likes a fast-paced, challenging environment.
- Visionary: creative and strategic thinkers.

If you use the DISC system for behavioral assessments, make it a point to learn the four types of behavioral traits:
- "D": Direct in how they approach problems. They are the controllers of people and situations. They tend to be energized by taking charge of the problem-big or small.
- "I": Influencers; they are the persuaders. They tend to be energized by influencing other people. This dispositional type is more energized by talking more than listening.
- "S": Steadiness; they are the accommodators. They prefer a stable, constant environment. They are patient and loyal.
- "C": Conscientious; they are good followers of procedures set by other people. They represent the compliant types. They tend to be energized by complying with procedures and process.

Be alert of the most common interview process problems. Statistics reported from studies made:
- In thirty-nine percent of interviews the interviewers are not well prepared or not focused.
- In thirty-eight percent of interviews hiring managers don't give timely and fair feedback.
- In thirty-seven percent of cases the job description lacks details or is inconsistent.
- In twenty-four percent of interviews the applicant is kept waiting too long.

- In twenty-three percent of interviews the next steps are not clear.
- In seventeen percent of interviews the process is too long or complicated.

Hiring Within the Law

Are you exposed? Some of the regulations are dependent on the number of employees you have. If your company has more than 15 employees it is under EEOC jurisdiction that protects for gender, race, religion, origin, race and disability. If you have fewer than 15 employees you are not under the requirements of the EEOC but you can be sued by the employee(s) for contract, tort, emotional personal injury or other reasons not connected with EEOC.

To protect yourself and your company make sure the job description lists core duties and requirements but doesn't stereotype or embellish the job. Also, the application must have only requirements for job-specific information and avoid any personal information that may be considered discriminatory. Make a list of unacceptable questions and have your staff memorize it.

After You Hire

After you hire the candidate(s) you can ask certain questions that may be related to the job. Draw a contract to be signed by you and the new employee. The contract must include its purpose, compensation including bonuses and commissions, compliance to company's policies, reasons conditions for termination including indemnification, ownership of materials, confidentiality requirements, and any obligations surviving termination (for example, clause not to compete).

To optimize the chances for success make sure you and the new employee agree on the standards of measurements, or how his/her performance will be graded. Ensure the new employee has adequate learning time and the proper training, but also the opportunity to learn all company policies.

Introduce the new employee to the rest of the organization and allow him/her to get to know them and particularly those with whom he/she will work. If appropriate have business cards ready for him/her and make sure his/her work station or office is properly equipped. Assign a mentor to work with the new employee and use the buddy system to give him/her confidence in the new environment.

Finally, clarify all expectations up front to eradicate all misconceptions or misunderstandings. Give the new employee the big picture and make sure he/she understands and buys into the goals and the vision of the company. And clarify career path opportunities for the new employee.

My book "Fundamentals of Job Interviewing For Managers" [9], available at Amazon.com, gives suggestions and ideas to make the job interview effective while also making it pleasant. Using the tips included in it you will ensure a good selection by learning as much as possible about the candidates.

The Team Peer Review— Example

For all questions, answers are given on a scale of one to ten (with ten being highest). If the question doesn't apply indicate it with NA.

Non-Managerial Performance Review

1. Company Mission and Values

- Demonstrates high ethical standards and personal integrity

2. Customer Service and Quality Control

- Consistently sets and meets high standards of quality, gets the job done right the first time
- Responds quickly and effectively to clients' needs, goes the extra mile.
- Constantly looks for ways to add value to our services and/or products.
- Supports the Quality/Productivity service team.

3. Problem Solving/Judgment

- Sets specific, challenging and achievable goals and action plans
- Provides a logical and effective course of action for him/her to see that established goals are achieved.
- Exercises sound judgment.
- Visualizes and anticipates new problems and develops practical solutions
- Analyzes problems accurately; properly distinguishes their component parts.

4. Production

- Consistently completes expected workload on time.

- Exceeds normal requirements when necessary.

- Works with accuracy, thoroughness and effectiveness.

5. Work Style

- Perseveres with enthusiasm.

- Adjusts to new situations and deals well with ambiguity and stress.

- Is a self-starter, takes appropriate independent action, finds solutions.

- Supports change.

6. Resource Management

- Seeks better ways to complete tasks.

- Vigilant in minimizing expenses.

- Effectively uses computer systems and other technologies.

- Supports the Human Resource service team.

- Supports the Information Systems service team.

- Arranges work for most efficient handling.

7. Communications Skills

- Identifies the right issues to be communicated and the appropriate audience.

- Writes clear well organized, logically developed memos.

- Makes effective and persuasive presentations, both oral and written.

- Interacts effectively at all levels within the company.

- Keeps others informed as appropriate.

8. Business Organization Knowledge

- Develops competence in one or more professional discipline(s) and is increasingly recognized and sought by others.

- Understands the company's mission, products and services.

- Understands the company's culture and knows how to get things done.

9. Teamwork

- Develops effective working relationships with peers and superiors.

- Invites information, constructive criticism and cooperation from others.

- Positive influence with co-workers.

10. Excellence Criteria

- Personal accountability.

- Attention to detail.

- Assessment.

- Teachablilty.

- Commitment to personal growth.

- Risk taker.

- Positive outlook.

- Value driven.

Leadership 360 Degrees Survey

This survey provides feedback about a person on areas critical to the person's success at this company. The statements listed below describe the behaviors required for performance excellence. It is important that you provide thoughtful and candid feedback.

Grade the person you are reviewing in each of the points on a scale of 1(lowest) to 10 (highest). If a question doesn't apply to the person you are reviewing, write NA. Add comments in each section to reinforce or explain ratings.

You are giving feedback for:
_____ Date: _____

QUESTIONS

Decision Making

1. Analyzes financial implications of business decisions.
2. Analyzes relevant data and information in appropriate amounts when making decisions.
3. Involves those that will be affected by the decisions they make in the decision making process.
4. Makes decisions without undue delay.
5. Carefully weights the pros and cons of alternative solutions or course of action before making decisions.
6. Recognizes the impact of decisions and actions on other areas of the business.

Comments:

_____

_____

_____

Developing others

1. Coaches employees and helps them improve overall work performance.

2. Puts people in challenging, learning situations, specifically to build skills.
3. Takes the time to share job-related knowledge.
4. Provides support and guidance to employees to ensure their ongoing development and success.
5. Ensures employees have the resources needed to get the job done.
6. Provides appropriate level of independence to staff and lets them take responsibility for their actions.
7. Gives others discretionary authority to handle the tasks the way they see fit.

Comments:

_____

_____

Results Orientation

1. Addresses situations requiring immediate action in a timely manner.
2. Demonstrates personal commitment and persistence in achieving goals.
3. Follows through on action plans and deliver results.
4. Holds people accountable for achieving timely results.
5. Expends extra effort when required to get the job done or meet commitments.

Comments:

_____

_____

Innovation

1. Involves appropriate parties in identifying process improvement changes.
2. Challenges conventional ways of doing things to improve organizational performance.
3. Fosters an environment that encourages innovation and the development of new ideas.

4. Promotes the use of best practices that lead to improved fiscal performance.
5. Thinks "outside the box" to make organizational improvements and achieve organizational objectives.
6. Takes well thought out risks.

Comments:

_____

_____

Communication

1. Actively listens to others to gain an understanding of the problems/situations they are facing.
2. Keeps people informed about organizational plans and developments.
3. Provides others with timely information on issues and decisions that affect their day-to-day work.
4. Uses effective presentations skills and techniques when delivering information or ideas.
5. Displays confidence when presenting ideas or expressing opinions to others.
6. Adapts own communication style to meet the needs of different people and different situations.

Comments:

_____

_____

Influence and Persuasion

1. Identifies and involves influential others to ensure the success of initiatives.
2. Develops good working relationships with the key people necessary for the accomplishments of project goals.
3. Develops alliances within the organization to further organizational goals.
4. Sells ideas and initiatives to both peers and management.
5. Acts as strong advocate and representative for the staff they lead.

Comments:

_____

_____

Integrity

1. Sets a strong example of integrity, dedication and fairness.
2. Communicates honestly with people at all times.
3. Accepts responsibility for actions.
4. Follows through on commitments made to others.
5. Stands up for values and principles.

Comments:

_____

_____

Resilience

1. Effectively balances work pressures with a healthy family/social life.
2. Remains calm and focused on stressful situations.
3. Communicates optimism regarding organizational issues and challenges.
4. Remains positive and optimistic despite setbacks and frustrations.
5. Clarifies priorities and direction during chaotic times.

Comments:

_____

_____

Open-Ended Comments

_____

_____

_____

Leadership 360⁰ Survey – Second Example

This survey provides feedback about a person on areas critical to the person's success at this company. The statements listed below describe the behaviors required for performance excellence. It is important that you provide thoughtful and candid feedback.

Grade the person you are reviewing in each of the 60 points on a scale of 1(lowest) to 10 (highest). Add comments in each section to reinforce or explain ratings. For points 61 through 65 be clear and appropriately expansive in the descriptions.

You are giving feedback for:

_____ Date: _____

Leadership

1. Is visionary and thinks strategically rather than "the idea of the week".
2. Handles stressful situations well without losing focus and direction.
3. Builds teams and motivates team members.
4. Accepts responsibility for problems instead of blaming others.
5. Sets an example of the type of behavior needed to enforce the culture of the company.

Comments:

_____

Management

6. Delegates effectively and holds people accountable.
7. Sets fair expectations and standards.
8. Places emphasis in staff development, training and coaching.

9. Brings out the best in people in achieving results.

10. Promotes team productivity.

Comments:

Business Focus

11. Sets a clear vision and direction for his/her organization/department.

12. Anticipates the key changes affecting our company and industry.

13. Exhibits good judgment regarding business direction.

14. Sets realistic goals and allocates sufficient resources to achieve them.

15. Understands how performance impacts the bottom line.

Comments:

Customer Focus

16. Sets high standards of excellence for serving customers.

17. Understands and serves customers' needs.

18. Finds new ways of serving the customer through creative solutions.

19. Identifies new markets, industry trends and opportunities to grow.

20. Maintains excellent relationships with key customers and stakeholders.

Comments:

Quality Focus

21. Strives to deliver superior results in all areas.

22. Emphasizes continuous improvement.

23. Develops and manages high expectations and standards.

24. Takes personal accountability for the organization's overall performance.

25. Takes timely corrective action for unsatisfactory performance.

Comments:

Corporate Development

26. Develops and implements systems and procedures.

27. Implements and enforces company policies.

28. Is sensitive to and helps develop company culture.

29. Promotes continuous improvement throughout the organization.

30. Maximizes efficiency of human resources.

Comments:

Communication

31. Provides candid feedback without offending or patronizing people.

32. Addresses conflict and disagreement effectively.

33. Presents opinions in a way that makes it safe for others to disagree.

34. Is persuasive, frank and a good listener and shows empathy for others.

35. Good at written communications, presenting and reporting.

Comments:

Decision Making

36. Considers relevant sources of information before making important decisions.

37. Empowers others in making significant decisions affecting their work.

38. Demonstrates good judgment and common sense.

39. Makes timely decisions and course correction without delaying action.

40. Demonstrates problem solving skills; is analytical and thorough.

Comments:

Self-Development

41. Looks for self-development opportunities.

42. Is aware of weaknesses and works to eliminate them.

43. Is open to new learning and feedback without becoming defensive.

44. Identifies lessons learned with his/her team to improve results.

45. Seeks advice, knowledge and coaching to expand own views.

Comments:

Planning & Organization

46. Develops plans and schedules and manages them effectively.

47. Keeps people focused on the organization's priorities.

48. Manages resources to meet schedules.

49. Constantly accommodates workload to improve efficiency.

50. Uses time effectively.

Comments:

_____

Interpersonal Skills

51. I can trust this person to represent my interests even if I'm not present.

52. Treats people with fairness and respect and shows emotional maturity.

53. Is respected by others for who he/she is and his/her contributions.

54. Fosters energy, enthusiasm and commitment in others.

55. Has productive one-on-one relationships.

Comments:

_____

Technical Skills

56. Is an expert in his/her area of responsibility.

57. Stays current with the latest technologies and advances in our industry.

58. Balances short term results with long-term competitiveness.

59. Actively seeks to use technology to build the organization's capabilities.

60. Demonstrates sound technical savvy in making business decisions.

Comments:

_____

Overall

61. Overall, I rate this person's business skills and abilities as

_____

62. Overall, I rate this person's relationships with others as

_____

63. Overall, I rate this person's contributions and achievements as

_____

64. Describe this person's greatest strengths as a leader.

_____

65. Describe specific things this person could do to become a better leader.

_____

References:

1. Jack Welch and Suzy Welch, *Winning,* (Harper Business; 1st edition, April 5, 2005).
2. Michael Gerber, *The E-Myth Revisited,* (HarperCollins; 1st edition March 3, 1995).
3. Ray Brun, *How Small Businesses Capture Talent; 164 Strategies for Recruiting and Hiring Winners,* (Outskirts Press, February 1, 2008).
4. Leigh Branham, *The Seven Hidden Reasons Employees Leave,* (AMACOM; 1st edition, January 3, 2005).
5. Towers Perrin, Global Workforce Study, www.towersperrin.com/tp/showhtml.jsp?url=global/.../gws/.
6. Liz Wiserman, *Multipliers: How the Best Leaders Make Everyone Smarter,* (HarperBusiness; 1st edition (June 15, 2010).
7. Patrick Lenzione, *The Five Dysfunctions Of A Team,* (Jossey-Bass; 1st edition April 11, 2002).
8. Peter Drucker, *The Practice of Management,* (Harper Paperbacks, October 3, 2006).
9. Oswald R. Viva, *Fundamentals Of Job Interviewing For Managers, Improve Your Hiring By Improving Your Interviewing,* CreateSpace, SkillBites.net, January 8, 2013.
10. Oswald R. Viva, *Performance Reviews; The Bad, The Ugly, ... The Alternative",* CreateSpace, Amazon, March 2014.

Chapter VIII - Communication

"Nothing can cripple an organization more than a work environment where information is on a need-to-know basis"

Justin Martin

Some people think that communicating is easy; I disagree. Communication, defined as an exchange of ideas or sentiments with another person, requires skill. This type of exchange demands that we listen and speak skillfully as a two-way relation, not just talk unilaterally.

Good communications in the business world applies to internal as well as external communication, communication between management and employees, between employees and customers, between U.S. based employees and foreign associates, between any business related person and those for which English is a second language in which they are not proficient, and between any people related to a business.

This is a book on coaching small business leaders/CEO and thus, while all those communication opportunities listed above are important, here we will only deal with internal communications and primarily between management and employees. It is an essential trait for all business leaders to be good communicators and to not treat it as such is risking more than just misunderstandings.

Communications Skills

The importance of communication skills plays an integral part in business. In every employee's survey ever done communications was identified as the #1 complaint issue. When employees are asked what traits they value in their managers, they consistently cite preferring working for supervisors who foster an environment of open communication in the workplace. Employees prefer working with managers who listen to them and who share information with them on a regular basis.

Research found that companies demonstrating poor performance in communications have nearly twice the employee turnover, and even slight improvements in organizational communication and giving employees access to information has a profound impact on employee turnover. These findings should motivate you to measure your communication practices and strive to improve.

Communication is a basic skill that is needed to work with people. Leaders set the tone and create the environment where communication is open and a sharing of ideas occurs or they can set the opposite where there is no communication and the organization fails. The culture of your company should include the rule for open and true communications where communication that promotes team work and a friendly environment is rewarded, and belligerent or dividing attitude is penalized.

Without the ability to communicate effectively your personal effectiveness will diminish. By limiting the information available to employees you risk the creation of internal silos and turf wars that will eat the heart out of your business. As a business owner it's important for you to spend time thinking about the needs and expectations of the individuals who work for you to be informed of everything that goes on in the business.

Yes, I understand the need to keep some things confidential, and as the owner, it is your prerogative to do so, but don't discount the benefits of communicating all that can be communicated.

As weak communications are a major problem within organizations, good communication skills are major assets for people and for business. The ability to get the right message across in a simple, effective manner offers crucial benefits in the form of improved effectiveness. If a strong, clear message is given, it leaves no doubt as to what was meant. This principle applies to communication at a one-to-one level and even to company-wide messages.

Employees Need To Know, and You Have a Need Too.

If you only tell employees "what they need to know" related to their individual jobs, but don't share information about the goals, vision or mission of the organization you will have workers who feel confused and uncertain about their role in the organization. By giving employees access to information about the company's goals and performance, it allows them to develop a deeper understanding of where they fit in the big picture.

As a leader you may be tempted to feel that those who report to you only have a responsibility to listen. But if you believe this, pretty soon conversations in the workplace take the tone of a lecture instead of a free flow exchange of ideas. It will lead to employee discontent and as a result, to low retention, but more importantly, it may lead to the failure of your businesses to achieve its potential and, in extreme cases, to failure of the business.

People have a basic need to know what is going on around them but many business owners make the mistake of assuming that employees aren't concerned with the big picture of how the organization is doing. And besides the need to know, employees feel comfortable with managers that share relevant information with them about the company, and about their performance and about their position within the organization. They are able to more directly see why their roles are important and are more likely to be committed to and engaged in working toward the company's long term success.

Just as the employees have a need to know, you as the owner/CEO also have a need to know what's going on in your company. Don't be naïve and believe that all the news will come to your door; you need to look for it. How you act and how you communicate will either encourage employees to come to you, or motivate them to hide information.

Nobody likes to be the envoy of bad news (unless they do it as a vengeance) but you need to know both good and bad news. If you retaliate (in actions or in words) against the messenger, you will not get any more messages from that person. If you thank them for their candid approach to bring the information and take measures to correct whatever issue caused the problem, you will be a trusted recipient of news.

Having an open door policy will not assure you of getting all the information that you need. You are the boss and people will naturally be shy about communicating with you. You need to go out and look for it; walk the floor, ask probing questions, listen to comments, observe attitudes of employees, and pay attention to even the smallest details and you will increase your chances of knowing what's going on around you.

Giving Feedback

Whether it is as part of a performance review or a casual interaction, what you tell an employee can be the difference between being respected by the employee (or even admired) and being considered cold, not caring or, worse yet, mean spirited. In their eyes your feedback is a reflection of their persona, not just of their capabilities, and if it is negative it can be taken as offensive.

Always make your feedback positive, unless of course when you have to reprimand someone, but even then try to make it in a positive tone, one suggesting actions to improve or not to repeat the wrongdoing. If you have to give negative feedback, balance it with some positive comment. Consistent negative feedback turns people off and closes future communication.

When treating behaviors or attitudes that you want to change, explain why you want the employee to change them. Never use the "because I say so" posture. Suggest or propose alternate behaviors and explain also the consequences of not changing.

Be in control of your emotions; even when confronted in a less than desirable tone, don't talk back in the same mode. Don't talk down to others or underestimate their feelings. If you are angry and you let the anger dominate your emotions, you will end up in an uncomfortable situation of no return. Change the atmosphere to a positive tone and save the relationship (and your reputation).

When you are giving a performance review, plan ahead. When you adlib without previously thinking what you will say, your words may come out differently from what you intended. I don't mean to give a rehearsed speech because that would not be perceived as sincere, but plan the context of what you will say. Present it as structured but honest comments and complement them with suggestions to improve, even if the review is for good performance.

Be specific in your comments; don't ramble on or "beat around the bush". Make your comments self-generated; never attribute negativities to others. If you are suggesting or demanding change, give ideas as to how to change; propose a plan and define outcomes that can be measured or identified. Propose a follow up review to check progress and be absolutely clear in what you expect.

When covering multiple issues don't present them as a total package of negativities. Pick the most critical and concentrate on those; after they are covered to your and the employee's satisfaction, decide if it is worth going on to the others. If you try to tackle all of them in one session it may be overwhelming and upsetting to the employee.

Open Communications

CEOs who communicate authentically, candidly, respectfully, consistently, and frequently will be viewed as trusted leaders by employees and colleagues. To communicate authentically means to be you.

Whatever you write or speak should be genuine; if you try to adopt an approach to communication that doesn't fit your personality, your message will not be trusted. You should be candid and tell the truth even if it is difficult to do so. Self-deception in leadership contributes to miscommunication.

Every aspect of a company is governed by communication. Effective communication between managers and those that do the work is essential to ensure that the right work is being done. But you need to realize that effective communication is a two-way exchange and you need to not just "hear" what the other party is saying, but to really listen. If you do this you will benefit from nuggets that lie dormant in the minds of their team members. A lack of communications skills can affect the bottom line.

> *Coaching suggestion: when you give instructions to someone, to be sure that the other party understood what you said ask them to repeat the instruction to the outmost details. While this may be a little uncomfortable at times, it gives you and the other person the confidence that your message was received accurately. Since there is no miscommunication, there won't be any excuses related to it if the job is not done right.*

You are the boss but you don't have to have all the answers. It's OK to say, "I don't know." In fact, you will gain respect when you admit it. If you want to find the answer, say so, and then follow up to share your findings. You may also decide to offer the employee to work on the problem together to find the answer. By doing this you will gain the trust of others because they'll know that you don't "fabricate" the answers.

In a dialogue (not in a monologue), look for common ground instead of focusing solely on the differences that may be between you and the other party. If you are proposing change, remember that change is stressful for most people, particularly if your activities affect them in a way that they can't control. Reassure them by telling them how what you're doing or proposing will benefit them.

A must rule is that your message needs to remain the same if it is given multiple times. If different parts of an organization are hearing conflicting messages you will be in danger of losing your credibility within the organization. Make sure you communicate the same key messages every time you are communicating on the same topic. Details may change depending on the audience and what they need to hear, but the core of the message cannot change.

Listening is a Key Part of Communication

Most people think they listen well, but the truth is that most people don't listen at all; they just speak and then think about what they're going to say next. Good listening means asking good questions and acknowledging what you heard. Understand that most people have a self-serving agenda but don't assume that someone will share or even agree with your agenda, so explaining what's most important to you and asking what's most important to the others, can help build a solid foundation for a two-way conversation for mutual benefit.

To give the other party the assurance that you listened and heard what they were saying, acknowledge the message and if necessary ask them to expand on it; for example, "tell me more about your concern" or "I understand your frustration". Share responsibility for any communication in which you're a participant.

Understand that people want to feel heard more than they care about whether you agree with them. I'm sure that for you it is important that people listen and care what you say; it is also important for others to know that you listen and care. Show that you're listening by giving others your complete attention.

Some situations can be confusing or difficult to "read" and you must be careful not to misinterpret what is said. When you listen to employees, learn to distinguish between reasoning and your guess work; between a disgruntled employee and one who is unhappy for personal reasons; between an employee who is fearful and covers up with bravado and one who challenges authority for other reasons; between important and incidental data; between related and unrelated incidents. List and evaluate every important factor in each situation. Carefully observing and checking the evidence will tell you what you need to know.

To get to the bottom of someone's real concern or agenda ask clear and direct questions. Only by understanding their concerns or agendas you can have a truly rich, beneficial conversation. Listen to the answers to your questions and proceed accordingly.

Communicating News

If your company has good news, it's important to share the celebration with employees. Alternately, if the news is not good, it's important to be honest with employees about what happened and what the organization is doing to counter the ill effects.

Often, when faced with a crisis, small business owners stop sharing information with their employees. Management may think that it's best not to talk about what has happened until there is a solution. The problem with this approach is that silence from management leads to employee speculation about what the problem might mean for the future of the organization.

If management isn't talking, employees usually assume the worst. When transmitting news, the message must be clear or it can be misinterpreted. I've seen it happen—good news can be delivered so badly that it sounds like bad news.

It's better to let employees know what's going on, and assure them that you are working to remedy the problems. Don't try to make the news more palatable by improving the facts. Don't disguise the news with a false picture; if you don't tell it like it is, employees will find out and will become even more concerned.

Remember that employees are smart and that eventually they will discover the truth. Instead, be honest and open. Let your employees know what you're doing and make them participant of the solution. By communicating openly with your workers in good times and in bad, you'll develop loyal and committed employees.

Always communicate respectfully and treat every employee with dignity. If you are disrespectful in your communications, they will be disrespectful towards you. You must place a priority on communicating consistently and frequently with your staff. A trusted leader communicates with stakeholders all the time, not just when he or she needs something.

Skillful communication guards against surprises occurring that catch employees off guard or feeling not prepared. Information needs to be shared with all members involved in a situation or new process. Even if some of the information is negative, the effects of not sharing that information can have a devastating effect on the organization. Employees do not like surprises or being kept in the dark. If you are not telling employees what they need to know, someone else will and you may not like their version.

Of course you don't like being kept in the dark either, and if you are it may be more damaging than keeping employees in the dark. They say that "bad news travels fast", but this is not necessarily true in the workplace. If something bad happens you may be the last to know; conversely, good news will make its way to your office really fast.

This "phenomenon" can give you a false sense of security of everything being OK. You need to make a special effort to find all news, good and bad, and you can do it by frequent conversations with employees at all levels and by practicing MBWA (managing by walking around) visiting the various departments.

Communication in Meetings

Clear and open communications in meetings are critical to the effectiveness of meetings. A few years ago Microsoft conducted a survey of thirty-eight thousand employees in two hundred countries; it highlighted that poor communication wasted significant amounts of time. Ineffective meetings were singled out as a particular problem.

Organize meetings to be what you intend them to be and don't allow poor communications to deviate from the agenda and the subjects to be discussed. Don't allow disruptions generated by personal disputes or animosity; kill any oral quarrel diligently and work to find consensus in the discussions. Set the rules beforehand and stick to them.

Coaching suggestion: have no less than quarterly meetings with the entire staff and present a "state of the company" with triumphs as well as challenges. If you report bad news, make sure that you also explain how the company will recover and what actions you are taking to do it. If the news is good, make them participants by explaining what role they played in the success. Always give a report on the business side and, if appropriate, how they will benefit by it.

Communications with your direct reports should be much more often; weekly staff meetings are recommended, but keep them productive; don't allow them to digress into non-

effective subjects. Keep them short and interesting. Your direct reports should do the same with their staff. Always have an agenda for the meetings and always decide and publish action items resulting from the discussions.

From my bag: *many years ago I was managing a large engineering group. The staff meetings invariably extended to an excess because—typical of engineers—the discussions drifted to a lot of details. In order to improve the quality of the meetings and to keep them relatively short, I removed all chairs from the room and enforced a "standing only" policy for the meeting. They definitely got shorter!*

Do You Need a Shield?

Think about what characteristics have to be present for you to feel totally safe, so that you can be completely honest and open with those around you. Do you need to use a "shield" to protect yourself from words spoken to you or about you? What does the shield look like? We all use protection from time to time to defend ourselves. When a person uses protection in this way, it usually causes the other person to defend themselves and as a result communications break down.

The better you are at recognizing the shield in yourself and others, the easier it becomes to disarm the other person. Realize that you have much to benefit as we take off your armor and establish openness in the communication.

The best way for an employer to avoid misunderstandings and potential disruptions to productivity is to recognize the need for clear, unambiguous communications without the color of cultural bias. If cultural bias appears in oral or written communications, it is quite likely to have a negative effect on employee morale and adversely affect business productivity.

The effective communicator in business takes into consideration the cultural difference of those they interact with. Be alert of these differences, particularly if you have a work force composed of various cultural backgrounds, and if needed get help from specialized consultants to learn the peculiarities of communications of various ethnic cultures.

Improving Communication Skills

There are many things you can do to improve your communication skills and therefore improve your business and personal success. Things such as active listening, eye contact, and clear speech all help with your ability to effectively convey your thoughts and point of view. You cannot try these skills out one day and expect an immediate difference in the eloquence of your speech. Like with all things in life, you have to practice these skills before you can perfect them.

When a manager is briefing employees about a new task, he must plan what and how he is going to say it. This might only take a few minutes, but it can lead to a message which is clearer and more effective than a rambling, off-the-cuff, briefing which can leave the employee confused, and result in an uncompleted or badly executed task.

Coaching suggestion: when you want to get to the bottom of an issue; for example to find the source of a problem, use the "five whys" practice. It works like this: ask a question, for example, "why did we ship a non-conforming product?" You will get an answer such as "it skipped final inspection", to which you reply again with "why?" The answer will come back something like this: "it was not specified in the traveler". So you come back again with "why?" and a new response will say "we used the old traveler". Your next "why" will get the answer "according to the production order that is what was to be used", and the next "why" will get you "the order entry document called for spec xxx". Now you are getting to the root cause of the problem and one more "why" will get you there and will give you the opportunity to fix the problem by addressing the root cause.

Technology

Technology may be detrimental to the effectiveness of good communication skills. As Joseph Priestly [1] said: "The more elaborate our means of communication, the less we communicate."

Unfortunately, nowadays people trend to move away from face-to-face communications, using instead technological tools to communicate. E-mail, phone voice messages, texting and other means are serious detriments to good communication.

Even if by using these tools people can express what they want to say, they cannot see or appreciate the impact that what they say has on the other individual; they cannot read body language or detect emotions.

Technology also plays another harmful role in the corporate environment by giving disgruntled employees a vehicle to transmit their discontent. Let's say that you give an employee a bad review (in private of course) and he/she is understandably unhappy; it is likely that there will be e-mails flying around telling the world (internally) what a bad boss you are and how unfair the review was. How do you prevent this? In reality, you can't, short of controlling all e-mail, texting and other communications.

Written communications between management and employees make up a much of the corporate communications, thus clarity of written communication is of utmost importance. Consequently, to prevent misunderstandings or misinterpretations, it is vital that people learn how to get their points across in a clear and straightforward way.

Because written communications lack the sensitiveness of verbal intercourse, and the writer cannot visualize the emotions it will generate, it is critical to do it such that it still maintain good management-employee cooperation.

Benefits from Employees' Ideas

In the fast paced moving environment that occurs in organizations, an open exchange of ideas is critical to a successful organization. Employees should be encouraged to contribute ideas. Giving value to employee ideas is a key element in fostering open communication. In turn the leaders of any organization need to listen to their ideas and encourage and thank them for their contributions.

They need to set a tone of acceptance by consistently getting out the message that employees' ideas and contributions are appreciated and should be part of everyone's job in the organization. The exchange of ideas is really what the basis of all communication for business is all about.

Simply because you are the leader, employees may have a perception that you only care about getting what you want. You need to do a self-assessment on how you respond to ideas and suggestions. When employees contribute ideas, be careful not to say anything negative about them, such as "That will never work", because it can send out the message that you are not interested in other people's ideas.

Communication is a basic skill that you need to work with your employees. You as the leader must set the tone to create the environment where communication is open and a sharing of ideas is encouraged.

Employee Handbook

An effective communication "system" is one of the best ways to have a happy and effective workforce, and a good employee manual is an effective vehicle to communicate company policies. All businesses, regardless of size must have an employee handbook. It provides the play book and rules for the employees. If employees know what to expect, then they will be able to focus on getting the work done that makes them proud and their employer successful.

As a "must have" tool it is also useful to set up defenses if you are sued by an employee or audited by an administrative agency. However, without the right policy, or wording in the policy, the defenses may be lost. You must be knowledgeable of and stay current with rules and regulations, both federal, state and any others. And if there are overlapping federal laws and state laws, the handbook must haves clarify for the employee how the overlapping laws will affect them.

Coaching suggestion: using the DISC assessment evaluate your employees' personalities and communication behaviors, and teach them to use the reports to learn how to communicate with each other, considering each person's personality.

Published Citations

The *"The CEO's Secret Handbook"* by Bill Swanson, former CEO of Raytheon, includes *"Swanson's Unwritten Rules of Management"*[2] originally part of a PowerPoint presentation the CEO made to engineers and scientists at the Waltham, MA defense giant several decades ago. Those rules include several pertinent to communication, and they are:

- Unwritten rule #1; Learn to say "I don't know". Is used appropriate it will used often.
- Unwritten rule #5; Presentation rule: when something appears on a slide presentation, assume the world knows about it and deal with it accordingly.
- Unwritten rule #11; confirm the instructions you give others and their commitment in writing. Don't assume it will get done.
- Unwritten rule #12; don't be timid, speak up, express yourself and promote your ideas.
- Unwritten rule #14; strive for brevity and clarity in oral and written reports.
- Unwritten rule #15; be extremely careful in the accuracy of your statements.
- Unwritten rule #18; never direct a complaint to the top; a serious offense is to "cc" a person's boss on a copy of a complaint before the person has a chance to respond to the complaint.

In *"What Got You Here Won't Get You There: How Successful People Become Even More Successful"*[3] Marshall Goldsmith and Mark Reiter's primary insight is that good manners is good management. The book is not actually a corporate book. It is an etiquette book more centered on basic interpersonal behavior than refined managerial technique.

The meat of it is thus his elaborate and revealing discussion of the *"Twenty Habits That Hold You Back from the Top."* Although they are intended for employees in general, they also apply to management. Some of them pertain to communication and they are:

- #3. Passing judgment: "It's not appropriate to pass judgment when we specifically ask people to voice their opinions ... even if you ask a question and agree with the answer."
- #4. Making destructive comments: We are all tempted to be snarky or even mean from time to time. But when we feel the urge to criticize, we should realize that gratuitous negative comments can harm our working relationships. The question is not, "Is it true?" but rather, "Is it worth it?"
- #5. Starting with "No," "But," or "However." Almost all of us do this, and most of us are totally unaware of it. But Goldsmith and Reiter say if you watch out for it, "you'll see how people inflict these words on others to gain or consolidate power. You'll also see how intensely people resent it, consciously or not, and how it stifles rather than opens up discussion."
- #7. Speaking when angry. Never engage in discussions when you are angry. Give yourself some time to cool off before facing your listeners.
- #8. Negativity, or "Let me explain why that won't work": Goldsmith and Reiter call this "pure unadulterated negativity under the guise of being helpful."
- #9. Withholding information: This one is all about power. Goldsmith and Reiter focus on ways even the best-intentioned people do this all the time. "We do this when we are too busy to get back to someone with valuable information. We do this when we forget to include someone in our discussions or meetings. We do this when we delegate a task to our subordinates but don't take the time to show them exactly how we want the task done."
- #15. Refusing to express regret: "When you say, 'I'm sorry,' you turn people into your allies, even your partners." The first thing Goldsmith and Reiter teach is

"to apologize—face to face—to every coworker who has agreed to help them get better."
- #16. Not listening: This behavior says, "I don't care about you," "I don't understand you," "You're wrong," "You're stupid," and "You're wasting my time."

Goldsmith and Reiter's message is, ultimately, a very straightforward one: "The secret to corporate success is that one must be able to work well with others. If this sounds an awful lot like kindergarten criticism, that's because it is. But it's also the stuff of top-level corporate coaching, and for good reason."

References:

1. Joseph Priestly Quotes, http://en.thinkexist.com/quotes/Joseph_Priestly/.
2. Bill Swanson, *Swanson's Unwritten Rules of Management*, (Raytheon 2005).
3. Marshall Goldsmith and Mark Reiter, *What Got You Here Won't Get You There: How Successful People Become Even More Successful*, (Hyperion; 1st edition, January 9, 2007).

Chapter IX - Culture

Create the right culture and you'll have an enjoyable place to work.

I'm always unsure of what should be covered first, the development of the organization or the development of the culture. Both go together and cannot be treated individually without covering both. Nevertheless, it must be clear in your mind what culture you want to institute in your company, so the organization is built within this culture.

Corporate culture can be described as a blend of the values and practices that all companies develop over time. It describes and governs what and how owners and employees of the company think, feel and act. It is the environment prevalent at work; it is a powerful element that shapes the environment, internal relations, interaction of people and departments and how or if they collaborate as teams.

One of the key assessments when interviewing prospective employees is where the candidate is a "good culture fit". Culture is difficult to define but you generally know when a candidate appears to fit your culture; it just "feels right". Culture is the environment that surrounds everyone at work all the time, but you cannot see it except through its physical manifestation in the work place.

The culture of an organization is made up of the values, beliefs, underlying assumptions, attitudes and behaviors shared by a group of people. It is the behavior that results when a group arrives at a set of generally unspoken and unwritten rules for working together. It combines all the life experiences everyone brings to the organization, but it is mainly influenced by founders and leaders because of their role in decision making and strategic direction.

The culture of your company determines to a large extend how well your business will do. If you fail to implement the "right" culture in the company, you are risking serious consequences for the business.

Tolerating poor performance or exhibiting a lack of discipline to follow established procedures, or ignorance of systems, will negatively affect the performance of the business. Accepting misbehavior of employees, lack of team unity, disregard for quality, breaking confidentiality, and even poor personal presentation are signs of a less than optimum culture.

The culture will determine what people do and what they won't try; who will stay and who will leave; how business will get done. It starts with you; decide how you want people to act and set the example. A company culture that is aligned with your goals and helps you anticipate and adapt to change will help you achieve superior performance. Stay connected to what happens around you. Acknowledge people and success often.

Creating the "right" culture is part of your development as CEO. You must establish it early because it is very difficult to change once it is predominant, so you want to make sure the "right" culture is driving the organization.

It is also difficult to measure; someone said that to measure the culture you should count the smiles of the people, but this may be misleading. Nevertheless, a good measure of culture is to look at the behavior of employees; how do they act and what do they do? Also, listen to your employees, suppliers and customers and look for common behavior.

> **Coaching suggestion:** *Practice the MBWA style of management (management by walking around). A "good morning" and a smile first thing in the morning can go a long way to make people feel "part of it". Learn the names of all your employees and greet them by name; ask about their family and remember special occasions such as birthdays. Practice this type of people management and you will have a happy workforce and the basis for a good culture.*

The Gallup organization has interviewed more than a million employees of American companies. Using the results of those interviews they set out to identify those questions where the most engaged employees—those who were both loyal and productive—answered positively and everyone else answered negatively or neutrally. They concluded that the following twelve questions are the simplest and most accurate way to measure the strength of a workplace.

1. Do I know what is expected of me at work?
2. Do I have the material and equipment I need to do my work?
3. At work, do I have the opportunity to do what I do best every day?
4. In the last seven days, have I received recognition or praise for doing good work?
5. Does my supervisor (manager) seem to care about me as a person?
6. Is there someone at work who encourages my development?
7. At work, do my opinions seem to count?
8. Does the mission/purpose of my company make me feel my job is important?
9. Are my coworkers committed to doing quality work?
10. Do I have friends at work?
11. In the last six month has someone talked to me about my progress?
12. This last past year, have I had opportunities at work to learn and grow?

A primary factor in the culture must be your values as they are the most important thing that you have and that you can implement in your company. So, establish your values as the core values that will drive the company and then allow your values to drive your decisions; when you do this, the decisions will be easier.

Establishing the right culture will result in clarity of the Vision because you will know what "type" of company you want to get you to your destination. It should be a company with high motivation and productivity, with a strong team and team work with cross-functional cooperation and high accountability standards.

For this, you will need to have employees that are highly motivated and engaged in the Vision of the company. You should also build or transform the organization into one that not only welcomes but also initiates change.

Company culture tends to change over time. Employee turnover affects these changes; as employees leave and replacements are hired, there will be changes; however, the stronger the culture the less the changes affecting it. Also, as the company grows, employees are added and systems change, the culture tends to change too. It is very important for you to be aware of these changes and to do what must be done to maintain the culture that you want in your company.

While all the above discussed conditions are important and necessary, perhaps the most critical one is the one pertaining to accountability. Accountability plays a role in all the others, as without accountability there is no assurance of performance or motivation. I'm referring to accountability at all levels and in all practices. As such, accountability deserves a chapter by itself and we cover it separately.

If you are the CEO of an existing venture I urge you to do a self-evaluation of the culture in your company. You need to answer the following:

- What are the elements of your current culture?
- How strong is your culture? There should be no doubts as to the culture reigning in the company. Everything and everyone should say "this is our culture" and obey by it.
- What are the beliefs about the way it is and how to behave? "This is how we do business here" should not be just a statement but it must be the way of life and it must be documented and followed like a religion.

- What new behaviors are needed for your company to succeed in the future? Analyze what you are lacking or needs improvement and act on it as soon as possible.
- How do the shortcomings affect the strategies? As the culture guides the company, shortcomings in it may affect strategies developed to evolve the company, and thus they must be corrected.
- Who in the organization exhibit the needed behavior? Or more importantly, who doesn't? Identify the culprits and take whatever action is necessary. In some cases, when there is a misconnection with the culture, dismissal may be necessary.
- What realignment will be needed in the organization? There may be cases where the alignment of the organization causes conflicts that are not conducive to keeping the right culture, and therefore a change in mandatory.
- How will you engage employees to understand the need to realign? Everyone must understand that maintaining the desired culture is a prerequisite in the organization and that whatever changes are needed to maintain it will be done.
- How will you communicate success in support of the new or revised culture? The success of it should be obvious, but repeated communications to reinforce it will convey the message of the importance it has.

Coaching suggestion: Do a culture audit consisting of the following: Assess the values of key individuals to see how they match with your values and the values you instituted in the company. Using proven instruments assess and profile the senior team with respect to the culture they practice and implement in their departments. Do a 360 degrees survey for key individuals to get feedback from peers, supervisors and subordinates. Also do an employee survey structured around culture issues, for all employees. Obtain and use feedback from exit interviews and from performance reviews of all personnel as valuable information regarding culture issues.

It is much easier to establish the "right" culture than to change an established culture. This is the prime reason why many company mergers fail, because merging to vastly different cultures is extremely difficult. The differences between cultures will create differences between the two organizations and develop the "us vs. them" syndrome that kills many businesses.

One of the two merging organizations will need to unlearn old values and behaviors and then learn the new values and behaviors demanded by the other. The larger the organizations, the more difficult the amalgamation of the two cultures; the end result typically is unhappy employees and a less than efficient business.

I go further than that: If you are considering an acquisition or a merger, before you get to the final negotiations you should do an analysis of the culture prevalent in the company that you are considering to acquire or merge, and if the results of the analysis show a culture vastly different from yours, forget the acquisition or merger; it would never work. You will save yourself much aggravation and headaches and even possible failures.

If a culture is to change, owners and managers must support the change in practice, not just verbally. They must lead the change by changing their own behaviors and practices and they must be consistent in these changes. Both organizations must go to extended training to clearly understand what is expected of them and what is not acceptable. The training is for both organizations because if you single only one of them, you are contributing to the problem of culture differences.

Make sure you review all your systems for alignment to the desired culture. Also review the organization structure and reporting lines, employee selection and hiring, review process and rewards, and all practices related to human resources.

Make the changes or adjustments that you see necessary to align the culture—or cultures if you are dealing in a merger—to your values and business goals. Changing the organizational culture takes time, commitment, planning and the right execution, so plan ahead and go for it; it isn't easy but it can be done.

As stated, it is much easier to establish a culture than to change a culture, but if you must change the culture of your organization, follow these points:

- Ensure the changes are supported by the team.
- Ensure understanding of the changes by all involved.
- Create value and belief statement.
- Practice effective communication.
- Evaluate possible changes to the organization as demanded by the changes in culture.
- Review your approach to rewards and recognition.

Coaching suggestion: *If you or your teams decide that employees spend too much time agreeing with each other rather than challenging (in a good way) decisions or data generated by other team members, is a sign of a cultural problem. If employees become solely "yes" respondents to your word rather than challenging you or contributing with their own suggestions, is a sign of cultural problems. If you and/or the organization accept less-than-satisfactory performance, is a sign of a cultural problem. If individual agendas are promoted to the detriment of cohesive team work, is a sign of cultural problem. If people, including you, are not held accountable, is a sign of a serious cultural problem. You better act on these and other signs and change them, or your business will undoubtedly suffer.*

Some companies have achieved success by replacing the traditional top-down management model in favor of an open structure that incorporates elements of an ownership culture. They share the responsibilities and rewards of the company with all employees. They provide a planned ownership stake for employees, opportunities for employees to participate in most critical decisions and contribute with input about their own jobs. To do this the company must provide information and training in how to make these decisions.

You, the owner/CEO have another responsibility in your job description: you are in charge of culture. You can help create the ideal culture by a genuine commitment to form a work environment in which employees are given the tools, training and opportunities to actually think and act like the key participants that they are.

Don't isolate yourself; break down the barriers represented by the walls of your office and by your title and position. Without becoming everyone's friend be friendly with everyone while maintaining the line of respect. Show concern for their problems and offer your assistance to resolve them. Show empathy for their feelings and contribute words of advice or support.

Listen to your employees, their suggestions and even their complaints. Ask for their opinion about many things and let them know you value their opinion. If you see value in what they say, go ahead and implement the idea but without fanfare. Listen to what they say but also listen to what you say, because you may unintentionally say something that gives the wrong impression or sends the wrong message. Always add "what can I do to help" in any conversation, particularly when you are asking people to do things.

Give credit where credit is due but be careful not to ignore someone in favor of others. Use the "mirror and the window" concept explained somewhere else in this book, giving credit and accepting blame. Watch for other signs as well, such as unspoken words or actions that may indicate unhappiness or discontent.

All of the above is very important to develop and maintain the right culture, but what is more important is to create a culture of fairness and accountability. You will not lose the respect of the employees easily than by showing signs of unfairness, favoritism and lack of accountability. Not firing bad or low performing employees or rewarding non-deserving ones will create more discontent than possibly anything else. Be strict, be understanding and, above all, be fair.

Creating this environment may be challenging but it will yield the culture that will drive success for your business and happiness for all involved, including you.

Coaching suggestion: *I know that people don't like meetings and that you probably have too many meetings already, but I suggest you and your team meet at least once a* *month for the purpose of reviewing the culture of your organization. Discuss and reinforce communications, team work and accountability under the premises of what is discussed above. Also use this opportunity to communicate company news or a business update. In addition, I strongly recommend a company-wide quarterly "state of the company" meeting to inform all employees of progress, challenges and opportunities facing the company, as well as celebrating accomplishments.*

Leadership Alignment

Creating the culture that supports your vision and being an effective leader go hand in hand. Developing the most effective work environment that stimulates creativity and innovative problem solving and supports your strategic objectives is a key leadership responsibility. However, there are far too many instances where a leader will chase the latest fad or try something that a successful executive wrote about as the reason that person achieved success.

Unfortunately, what works in one organization and industry with a unique culture may not work in another. The lack of understanding of the connection between one's culture and leadership behaviors is one reason organizations fall short in achieving their objectives. They fail to align their leadership behaviors in support of the desired culture.

The Solution

Grade yourself in each of the following questions and determine your score in your leadership behavior. Use a scale of 100 where the maximum score represents full compliance with the subject.

Employees are quick to identify gaps between words used to describe how leaders want a firm to operate, and how the leaders are actually behaving. And, as the adage goes, actions speak louder than words. You need to examine these questions for your organization:

- Have you clearly established your direction, creating the vision, values and strategies needed to achieve you goals? Are they institutionalized?
- Has the leadership team clearly identified the desired culture and the supporting business case?
- Have you clearly and frequently communicated the vision and strategies to insure people understand and know what part they must play in achieving the goals?
- Do you delegate responsibility and authority, involve people in some of the decisions, motivate and energize them to be resourceful and overcome typical bureaucratic barriers?
- Do you help to create change by supporting the free flow of ideas and implementing processes and resources that are consistent with the culture?
- Is there full buy-in by the organization on the target culture and strategic goals?
- Do you find ways to satisfy the basic needs for achievement, belonging, recognition, self-esteem, a sense of control over one's life, feedback and role modeling?
- Have the leaders and managers analyzed how they need to change their behaviors? Do you know what behaviors must change throughout the organization? Are they visible role models?
- Is the organization prepared to provide any necessary training and coaching and hold people accountable for those behaviors?
- Do the leaders establish good working relationships with many people in the organization to create a collaborative, participatory environment where there is shared vision and goals?
- What actions need to be taken to support the culture and direction of the organization?

Your score

1 to 20: You are not the leader that the company needs to achieve your vision. Work with a coach to start developing your behavior.

21 to 40: You probably have the capabilities to develop your behavior in favor of the right culture, but you are consumed by the urgent issues and don't work on the important issues.

41 to 60: You are doing a good job but can improve it by identifying your shortcomings and applying the actions to correct them. You must establish clear objectives and getting senior team buy-in

61 to 80: You have a good handle on the leadership alignment of your organization. Competent leadership is emerging and most strategic goals are being achieved.

81 to 100: The direction of the organization and identification of the efforts to achieve the strategies are clearly established, communicated and supported throughout the organization. Leadership and culture are aligned and support each other.

The Outcome

The direction of the organization and identification of the efforts to get there are clearly established, communicated and supported throughout the organization. Leadership and culture are aligned and support each other. Strong competent leadership is emerging throughout the organization. Strategic goals are being achieved.

Establishing clear culture objectives, ensuring senior team buy-in, and identifying and communicating examples of behavioral alignment speed your way to achieving the culture that will support your success.

Chapter X - Delegation

"The single greatest cause for failure in managers is their inability to delegate."

—J.C. Penney

"Wise is the person who realizes early in life that what they can do by themselves is relatively small. A person's success is determined, in large measures, by what they are able to get other people to do."

—Lee S. Brickmore

What is delegation? Appointing someone else to act on your behalf. Acting on your behalf means that you are assigning the authority and responsibility to another person to carry out certain tasks or activities that you usually do.

Effective delegation is the most powerful activity in management because it enables you to direct your focus and energy to those activities that are the responsibility of the CEO and only you can do.

Stephen Covey, in his book *"The Seven Habits of Highly Effective People"*[1], suggests two types of delegation:

- Gopher Delegation is telling employees what to do, how to do it, when it needs to be done, and then sitting at their elbow and making sure they are doing what you asked. Under this type of delegation, employees' opportunity to develop professionally is limited.
- Stewardship Delegation is focused on results, not methods. It allows the other person to choose how to accomplish the assignment and holds him or her responsible for the results (accountability).

For you as the CEO, it should be obvious which the preferred method to adopt is. Stewardship delegation requires trust in the people you are delegating to, and trust is the highest form of human motivation. Sure, this involves more time than doing the task yourself, but this is time well invested because you are investing not only in the growth and development of an employee but also in the firm and in yourself.

When should you consider delegating? The short answer is *always* if you want to grow your company and yourself, but particularly when the following is evident:

- When you reach a point in your business where you are juggling too many balls and you begin to drop them.
- When you want to free yourself of areas that are not your strengths or which you do not enjoy.
- When doing certain functions takes away from you doing your job of CEO.
- When you have to deal with time management issues.
- When you need to create free time to strategize your business.
- When you need to work on your business not just in it.
- When you need to reduce the amount of time you are working, not only in hours but days.

You need to delegate to:

- Create growth in your company. The greatest value to a company is in its management team, and you need to delegate—and empower people—to make your team valuable.
- Protect yourself and the company in case of your incapacity. If you become incapacitated even for a short time, you need to have others ready to assume your functions.
- Prepare your business for an exit strategy. The value of your business will be greatly increased if you have a full team capable of running the company at its full effectiveness. You need to delegate now as much of your functions as possible in order to create that value when you are ready to exit.
- Reduce stress. If you are the only one that can do—or want to do—certain functions, you are creating stress for yourself. If you delegate you will still be responsible, but you won't have the stress of having to do it all yourself.

You must realize that your staff isn't the source of your problems; they are the solution to them. Don't look at your employees as a time consuming obligation that you have as CEO; if you choose your staff carefully and hired the right people, they should be the help that you need to be effective as CEO. Your ability to delegate will make the difference.

How much of your to-do list you could delegate? Dedicate your efforts to identify what you can delegate and what you need to have in order to be able to successfully delegate. Delegating correctly is not passing on the work to others; the more you can delegate, the more time you will have to dedicate to your people.

Some things you cannot delegate; namely your (the owner's) enthusiasm for the business and the drive towards your Vision. As dedicated as your employees may be, they will never have the desire and motivation that you have. The sooner you realize this, the better it will be for you and for your company.

> ***Coaching suggestion:*** *Draw a table with four columns. In the first column list all the tasks that you do today; in the second column list those tasks that you enjoy; in the third column list the tasks that you can delegate today counting on the people that you have, and in the fourth column list the tasks that you could delegate if you had the right people. You can also make a fifth column listing the time that must dedicate to each task. When completed, it will suggest the alternatives to delegate tasks, keeping those that you want to keep (enjoy), and how much time you would save by delegating; time that you can dedicate to more CEO related duties, to improve yourself, or to balance your life. It will also suggest what you need to do to be able to delegate more.*

> *"No man will make a great leader who wants to do it all himself, or to get all the credit for doing it."*
>
> —Andrew Carnegie

Delegating is Difficult

I've always said that delegating is the second most difficult job for a small business CEO to learn, but the good news is that it can be learned. What is the first most difficult job you ask? It is delegating with accountability, but we will cover that next.

Why is delegating so difficult for small business owners/CEO? It is for a variety of reasons.

- "Nobody can do it as well as I can". You started a business because you knew how to do something very well, and it is probably true that you are still the best at it, but unless you learn to delegate you will always be doing "that" job and not the job that you should be doing, the job of the CEO. As a result your company will not grow and you will not grow either.
- "I know I should be delegating but I don't have time to train someone now". Well, guess what? If you don't take the time to train someone to do it, you will be doing it forever. How long does it take for you to train others to do it? And how much of your time it takes for you to keep doing it? If you don't invest the time to train now you will continue to waste all that time doing "that" job instead of what you should be doing.
- Lack of confidence in employees for either of two reasons: a) "I don't believe I have anybody capable of learning the job". If is true, it's your fault, because it means that you hired the wrong people. Or b) "If I teach them this job they might find another employment"; another example of insecurity. Both are very poor excuses not to delegate.
- Perhaps the worst reason, and one that people will never admit to, is the reluctance to give up being "the expert" on certain jobs. If he teaches others how to do it, he won't be the only one knowing how to do it anymore. Like I said, people won't admit to this but I have seen it happen numerous times. It is a sign of insecurity.
- "Why should I let someone else do it when this is something that I truly enjoy doing". I tell you why, because if you keep doing "that" you are not doing your job. Find a way to do "that" as a hobby, but not taking valuable time from your job.

And even more excuses used to avoid delegating:

- Avoidance of change.
- Concerns about acceptance of others.
- Fear that the employee will do it better than you.
- Paranoid about sharing "your" systems or methods.
- Your lack of desire to take risks.
- The quest for perfection.

If your organization does not delegate properly it is severely limiting its effectiveness to the talents and energies of an extremely limited number of individuals (you and perhaps a few others). With this culture it will be very difficult to expand and grow the business on a profitable basis. You must take it as a fact that you can't do it all and succeed in your growth plans.

If you don't delegate effectively most of the staff will find itself with limited energy, low motivation and below par performance. Conversely, by practicing effective delegation, you'll give your employees additional job satisfaction and your organization will be able to utilize the energies and abilities of all its members and channel that energy toward the growth of each member and of the company. Just as important, you will be able to run the business rather than it running you and you'll have more personal time to enjoy life.

Delegation of responsibility requires equal delegation of authority but not of responsibility. The person you are delegating to is responsible for completing the task or executing the function properly, but in most cases you are still ultimately responsible for it or them. Authority means the right to direct, coordinates and decide, but it does not imply autocracy.

Learn the difference between delegating and abdicating. Abdicating is defined as to give up a position with no possibility of resuming it. To abdicate implies a giving up of power or sometimes an evading of responsibility. This is definitely not your position.

Coaching suggestion: If you have trouble delegating do not try to learn it all at once. Pick two or three relatively easy tasks to delegate and practice with those. You will soon find out what your weaknesses are in delegating, and by following the coaching of this book make the adjustments to your behavior needed for successful delegation. It is a good idea too to retain some control over the project to boost your confidence. As you become more proficient and develop the confidence, add more tasks or projects to be delegated. Try to add projects that require more people involved, more time to execute, and/ or more complexity. You will soon see a change in your attitude regarding delegation. Use this suggestion to teach others to delegate.

From my bag: *The CEO of a small (eight million dollars) company I was coaching used to take home every night a sizable amount of work that he claimed didn't have time to do at the office. The hours he was putting in at home was causing stress in his family life, with his wife and two young children complaining that he was never available for them. You guessed it; he did not delegate. Part of the problem was his lack of knowledge on how to do it, and part of it was that he didn't trust his staff. I started worked with him by having him complete the exercise discussed above under "coaching suggestion". From that table we selected a few things he could delegate and as he became comfortable with them we added some more. The end of the story is that he became a good delegator and found renewed happiness at home.*

Delegation is a Contract

When you are delegating you are in effect setting a contract with the employee or person you are delegating to. As a contract it must include rules, expectations and commitments. The rules are those that you institute to ensure that the task or function will be done right. The expectations are those that you set for the outcome of the task or function. The "contract" can be just a verbal agreement between the two parts, but in essence, if the employee accepts the challenge he/she is giving his/her word and thus making a commitment to you.

The commitments are from both you and the person you are delegating to. Yours is that you will empower the person and will provide the tools for him/her to accomplish the task or function according to your expectations. And the employee's, is a commitment of dedicating his efforts to meet the objectives and goals of the tasks or function.

When the employee accepts the delegation he/she is assuming ownership of the project or task. To assume ownership there must be empowerment so that the employee sees him/herself owners of the project or function, and have the authority to make decisions concerning the job. With ownership come responsibility and the authority to act. By delegating responsibility you are letting authority flow from you to the employee; however, accountability flows from the employee to you. To avoid misunderstandings with other staff members, the levels of authority should be clear and known by all involved.

For an effective delegation the employees need to understand why they are doing what they are doing, what results and standards are expected, and how their responsibilities for the task, project or function fit into the long term plan of the company. It is not enough to tell the employee to do something, that's not delegating, that's giving an order to comply. The employee needs to know the details and why the task is to be completed; moreover, the reasons he/she was selected to do it, and the conditions for the delegation.

Identify and transmit your expectations clearly, understanding that expectations are not goals. Goals are the ultimate results that you are aiming to achieve; expectations are the processes and activities needed to reach the goals. Communicate the expectations and make sure they were understood by soliciting questions from the person or persons that you are delegating to.

To be successful in carrying out the assignment the subordinates must be given guidelines and standard of performance, time schedules to be followed, and rewards/penalties for performance. You need to make sure the employee is trained to do the job or provide extra training and coaching. He/she must know exactly how he/she is expected to perform, or if it is up to the employee to set the guidelines, what are the rulers to follow. Lastly, the employee must know how he/she will be rewarded for doing a good job (it could be just as simple as a thank you) or the consequences if the outcome is not acceptable.

Subordinates also need:

- A detailed job description of the job assigned.
- A written system or process to be followed.
- Objectives that can be measured, explaining how they will be measured.
- Objectives that are achievable, not impossibilities to "test them". *(Remember the SMART goals discussed)*.

The Delegation Process

Like with most things in business there must be a system to delegate and a process to follow.

- Identify the need. Make sure you have identified a need to do what you are asking others to do. You are not assigning chores just to keep people busy; that's not delegating; when you delegate there is a need to accomplish something and the need is desired, if not critical, for the success of the business.
- Select the person that you will delegate to. "Select" is the key word here; don't just pick whoever is not busy at the moment. Chose the employee(s) that because of their capabilities will perform as needed.
- Plan the delegation. Be sure to cover all the what, when and how of the job and be sure you have enough information to transmit to the employee. Don't make the mistake of telling the employee exactly how to do it. Also, retain some control over the project, whether supervisory or for approval.
- Hold a delegation meeting. Whether it is a one-on-one or with a team have a formal delegation get together in which you explain everything that is involved, and you give all the instructions necessary. If needed, give the instructions in writing so there are no misconceptions or misunderstandings later.
- Create a plan of action. With the employee develop a plan detailing how the job will be done. Keep in mind that the plan needs to be "the employee's plan", even if you developed it. Drive the employee to buy-in the plan

so it becomes his/her plan (in the employee's perception).

- Review the plan carefully with the employee making sure (double sure) that he/she understood all instructions and outcome expected. Putting things in writing can help with the understanding.
- Implement the plan. Once you are comfortable with the delegation and with the understanding of the employee, give him/her the green light to start.
- As part of the plan, schedule periodic review dates to check on the progress made. The frequency of the reviews will depend on the length of the assignment, but do not wait until it is too late to make necessary adjustments or repair what is already damaged. It is also very important that you keep the dates scheduled, because if you don't you are sending the message that "it is not important". *(See the Accountability section for further details on this).*
- Butt out! Yes, once you completed the delegation process, get out of the way and let the employee proceed without your meddling. Supervision yes, meddling no. Make sure you know the difference and when to step in to help or advice and when to stay out. Give the employee(s) the opportunity to learn from mistakes—as long as they are not critical.
- Follow up.
- Follow up.
- Follow up. Cannot stress enough the importance to check on the progress and compliance of the project, task or function, and if necessary make adjustments as you go. Work with the employee to set interim goals and check marks. Together set check points to review progress and keep those dates religiously to emphasize the need for accountability.

If you or a manager of the subordinates invades into their area of authority, it will effectively relieve the subordinates from their responsibility. If you allow this you will generate confusion, loss of effectiveness, reduced productivity and loss of morale among the staff. These actions are typical of organizations with high employee turnover rates.

The Delegation Exercise at the end of this chapter can help you identify those tasks that you can delegate and the advantages obtained from it.

Levels of Delegation

Depending on the criticality of the delegated plan and on the seniority of the person to whom you delegated, there are different levels of authority and responsibilities given. For example:

- A basic level: Report facts back to me and I will make a decision on what is to be done. This is more of a job assignment than a delegation.
- Give me alternative actions, with pluses and minuses of each and give me a recommendation of the best option. Now you are giving the employee a little room to participate in the decisions.
- Advise me of what your plan of action is; don't take action until I authorize it. OK, you are saying use your initiative but I don't trust you enough to give you the full green light.
- Advise me of your plan; proceed with the plan unless I tell you otherwise. One step further up the ladder of delegation; I trust you but I reserve the right to stop you.
- Activate your plan and advise me of what was done. Full green light but let me know how well you did. Assuming that you know what the plan was, this is a good place to be because you need to know the outcome in a timely manner.
- Activate your plan to solve the problem and nothing is required of me. This is great delegation, but in practice

I much prefer the step above because you need to stay informed.

As we will discuss in the Accountability section, subordinates should be accountable for their performance of delegated tasks. Evaluate their performance based upon subordinates staying within authority boundaries as transmitted during the delegation planning. Measure performances based upon desired or expected results and results achieved. Another performance measurement, if appropriate, could be how he/she got his/her subordinates involved and used accountability measurements with them.

Causes of Ineffective Delegation

Of course we could name a litany of reasons that make delegation ineffective, but we will concentrate on the most common ones.

- Employee's lack of ability. Is the employee not knowledgeable enough about the project delegated, or does he/she lack the training necessary? Was he/she a poor hire or was he/she neglected regarding training? In either case, don't blame the employee as it is your fault. Perhaps the employee is a good employee but was the wrong choice for the project delegated; is it a case of elevating someone to their level of incompetence? Your leadership qualities and those of whoever is doing the delegation should tell you or the manager if the choice was correct and if so, what needs must be satisfied for the employee to be able to perform to your expectations.
- Employee lack of incentive. Again, you must question your choice of the employee; is lack of incentive a general problem with this employee, or is it only for this project? Why does the lack of incentive manifest itself at this time? Is it that the project being delegated is a bad match for the employee's interest and capabilities? Have you put any effort into motivating the employee? Does he/she know why he/she was chosen and what is the opportunity for him/her? If you plan the delegation correctly and had "the contract"

made very clear, this should not be a problem after the fact.

- Employee's unwillingness to take risk. This could be because of lack of motivation or drive, or because of insecurity; in either case, most likely is a bad choice for the project unless you see some talent in the employee that he/she doesn't recognize, and you want to help the employee by giving him/her this opportunity. Thread carefully, your magnanimity may not be rewarded.
- Employee's fear of punitive action. This goes together with the unwillingness to take risk. The employee doesn't feel capable of taking on the responsibility for the project and is concerned that he/she will be penalized for poor performance. Another clear case of choosing the wrong employee for the project.
- Unclear job duties or task assignment. The delegation process was not followed and you sent the poor employee to a sure losing game not knowing what the rules of the game are.
- Constant criticism of task results and techniques. Or to put it in other words, bad management. The employee needs coaching and encouragement, not negative criticism. As part of the delegation plan you should have reviewed the techniques to be used, so that was the time to make corrections.
- Lack of achievable goals or defined objectives. Are you asking the employee to do an impossible task? Have you clearly defined the objectives and goals to be achieved, or have you left inconclusive what is to be achieved?
- And last but not least, over controlling the employee. Are you delegating or are you distributing work? Are you empowering the employee or are you only assigning work? Remember the delegation process and the levels of delegation.

Delegating Criteria

To summarize the subject of delegation, to be successful in delegating you must accomplish the following:

- You are clear in your delegation and the chosen employee has demonstrated the capability to carry on the project successfully.
- The employee is seeking to take the responsibility. He/she takes on the assignment with enthusiasm and confidence.
- The objectives are clear to everyone involved.
- All the required resources are available. The employee has the tools, resources and training necessary to be successful.
- You have a high degree of confidence that the project will be successful when carried on by the employee.

Sources of Additional Information

"Who's Got the Monkey?"[2] is a classic article from Harvard Business Review published in 1968. It became the most reprinted article in HBR's history. It cleverly identifies tasks that are "delegated up" to the boss by his/her subordinates. It lustrates the different direction of delegating; i.e., up to the boss or down to the employees. It is a fun read with good lessons to be learned.

Management always runs out of time while employees run out of work. This has to do with management time as it relates to the interaction between managers and their bosses, their peers, and their subordinates. Most managers spend a great deal of time dealing with subordinates' problems. The article from HRB uses the monkey-on-the-back metaphor to examine how subordinate-imposed time comes into being and what the superior can do about it.

When a subordinate, openly or surreptitiously charges the manager with a task, he/she is passing the "monkey" to the manager's back. "Monkeys" are defined as the next move implicit in a task. To prevent being charged with them one must learn to identify tasks that are delegated up from the subordinates.

For example, some forms of up-delegation from subordinates:
- "I can't get that department to cooperate, could you talk to them for me?"

- "I'm not sure what to do next, could you take a look at what I've done so far?"
- "You know more about this customer than I do."

If a subordinate tells you "Boss, *we* have a problem" your response can be something like "We can't handle a problem. Either it's your problem, or it's my problem. Since I don't go to you with my problems, I have to assume that it's your problem we are discussing."

Every task has two parties involved; one to work it and one to supervise it. As soon as you agree to review it, follow it, decide it, or fix it, you just became the one working the task. All tasks should be handled at the lowest level consistent with their successful completion. Keep in mind that your staff has more collective time and energy than you do and they are closer to the problem, therefore, only those tasks that no one else can handle should be yours. As an added benefit, keeping those tasks out of your office allows you to help your staff more.

As you become really good at delegating, don't allow your employees to pass the monkeys to your back.

Final Thoughts

If You Can't Delegate, Your Company Can't Grow: The Seven Essentials [4]

It can be said that the basis for successful delegation is half knowledge, half attitude. The following seven key essentials of delegation illustrate this.

1. Realize that you are not the only person who can do things exactly right. As long as you retain the ultimate responsibility for all delegated tasks—and as long as you are available for consultation at various stages of the work—your company will retain your personal style.

2. Establish written descriptions of the tasks you are delegating, and be sure that your employees understand every detail. Descriptions of tasks should include: methods, goals, means of accomplishment (finances, employees, equipment, etc.), quality of work done, means to define that quality and timelines for completion of each stage of work.

3. You can retain varying degrees of control by requiring your delegates to provide written or verbal reports at specific stages of completion, or at specific time intervals throughout the course of a project. The amount of control you retain over a delegated project is determined by how often you meet with the people doing the work, or how often you require them to report to you.

4. When delegating a project to a team, assign responsibility to only one person. If you leave ultimate responsibility vague, your results could be vague.

5. Try not to tell people exactly how to do things. Sure, you have your own style, but even if someone does something a little differently than you would, the project can still be 100 percent successful.

6. Don't start by delegating large, extremely important projects. Take things one step at a time by starting with smaller, less important tasks. As your experience with delegating progresses, you'll feel more comfortable assigning larger projects, and you'll be better at the delegation process.

7. Look ahead to the time when your company has grown to such a point that even your delegates will have to delegate some responsibilities to others. This second stage of delegation is key for growing companies and requires that you will have to feel even more comfortable with the delegation process. It's important to train your key employees to delegate, so when the time comes they will feel confident and have the experience required.

Delegation Exercise

List all tasks that you do; then identify those that you could delegate to your present employees. List the time that you spend on each and the effect that delegating them would have. Extend the exercise to include tasks that you could delegate if you had the right resources (separately, you can identify those resources and the benefit that delegating to them would have to the company)

References:
1. Steven Covey, *The Seven Habits of Highly Effective People*, (Free Press; Revised edition, November 9, 2004).
2. William Oncken Jr., Donald L. Wass, Stephen R. Covey, *Management Time: Who's Got the Monkey?*, HBR Articles, Nov 01, 1999.
3. Oswald R. Viva, *Delegate to Succeed*, e-book; SkillBites, December 2011.
4. Business Week -- Release Date: 12 / 23 / 2004

Chapter XI - Empowerment

Without empowerment there is no commitment.

Empowerment: To give power or authority; to authorize, especially by legal or official means. To give or delegate power or authority. (Dictionary.com)

Business definition: Empowerment is the process of enabling or authorizing an individual to think, behave, take action, and control work and decision making in autonomous ways. It is the state of feeling self-empowered to take control of one's own destiny. As a broad definition empowerment means giving employees the power to do their job.

As we discuss how empowerment is very beneficial in business, we also need to consider the disadvantages of non-empowerment. Lack of empowerment of employees can significantly increase the cost of doing business.

A good example of this is organizations of customer service that because of non-empowerment of its employees, pass customers from level to level until someone is authorized to make a decision regarding a complaint. Empowerment could allow the first level employee to take action and satisfy the customer, thus saving a significant amount of money to the company and hopefully retaining a dissatisfied customer.

> **From my bag:** *A CEO I was coaching complained of being constantly "bothered" with interruptions to make decisions that other people should have been able to make. My analysis of the situation indicated that he had created a "culture of going to the top" for almost everything that needed a decision. This "culture" was not created by design; it had grown from a non-tolerance by the CEO of decisions made by others that he did not agree.*
>
> *It was clearly a combination of non-empowerment and a belief that he was the only one that could make the right decisions. It took some time and much coaching to change first his attitude toward others' decisions, and then for*

him to learn to empower employees to make those decisions. After the changes he became much happier and the organization much more effective and efficient.

In *"Empowerment Takes More Than A Minute"* [1] Ken Blanchard, John Carlos and Alan Randolph tell us not to manage employees minute-by-minute. Instead, create a more effective organization by giving your employees the information and authority to act and make decisions on their own, within a structured set of organizational goals and values.

By creating the culture of empowerment employees are free to use the knowledge they acquired, the experience gained by that freedom, and the motivation of being a true part of the business. Empowered employees feel a sense of ownership in their projects and functions with the resulting excitement and motivation to perform. As "owners" of their projects they become accountable for results, doubling the benefits to the organization.

Unfortunately, talking about empowerment is a lot easier than creating the culture to make it work.

The concept of empowerment was first introduced in business in the eighties. It promised much but because of the difficulties in implementing it, it didn't quite give great results. The difficulties were in implementing a change in management philosophy needed, and in understanding by both managers and employees of what it meant regarding responsibilities. The theoretical benefits were (still are) unquestionable, but in practice, the changes in mentality required were a barrier difficult to conquer.

Still today managers view empowerment as giving people the power to make decisions, and some employees view empowerment as being given the freedom to do what they want to do, without regard for position or authority. In reality it is a process to release the knowledge, experience, and motivation that is already in people but is being severely underutilized.

Employees gain through empowerment a happier work environment and a sense of personal growth; companies gain a more efficient organization and a chance for continuous improvement through employee involvement.

The Three Keys to Empowerment

In their follow-up book *"The 3 Keys to Empowerment"* [2], Ken Blanchard, John Carlos and Alan Randolph propose a concept a three part process to create empowerment. These three keys are:

- First Key: Share information with everyone. Is your responsibility as CEO to share all information on the business that can be shared. Unless they have the information employees will take empowerment as just another "management talk". By having the information, they will feel that management is making them part of the business and will develop trust in management. *(See the chapter on "Communication")*
- Second Key: Create autonomy through boundaries. It relates to the need for autonomy by establishing boundaries within which employees can determine what to do and how to do it. The boundaries are set by you, the CEO, and you declare off-limit areas that are the exclusive work of the CEO, such as the Vision and general management rules.
- Third Key: Let teams become the hierarchy. Calls for replacing traditional hierarchy with self-direct teams. Empowered, self-directed teams are quite different from semi-autonomous teams. They play a much more active role; they make and implement decisions and are accountable for results. These teams require members to learn to function within their different charter.

If you are implementing a culture of empowerment you will face some challenges. As with any cultural change and behaviors adjustment of both leaders and employees, the process will involve many ups and downs along the way.

To create a culture of empowerment, people must behave in different ways than would commonly occur in a hierarchical culture. This change of behavior involves a movement from dependence on the leadership of others to independence from, or interdependence with, external leadership, and these changes are not easy.

> *Coaching* **suggestion:** *To make your journey more palatable and to ensure its success, I strongly suggest coaching by third parties of both individual team members and teams. Perhaps this coaching can be in tandem with coaching on accountability, as the two subjects go together.*

Empowerment can be difficult to achieve and implement because of the requirement to create the culture, but if you undertake it, you must be patient and stay the course. Understand that you can't tell employees to act empowered and expect them to do it; they need to be trained and coached on how to make decisions and in accepting the responsibility for them. The process can be made easier if you start with and stick to the three keys of empowerment.

> *Coaching* **suggestion:** *get both books mentioned above and follow their teaching; the journey and the results will be worth the effort.*

The Benefits of Empowerment

There is no question as to the value of empowerment. Managers want employees who accept responsibility, have a proprietary interest in the company, and want to work hard to achieve good results. Employees on the other hand, want to feel valued, be involved in their jobs, and be proud in the work they do. Essentially then, managers and employees want the same thing, even if they do not realize it at first view.

In the book *"Employee Involvement and Total Quality Management"*[3], Ed Lawler and his colleagues in the University of Southern California support the claim of benefits to the organization, with a study they conducted. They report that when people are given more control and responsibility over their jobs, companies achieve a four percent greater return on sales than those companies that do not involve people.

While this is not necessarily a significant number, the benefits are much greater than that. Employee satisfaction and the corresponding lower turnover, improved team work, improved customer service and the resulting customer retention, are perhaps more important benefits.

Workplace Empowerment

By empowering employees you are providing them with opportunities and the freedom to make their own decisions with regards to their job. But providing freedom doesn't mean to leave them alone. For empowerment to work well you need to be involved … but not too involved.

If you are not involved at all, you are not communicating, measuring or coaching those who you are empowering, you are sending the message that they are on their own and you are giving employees a sense of insecurity. This is just the opposite of what you want. If the employee or the team fails, you are to blame for providing no guidance.

Conversely, if you are too involved, you are not demonstrating confidence in your employees. You are undermining their authority by meddling on their work and they become frustrated by your lack of trust. There is a delicate balance between the two situations and you need to be sure of how to act based on the personalities involved, the training they have and the complexity of their job.

There is a belief among business owners and leaders that employees don't care and always try to do for the company as little as they can get away with. For these owners to be able to implement empowerment, first they need to get over this thinking. The truth is that each case is unique, there is a wide spectrum of situations and of people and you need to know your employees, yourself, and the work environment well enough to know where on the spectrum it is appropriate to start the process.

To create empowerment, the management role must change from an in-control mindset to an attitude of assigning responsibility and providing the supporting environment for employees to have the opportunity to excel in the performance of their functions. People already have power in their knowledge and motivation; empowerment is releasing and focusing this power.

The key is for managers to understand that empowerment involves releasing the power people already have, and for employees to realize that empowerment also means greater responsibilities and accountability and opportunities to advance. If both parts adopt these concepts, both will benefit and together they will benefit the company. You as the CEO are responsible for teaching the concept to your staff and creating the culture to make it "the way we work here" philosophy.

You and your company have the responsibility to create the work environment that will foster the ability and desire of employees to act in empowered ways, and the responsibility to remove barriers that limit the ability. Unless empowerment starts at the top, it's going nowhere; it's up to you to make it successful.

Benefits of self-managed teams:

- Increased job satisfaction.
- Attitude change from "have to" to "want to".
- Greater employee commitment.
- Better communication between employees and management.
- More efficient decision making process.
- Improved quality.
- Reduced operating costs.
- More profitable organization.

The Process of Empowerment

Empowerment is a process that includes the following components:

- Your confidence in that the employee has the capabilities and resources needed to do the job.
- Set clear expectations regarding the job and expected outcome.
- Communicate work goals and department process and share all information you have regarding problems or challenges.

- Show your commitment and support to the employee by guiding him/her without interfering.
- Establish metrics in advance and make it clear what the department and company standards are.
- Hold the employee accountable; he/she is accountable for the solution and he/she learns from the problem or mistakes committed. How much support you give him/her will depend on the employee's level, knowledge and the complexity of the job.
- In order to get the most out of your staff, you need to learn how to empower employees effectively, and allow them to use their unique skill to solve problems. *(see chapter on accountability)*
- Listen to your employees. Because they work at their jobs every day, they can contribute with viable suggestions for ways to increase the efficiency.
- Establish the boundaries discussed earlier.
- Be willing to allow your employees to fail and send the message that you have given them the power, and that you are not going to second guess them. A second benefit is that they will learn from their mistakes.
- Remember that empowering employees does not mean giving up all control. You are still in charge, and you are still responsible for the final outcome. As such you need to retain some control and measure progress.

Empowered employees add value to your company, so by learning how to empower employees you are helping a strong business grow even stronger. Using the talents that are already on your payroll is one way to build competitive advantage over your competition.

> **Coaching suggestion:** *As the employees learn to be empowered and achieve success, you should give the employees more freedom to act and more responsibilities and/or more complex jobs. By staying involved, communicating with the employee frequently and measuring his/her performance against established standards, you'll know how much more he/she can handle and how involved you need to be. This is a commendable way to develop employees and as a result increase the value of your company.*

An article by Susan M. Heathfield titled *"Top 10 Principles of Employee Empowerment; Empower Employees Right to Ensure Success and Progress"*[4], lists the most important principles for managing people in a way that reinforces employee empowerment.

The Credo of an Empowering Manager

You want to create an environment for people to feel empowered, productive, contributing, and happy. Don't handicap them by limiting the tools they need. Trust them to do the right thing and get out of their way. (Trust but verify).

These are the most important principles for empowering people in a way that reinforces accomplishment, and contribution.

- Demonstrate that you value people. Help people feel that they are part of something bigger than themselves and their individual job. Do this by making sure they know and have access to the organization's overall mission, vision, and strategic plans.
- Share goals and direction. Empowered employees can then chart their course without close supervision. Trust the intentions of people to do the right thing, make the right decision, and make choices that, while maybe not exactly what you would decide, still work. When employees receive clear expectations from their manager, they relax and trust you.
- Delegate authority and impact opportunities, not just more work. Do not just delegate the drudge work; delegate some of the fun stuff too.
- Provide frequent feedback so that people know how they are doing. Sometimes, the purpose of feedback is reward and recognition as well as improvement coaching.
- Solve problems: don't pinpoint problem people. When a problem occurs, ask what is wrong with the work system that caused the people to fail, not what is wrong with the people.
- Listen to learn and ask questions to provide guidance. Guide by asking questions, not by telling grown up

people what to do. People generally know the right answers if they have the opportunity to produce them.

- Help employees feel rewarded and recognized for empowered behavior. The basic needs of employees must be met for employees to give you their discretionary energy, that extra effort that people voluntarily invest in work. For successful employee empowerment, recognition plays a significant role.

Coaching suggestion: don't empower employees only for the work they have to do; empower them too for some fun activities. Delegate and empower them for the important meetings, let them participate in product development and decision making, and get them involved in projects that other employees and customers notice. By doing this you will help them grow and develop new skills, but they will also feel more of an important part. You will have more time for your duties and you will gain the respect of all employees.

References:

1. Ken Blanchard, John Carlos and Alan Randolph, *Empowerment Takes More Than A Minute*, (Berrett-Koehler Publishers; 2nd edition, October 10, 2001).
2. Ken Blanchard, John P Carlos and Alan Randolph, *The 3 Keys to Empowerment: Release the Power Within People for Astonishing Results*, (Berrett-Koehler Publishers, April 15, 2001).
3. Edward E. Lawler , Susan Albers Mohrman, Gerald E. Ledford, *Employee Involvement and Total Quality Management: Practices and Results in Fortune 1000 Companies,* (Jossey-Bass Inc Pub; 1st edition May 1992).
4. Susan M. Heathfield, *Top 10 Principles of Employee Empowerment; Empower Employees - Right - to Ensure Success and Progress,* http://humanresources.about.com/od/managementandleadership/tp/empowerment.htm

Chapter XII - Making it Happen - Execution

"Vision without execution is merely hallucination"

The Discipline of Getting Things Done.

Execution is the most important set of activities for an organization. One of the signs of a good leader is the ability to take the goals they set for the company and convert them into results. Too many leaders though, fail to accomplish this; they create excellent plans but cannot implement them. Robert Kaplan and David Norton, authors of "The Balanced Scorecard" say fewer than ten percent of well-formulated strategies are successfully implemented.

Too often, I have seen beautifully presented strategies developed as part of a strategic planning process, with the leader feeling very proud of the "job done". Regretfully, the job is not done until those beautifully presented strategies are executed successfully.

When developing the strategic plan, execution of the strategies must be carefully considered. A good strategy includes an action plan that you can rely on to reach your business objectives. To get from goals to results the organization must execute all details of the action items.

In reality, execution marries all of the disciplines covered in this book. Leadership, planning, management of all resources, delegation, empowerment and accountability must play in harmony for execution to succeed. Moreover, accountability is the most critical piece of the package, because without it there is no successful execution.

What really drives results is the execution of strategy….even more important than market position, innovation or the quality of strategy itself. Execution is a discipline and the major job of a business leader; is a systematic process of rigorously questioning everything, being disciplined in what everyone does and ensuring accountability.

Your job as the CEO is not only to set strategies from the top and working with your team; you are not exempt from the details of actually running things and executing the strategies. Larry Bossidy and Ram Charan in *"Execution; The Discipline of Getting Things Done"*[1], contend that the reason for the failure to implement strategies is that "business people do not think about execution as a discipline or a cornerstone of a business' culture".

For a company to be successful, execution must be everyone's job and must be a core element of the business culture of the company, and as such, it must be embedded in the norms of behavior that everyone practices. Behaviors are what deliver results.

Incidentally, "Execution" like so many other business books is aimed at large companies and its teachings, while valuable, are appropriate for them but not necessarily for small businesses.

Leaders that do not realize what needs to be done to convert a vision into specific tasks, fail to involve themselves and people from all affected areas of the strategic plan and remain uninterested and uninvolved in the how of getting things done. This is more prevalent in large organizations but I have seen many CEO of small businesses being detached of the daily operational details and, as a result, efforts at creating and running an execution strategy fail from the top down.

Everyone is involved and responsible for execution, but execution does not just happen; it must be driven from the top. You as the CEO must create the framework for cultural discipline related to execution, and this discipline must include an open dialogue between departments and all their members as a crucial component.

Your culture must allow people to be involved in dialogues with an open mind and without prejudices or fear of conflict. Through this dialogue, all of the people accountable for executing the plan must help to develop and apply the operations plan.

Part of your responsibility is to evaluate if your organization is capable of executing the strategies. To be able to do this evaluation you must be intimately involved in what Bossidy and Charan call *"The three core processes of execution"*; people, strategy and operations processes.

This means to ensure you have the right people capable of implementation of the strategies developed, to make sure the strategies are reasonable and actionable, and that the processes in place are the recommended ones for the efficient and effective deployment of the strategies.

I have seen many examples of failures to execute because the company lacked the resources necessary to accomplish the tasks of the plan, or because the strategies didn't match the capabilities of the company. Be realistic in your plan and adjust it to what you have or are willing to spend.

Listen to your people; if they tell you that there is not enough of them to do what you want them to do in the time you want them to do it, do not ignore them. If they ask you for certain tools needed to do what they need to do, do not disregard their request. If they complain that the time you assign for a job is impossible to meet, do not discount their input.

Being dictatorial will not accomplish your goals, and if by chance you do, it will likely be with unhappy employees that feel unpowered, that their input doesn't count and they only do what they are told to do. Don't get me wrong, I'm not saying you should yield to their demands or complaints; only that you be open minded and think about what they are telling you; after all chances are they are closer to the work than you are.

> ***From my bag:*** *In my work with a manufacturing company in the high-tech industry with twenty-seven million dollars in revenues, it was painfully obvious that execution was lacking throughout the company. As a manufacturer it had the historical silos of Sales, Operations, Engineering, Financial, and supporting functions, with the unfortunate characteristic of not working in unison.*

Because the company had a target of becoming ISO9000 certified, we used this goal as the vehicle to instill team work and develop an actionable execution plan. We succeeded in both goals achieving ISO certification in record time and simultaneously creating a culture of execution and accountability that everyone was very proud of. And because they saw the benefits, they adopted team work as their operating mode. This is an example of marrying two (or more) goals to achieve a global goal that significantly improved profitability and created a culture of success.

From my bag: *I worked with an organization lead by a dictatorial new manager that the CEO had hired "to shape up the organization". This manager demanded employees to work weekends to execute jobs that he wanted to complete on a certain schedule in a plan that he had developed without anybody else's input. The logical unhappiness among employees had a number of negative effects.*

He lost the respect of employees (or never had it), lost some key employees unable to work under those conditions, deteriorated the culture of the organization into one with very unhappy employees, and—coincidentally— failed to achieve the goals. Fortunately the CEO realized his mistakes and fired the manager, but it took him a very long time and much anguish to rebuild the organization and its culture.

Implementing a Culture of Execution

A mediocre strategy well executed is better than a great strategy poorly executed.

Working to bridge the execution gap is not optional; it is a competitive necessity and should be a way of life for all involved, from the CEO to the last employee. When everyone works on bridging the gap, great things happen and making it happen is a source of pride for each.

The three core processes that Bossidy and Charan mention must be tightly linked with one another and you as the CEO must be well immersed in all three. All three are necessary for executing the strategies and all three must be prioritized at the same level because without any one of them execution will fail.

We covered the strategy process in the planning section, so we will talk here about the operation and people components of execution, as one, but considering the people process as the hub of the subject.

People with college degrees and managers in general know more about developing strategies than executing plans; they are trained to plan, not to execute. If you analyze most MBA programs, you will see that this is the case; graduates with good knowledge of planning only get a superficial look at execution.

Consequently, execution is learned by doing, on-the-job-training and the "school of hard knocks" instruction, with all its faults. It is up to you then, to make sure your people are trained in execution, or to implement an internal training program that will give them the necessary knowledge.

> ***Coaching suggestion:*** *To train your staff to execute make sure they understand what execution is (may sound silly but you'll find that many don't really know what it is). But beyond the definition of the term, you must ensure they understand **how** it is done. Execution is a discipline and as such you must "enforce" it (even if this is a little strong) in the organization. As a discipline it must have rewards and consequences; if you follow it you'll be rewarded and if you don't follow it you will be penalized. The degree of rewards and penalties is up to you and will depend on the importance of the task and the degree of accomplishment.*

The Making it Happen Plan

Execution is a method and should be treated as such. It is not the result of a single decision or action. It is the result of a marriage of a series of decisions and actions over time. As with all business processes, it must be anchored in a plan, and the quality of the plan will, to a large extent, determine its success. Thus, start with a plan as the cornerstone of your effective execution process. In the plan, translate the objectives that you and your team developed, into specific activities.

A good action plan should help you manage the work involved, measure and manage progress and communicate it to all involved. It should include clear description of all action steps with their tasks and activities for each, who has responsibility for each step, when each action will be completed, review dates for each action, resources needed to accomplish them, and the proper accountability responsibilities and consequences *(see chapter on accountability)*.

The plan should focus on only a few priorities so as not to overwhelm your resources or your people. Concentrate on those and don't let the daily distractions that are present in all businesses, take your attention away. Take them seriously and push others to take them seriously too, and follow through in regularly held meetings to ensure everybody does what they are supposed to do.

Reward the doers who produce specific results making sure you link rewards with performance. Teach your knowledge and experiences to your employees so that they can grow and expand the capabilities of the organization.

In developing the plan make sure that all components are connected and that you know what connects with what, when, where, how, and how much. In particular, the "what connects with what" is critical because unless this is clear it can lead to grave disassociations of efforts and the consequent failure of the plan.

Remember than in an organization, even in a small organization, people and departments have different sets of metrics, perspectives, and backgrounds and they are all different, presenting a challenge of alignment of efforts.

After developing the plan you must monitor its progress. You have identified targets and milestones; now implement measurements and periodic reviews on fixed schedules to monitor how well each action of the plan is executed. Don't hesitate to make corrections and adjustments as you go, but without postponing an action due to lack of accountability.

I have seen people (companies) redefining the objectives to justify delays or failure to achieve objectives. Perhaps because of issues that they consider out of their power they fail to execute according to the plan, but they still consider the plan met "because the failure wasn't their fault", this of course is wrong and can even be dishonest.

Define what the terms "on-track", "on schedule", "in process" and "completed" really mean and make sure everyone understand the definition. Then, when some job or task is determined to be on schedule or on-track, or completed, everyone will know what it really mean, and will also understand that the status doesn't allow for excuses.

If you need to make people or organizational changes, be firm, be impartial, be constructive, be supportive and be forward-looking, but also be prompt and make the changes that need to be made.

> ***Coaching suggestion:*** *Use simple dashboards to monitor progress of execution of actions. Keep items to be measured to a few critical parameters updated on a daily basis or at a frequency compatible with the actions. Develop the discipline to look at the dashboard and act promptly if corrections are needed. Teach your employees to do the same and to act on their empowerment to keep things moving in the right direction.*

The People Effect.

Because it is people dependent, execution is coupled with human resources. To gain confidence in meeting your objectives you may need to re-evaluate your leadership team—whether it is a team of one or of many—to see if they are capable of producing the results that you expect.

You need to be impartial in this evaluation and without favoritisms or prejudices, and if the evaluation tells you that you need more or different strengths in the team, do not delay the changes; the livelihood of your business may be at stake.

In the evaluation consider not just the short term but also where you expect the company to be in three or five years and how the team matches those future needs. This may tell you if you need to develop a "bench" or "pipeline" of leadership and what the bench should look like.

Assuming you have "the right people in the bus", position the right people in the right place for execution. What do I mean by this? Some people are better than others in the "doing" of a plan and you need to place them where they will play a more important role for what you are trying to achieve.

If you have low performers (and you want to keep them), focus on what they do well; set for them a modest goal that is relatively easy to attain and provide appropriate coaching and support, and the help they need to accomplish the goal.

Expect top performance from all your employees; remember that *"what you accept is what you teach"* as in a book by the same title by Michel Henry Cohen [2]; because you need everyone at your business working at full potential. To get top performance you must encourage top performance; make an effort to catch people doing something right and provide the recognition for it.

By providing this recognition for a job well done you will have a powerful effect on your people's ability to execute. Your employees will enjoy the recognition and develop a discipline of executing rightly. It is a fact that the best execution performers are those who are happy in their jobs.

Wayne Callaway of PepsiCo once said, "We take eagles and teach them to fly in formations." And my colleague Ray Brun said: "You can train turkeys to fly, but in the end they will still be turkeys, so if you want to soar with eagles, make it easier on yourself and just work with eagles." Of course, having the right people in the right places is not enough; you must give them the right tools to do their jobs.

A study conducted recently said that only forty-three percent of employees in Corporate America feel they are given the skills needed to fulfill their job responsibilities; while this may be better in small businesses, it isn't perfect and it is up to you to correct it.

It is difficult to change the business practices without affecting the attitudes and skills of your people. The good news is that it is possible to engage and connect people in a meaningful way to help you take the business where you want to take it.

You can build the competency and skills of your people so they are strategic and also effective in executing the strategies. However, they need to know that half effort is unacceptable and that only top performance and a sense of urgency will yield the results you expect.

As I said above, it is critical to have the right people involved in doing the work, but it is as important to have the right people involved in the decision making process. To improve the quality of decisions in your organization you need to understand what "delegate" truly means *(refer to the chapter on delegation)*.

Sometimes it is OK to be an autocrat and dictate what you want done, but other times you need to build consensus within the team or even within the entire organization. Do not let emotion or bias cloud the issues and do not simply resort to what you have done in the past; instead, try a systematic decision-making process and you will see execution coming to life.

Frequently there is conflict between doing the right thing for your company but the wrong thing for your employees. When such a conflict exists, "getting it done" becomes immensely difficult. All businesses, even small businesses, have departmental organizations where all departments rely on one another to get things done.

Management efforts to get different departments or groups to work together more effectively can be challenging as some times those efforts are thwarted because as soon as those people return to their "regular" occupations, they do what they are used to doing. This is not surprising because after all, they get paid to do "their job" or "what the boss tells them to do", not what someone in another part of the organization asks them to do.

Another potential roadblock is people's resistance to change. Frequently, people who need to step up and get things done are those most apt to resisting change, causing a negative effect in the organization. "Doing things" often mean getting out of the comfort zone and taking risks, and this may require changes in people's demeanor, which is not easy to do or even accept. This may require you to help employees believe in change and its benefits, and that without change, growth can't happen. Build "change readiness" and you'll see the difference.

Internal cooperation and collaboration are keys to success. Emphasize cooperation and common grounds for universal benefit. Demonstrate clearly that you want cooperation and show that everyone is working toward the same goals. This is where your talents as a team developer have an opportunity to shine *(see the chapter on Accountability)*.

Here is where I use my favorite word again: "accountability". Without it you will not have effective execution. You must assign responsibilities, empower employees to carry on with the work involved, and ... hold them accountable. Remember to clarify expectations, establish clear due dates, and schedule periodic check-ins so that you can enforce accountability.

> ***Coaching suggestion:*** *Regular meetings to review progress are essential to the success of your plan. There are different opinions as to the frequency of these meetings; for example, The Rockefeller Habits process recommends daily "huddles" in each department or group, for reviews at various levels in the organization. The Entrepreneurial Operating System (www.eosprocess.com) suggests ninety-day "Rocks" to focus everyone on what must get done in the next ninety days. My recommendation is to meet as often as the actions demand, but in fixed schedules, and to make these meetings a "must attend" affair because if you allow them to drift you are sending the message that they are not important and therefore meeting the goals is not important either.*

The Operations Effect

The operating plan provides the path and the tools to achieve the execution plan.

The operations effect is an integrated set of systems, processes and results, operating in a predictable fashion that allows all functions to be replicated to achieve reproducible results. The key words here being "a system to achieve reproducible results".

When no aspect of your business is left to chance, your ability to achieve your goals is greatly enhanced. To do this you need to create an integrated process for reproducing the same product or service consistently, and the discipline to use it all the time. Emphasize the power of systems to realize successful execution.

Michael Gerber in *"The E-Myth"* says: "If you want a business that truly works, then you need to make your business process dependent not people dependent." When something fails, don't think that someone failed, but that a system failed; then find what failed, fix it, document it, measure performance after the fix and if successful, adopt it as the new system.

In this process all steps of the operation are documented, all procedures for doing what the business does, the way everything is prepared to get the same results every time, and even a system for building the systems is documented. When you do this, your business will provide consistent and predictable value to all stakeholders and be totally organized in an orderly fashion.

The root of this way of thinking is the popular saying "Insanity is doing the same thing over and over and expecting a different result"; (attributed to Albert Einstein although there is no evidence to suggest that he made this statement.) Or the other saying from Einstein "You cannot solve a problem with the same level of thinking that created it". The meaning of these quotes is that every problem and every frustration is systemically occurring and will continue to occur until we change the way we do it or think of it.

Whether we think of it this way or not, it's happening. If you have developed and implemented systems in your company, and you enforce the discipline to use them, you are likely executing well. This is a key part of the operations effect to make it happen.

More on this in the chapter on Systemization.

Final Thoughts

To achieve good execution, you must have simple and clear strategies and the plan to make them happen. You must align the people and the operations with the strategies, instilling the team concept for all involved to act in unison.

You are responsible for forming the team, training every player on the team, providing the resources needed and managing the outcome. The plan and its execution must be grounded in economic reality so it supports and drives all actions of the company.

Observe results and make needed corrections. Good management always inspects what it expects and is never afraid to change plans and make needed corrections. An organization that can't deliver on its promises is doomed to fail, so it is essential to find ways to ensure a culture of continuing excellence.

Don't declare victory until you do frequent and thorough reviews of the plan and the results obtained on an ongoing basis. From *"Swanson's Unwritten Rules of Management"*; Rule Number 7— "Constantly review developments to make sure that the actual benefits are what they were supposed to be." Follow through is just as important as good decision making. When deciding on a course of action, set measurable objectives.

Assume that your decision may have second and third order effects. Monitor the progress of the actions you set in motion to make sure these effects are not counterproductive, and if they are, see that they are addresses early. It is essential that management uses these concepts to gain insight into the program and its progress and not simply as a "need-to-do routine".

Don't assume that by applying the concepts discussed—or any other concept for that matter—you'll ever be able to close the execution gap completely. There will always be room for improvement and you must continue to monitor and upgrade your practices to perennially achieve higher levels of execution. Dedicate effort to understand what is common to all of your execution related challenges so that you can work on improvements to each of them.

Successful execution will drive revenues and profitability by achieving effective and efficient operations, on-time delivery of your products and satisfaction of your customer's needs. If for no other reason, financial rewards should drive your efforts towards excellence in execution.

> **From my bag:** *Successful manufacturing company owned and run by two partners. The senior partner is the administrative and visionary type, while the junior partner is the operations expert. Plans are developed by both of them with the participation of the management team. Execution is the weakest link in the otherwise excellent company. The reason is that it lacks focus on getting things done, and the root source of the problem is that the partner in charge of operations does not impose the discipline of making it happen.*
>
> *What is the solution? Cannot fire the partner because he is a talented executive … and an owner; so, the solution is coaching. Working not only with the executive in charge of making it happen, but with the entire organization to "educate" them in the value of execution and how to optimize it, and in how to apply the discipline for it.*

References:
1. Larry Bossidy and Ram Charan, *Execution; The Discipline of Getting Things Done,* (Crown Business; 1st edition, June 15, 2002).
2. Michael Henry Cohen, *What You Accept is What You Teach: Setting Standards for Employee Accountability*, (Creative Health Care Management; 1st edition, December 1, 2006).

Chapter XIII - Accountability

Is the willingness to answer for results.

Delegation without accountability is just distributing the work

Consequences of one's actions or lack thereof. From *"Accountability; a Little Clarity Please"* an article by Lawrence E. Wharton & Richard Roi.

Webster's definition: "subject to having to report, explain or justify; being answerable, responsible."

I said earlier that delegation was the *second* most difficult thing for small business owners to learn; allow me to say here that accountability is **the** most difficult thing to master for owners and for management too. Sadly, most small business owners don't have a clue about how to hold people accountable, and ... to hold themselves accountable.

Why is this? Why do most leaders have difficulty exercising proper accountability?

- They are used to working in a culture of conflict avoidance. It is much easier to let" things go" than to try to hold people accountable and face conflicts.
- Lack of skills to deal in accountability. Not to repeat myself, but because it is a difficult thing to learn, most people don't have the skills needed.

The Culture of Accountability

There is one core cultural value that no truly successful organization can do without: personal accountability. Personal accountability requires team members to take responsibility for their own actions and help other members to take similar responsibility. They also contribute to improve the performance of the organization by focusing on actions to take at the individual level. Organizations that master this value consistently have higher levels of employee morale and significantly outperform organizations that do not embrace it.

Accountability—like most things—starts at the top. You have to hold yourself accountable and set the example before you can expect to hold others accountable. What makes accountability so critical is that without it you and your company will suffer. Without accountability throughout the organization, the result is chaos.

Building accountability at all levels of the company is key to making a business sustainable. Accountability is not something you "make" people do; you must implement the culture and you have to have people accept and "buy into" the concept. You need to understand that this may be a new, unfamiliar way to work for your employees, and therefore, you need to teach and coach the concept as a benefit and not as a penalty.

In a company that has a culture of accountability people do what they commit to do. Conversely, if an organization lacks accountability there will be a tendency to live by a flood of excuses for not meeting objectives. If "good enough" is accepted as good and meeting objectives and "no one will notice the difference" is an acceptable mantra, or worse yet, a feeling that objectives are arbitrary and stupid, the company can suffer the consequences of low morale, low quality and higher costs.

With accountability comes a measure of discipline. Accountability is a synonym of responsibility and the opposite of permissiveness. Holding people accountable is really about discipline and the distribution of power. Individuals have more purpose when they have the power of responsibility and accepting accountability. When people become more responsible, they can have more freedom.

Creating the environment where accountability can take root and blossom isn't easy, but you don't have to make it harder than it is. You need to understand what motivates people to become more empowered, responsible and accountable without the need for punitive measures. With this knowledge you coach them to accept the fact that being accountable means to have more power over what they do, and the satisfaction of being "their own overseer" with respect to the completion of projects and the quality thereof.

The accountability that we are discussing here has very little to do with titles or positioning; it has everything to do with responsibility at all levels of the organization, not just managers or supervisors. No employee can be content with letting management assume all the responsibility for the performance of the organization and affixing blame and offloading personal responsibility for mistakes to those in lower ranks.

Position-based, command-and-control management is completely obsolete when accountability is the culture. Don't get me wrong, there are still reporting levels and levels with varying degrees of responsibility, but in this culture everyone is accountable for their projects, regardless of how the project was assigned.

Within this culture team work is fomented because the actions and results of each member affects the team and thus each member is motivated to go the extra mile to help co-workers, but also to drive coworkers to be accountable.

Holding team members accountable or driving them to be accountable can be a challenging interaction because these conversations have the potential for strong emotions. These conversations require courage because they can jeopardize the quality of relationships with co-workers. But if a team member chooses not to meet a commitment, he/she is hurting him/herself but also the team and likely the entire organization.

On the other hand, holding others accountable can help build stronger relationships, if done right. Holding others accountable is not about blaming or faulting them, or accusing them with what they should have done; it is about expecting the best from coworkers, but also offering help to achieve the goals.

Am I proposing a hypothetical organization? Would this be an impossibility to achieve? Most definitely not. It is very achievable if you as the CEO put the emphasis in the culture and you dedicate the effort to educate all employees (and yourself) in the requirements and benefits to be enjoyed.

The use of an experienced coach would help because— aside from the expertise that he/she would bring in—it would be easier to implement with one-on-one and team coaching from outside.

Clarity is Key and Starts With You

As I already said, owners are among the biggest offenders when it comes to accountability, but also to establish clear, well-defined performance objectives. Accountability means little if specific goals are not clearly communicated. Not knowing exactly what or how to do it can be frustrating for employees; unclear marching orders can be exasperating and demoralizing, but it gets worse when after finishing the job they get a "that is not what I wanted" from the manager, leader or owner.

Employees should speak up and demand clear instructions and expectations, and should not accept blame or finger pointing. If everyone acts this way it would force the culture to develop and become "the way it's done".

From my bag: I coached a VP level executive of a manufacturing company who frequently created organizational and operational problems because of his lack of clarity in assigning projects. He believed that if he hired someone to do a job, the person "should know what to do without me telling him how"; in other words, he assumed the employee knew how he wanted the job done.

For example, one time he asked a line manager to give him a report on a production schedule, without any instructions. When the manager produced the report my client said "that's not what I wanted", go back and do it again. Sure enough the second version was also not what he wanted, and the third version had the same result. He decided to fire the manager under the reason that he was unqualified and didn't know how to follow directions.

I had to spend a sizable amount of time coaching him in delegation and accountability until he learned that people are not mind readers and if you want them to follow your way of doing something, you need to explain to them what that way is.

The instructions to be given at the time of assigning the job should include expected outcome, what constitutes completion, when it is expected to be completed, what actions are to be taken upon completion, and anything else that management expects. If the project is long or extensive there should be requirements to report progress periodically to make sure the work is on track. These reviews should be scheduled at the time of the assignment and the schedules should be kept religiously; otherwise you are sending a message that they are not important.

If the project is assigned to a team, its leader is accountable for the overall performance of the team. It is typical in the case to give the instructions to the leader; however, depending on the circumstances, the entire team should receive the same instructions. If this is the case, it gives all team members the opportunity (and obligation) to hold each other accountable for performance.

Team Accountability

Patrick Lencioni, author of *"The Five Dysfunctions of a Team"*[1], has said that "ambiguity is the enemy of accountability." Many problems with accountability originate from a failure to create a level of clarity around tasks and not from inherently irresponsible or unqualified employees.

Often we assume that we have been perfectly clear in our verbal instructions, and we also assume that a tacit acknowledgement from the employee is proof that the message was well expressed and well received. This false sense of security can lead to performance breakdowns. Because of this, it is highly recommended that all instructions be given in writing.

This will also prevent disagreements of performance issues that can also create serious employee-employee or employee-management disputes. Writing clarifies thinking, helps to confirm understanding with others and saves time and expense by avoiding project rework and "restarts."

Lencioni identifies lack of accountability as one of the five dysfunctions, but in reality, if you analyze them carefully, all five dysfunctions are related to accountability. He defines accountability as "the willingness of team members to remind one another when they are not living up to the performance standards of the group".

Thus, if we go by this definition, it seems simple to just get team members "to remind one another", but in reality we must work through barriers presented by personalities, jealousy, ambition, drive, etc, to get team members to work as a team. It may be easy in some cases but not so easy in others; your talents as a leader are put to test to accomplish that. Don't try to do it in one day; it will take quite some time and a lot of patience, but you can do it.

From my bag: *One of my favorite clients was the CEO of a distribution company with approximately twenty million dollars in revenues. He was (still is) an excellent manager and had formed a valuable team of executives in various disciplines. Although the company was doing fine, the CEO was not satisfied because goals were not met and there was certain disconnect within the team.*

We proceeded to do an exercise of the Five Dysfunctions of a Team, and it became clear that the problem was lack of individual and team accountability affecting relationships within the team. After intensive training and coaching both at the personal level and as a team (including the CEO) the group started to function much better and the results of the company also improved. The coaching included behavioral assessments and discussions, so the drastically different personalities of the group could better understand each other. As an added bonus, the morale of the group also improved significantly.

The Absence of Accountability

How many times your company missed shipments, deadlines or goals because of someone or some department not doing what they committed to do? I'm sure this happened more times than you care to admit. How many times you received customer complaints because someone didn't provide the service that "customer service" should provide? Again, I'm sure that you are not happy about that. Now think of how strong is your commitment to accountability and your efforts to provide a culture of accountability; it could have been better, right? Now is the time to change that and get it right.

I'm sure that most of those instances happened because of lack of accountability. Pointing fingers and blaming or using excuses to justify a failure would only guarantee that the problems will repeat themselves. My guess is that you heard people saying "I did my part", or "I didn't have the right tools", or "I just followed the instructions in the traveler", or "John didn't give me the right spec", or ... well you get the idea. All those "reasons" are mere excuses that have no place in a well-run organization.

Of course, the problem is reflected on a negative impact on productivity, quality, revenues and/or profits, and moral in the organization. Of all those negatives, the most important is the effect on the moral of the people, because all others are easier to recuperate from than the moral.

If you try to implement accountability when a lot of problems were brought to the surface, people will see it as a penalty and will likely resent it. People will feel that they let the team down or missed an important item and now they are being penalized.

Introducing accountability can feel uncomfortable in the short term; employees will resent the idea as a measure by management to "tighten the reins" and identify culprits of bad performance. They are used to the practice that when things go smoothly nobody asks who is responsible for the success, it is only when there are problems that management wants to know who screwed up; this will not help your cause to create the right culture.

Generally speaking, employees want to excel; they want to be proud of their performance—whether it is for self-satisfaction or just "to be out of trouble"—but they also want to be liked by co-workers and want to avoid conflicts. Sometimes, holding others accountable means (in their eyes) to point fingers and "accuse" teammates and thus, they don't want to be known as betraying team member's loyalty.

Your challenge is to convince them that accountability means something totally different; it means team work and pushing together towards a common goal. Personal credibility and pride of achievement are gained through accountability.

> *From my bag: An Engineering VP of a manufacturing company was valuable to the company because of his technical talents, but he was bad at keeping commitments and meeting goals; in fact he was retained as an employee only because the company needed his knowledge. His problem was that he wanted to be liked by everyone and thus, he constantly spent time doing things for others that had nothing to do with his main job. As a last measure before letting him go, the CEO asked me to work with him.*
>
> *The focus of my coaching had to be making him understand that by tending to menial things for others he was not only jeopardizing his job, but he was also jeopardizing the company. The process wasn't easy but after severe "therapy" he improved in his accountability and his performance improved significantly. Because of his much improved performance, his peers respected him more and he became more popular than before.*

Implementing Accountability in Your Company

First you need to decide if accountability is missing from your organization or even in certain pockets of it. John Miller, author of *"QBQ – The Question Behind the Question"*[2], gives some guidelines in this respect:

- Is there a tendency in your company to assign blame? Is it always someone else's fault? This can be on an individual bases or by departments as in "we did it right, but they screwed up".

- Do some employees feel they are victims? Do you hear "why nobody tell us what's going on"? Or "why do we have to go through all these changes?; we are doing fine without them".

- Do they use procrastination as a weapon? Do people delay activities or push deadlines further away from the agreed upon date and justify it by saying "it doesn't matter because nobody will notice anyway" or "even if I keep the commitment I won't get any rewards".

- Do they make excuses for their performance by blaming it on incidentals, such as "how can I get it done when I don't have the right tools?" Or "is not my fault, I couldn't get any help from engineering".

- Do your employees look at work as a burden dropped upon them that they cannot escape from, rather than enjoying what they do? I don't mean to be altruistic, but unless employees show some signs of enjoyment or at least acceptance of their job, chances are they will resent being held accountable or working in an environment of accountability.

OK, now you know that you don't have the accountable organization that you need, so, how do you build company-wide accountability?

You need to start by changing or eliminating practices that undermine accountability, such as micromanaging, legislating the how's and what's and other activities not conducting to what you want to establish. Then start working on team development; eliminate person-to-person competition and promote person-to-person assistance.

Yes, I know, easy to say, not so easy to do, but remember that it is a process that won't be done in a short time. You allowed the culture to drift and now you have to change it; it's a marathon, not a sprint.

Working with the team as a team, develop goals in agreement with your vision and with the strategic plan. These goals will have metrics and schedules to meet, and they will have specific persons or teams responsible for meeting them. You are part of the team and you will have goals and measurements to meet too; this is your opportunity to set the example for the rest of the team.

Refer to the Chapters on *Delegation* and *Empowerment* as guides to develop plans and to make sure you are assigning jobs correctly.

If you can get your company to clearly identify, articulate, and execute the strategies and strategic goals you will be well positioned to be able to create organizational accountability. Decide what's important in the strategic position and develop the goals together with the systems that support the goals.

Now you are ready for the execution of the plan with each part of the team having the activities to support the plan. Don't overlook problems that may come up; work on them to find the root cause and work as a team to do it.

A blog in TTI's (Target Training International) site on 12/21/2010 listed *"Ten Steps for Creating a Culture of Commitment and Accountability"*. Other people have published somewhat different lists, but this is one to which I subscribe.

- Communicate to everyone that accountability and commitment are a requirement of the organization.
- Align every job description to your company's strategy and goals for the coming year. Ask everyone to commit to a shared vision of results.
- Make accountabilities clear for everyone by using the benchmark for their job to start a discussion about how their individual contributions matter.
- When you hire new employees, have job-related professional development planning already in place to help them reach their full potential.
- Build accountability into your company culture by using "what and by when" for goals and tasks planning. Project management can be very sophisticated, but the bottom line is "who, what, and by when?"
- Offer ways for employees to communicate obstacles and request the help or resources they need to achieve their goals. When you listen to them, recognize that what you're listening to is someone who is committed to producing results.

- Involve employees in an ongoing dialogue about how they can identify process improvements or otherwise increase the quality of their work and the team's productivity.
- Use small "course corrections" on a monthly or as-needed basis to guide employees toward behaviors and practices that are effective for meeting goals. Don't wait for the annual performance review. You wouldn't wait until arrival at a destination to notice a wrong turn along the way, would you?
- "Catch" people doing something right; give frequent, honest and positive feedback. As a general rule of thumb, a ratio of five positive interactions to one critical interaction will help managers build an open communication channel with direct reports.
- Identify ways to recognize and acknowledge employees company-wide when their actions exemplify an "above and beyond" commitment to company objectives. Success breeds success.

You must set clearly defined results. These can be sales numbers, profit levels, ROI, positioning in the industry or any other goal that is (are) part of the strategic plan. Once these goals are set, make sure that the entire organization, from top management to the lowest position, are clear in what the goals mean for the success of the company and how each employee can affect the goals. Now develop accountability measurements for each employee or department, and explain joint accountability.

Joint accountability means that even if individuals have met their goals but the team hasn't, accountability has not been reached. Individual success does not necessarily transmit to group success. Granted, individual accountability must be a reality before joint accountability can be reached, but you must promote both if you are to win the accountability battle.

The prevalent mentality must be to achieve results, not just do the job. I heard innumerable times—and I'm sure you did too—managers or executives say "I don't care how you do it, just get it done", but getting it done many times is not sufficient if you don't reach the goals. People believe they are getting paid to do a job and as long as the job gets done they are not concerned about individual results or the results of the team. Positioning within the organization and job descriptions have a lot to do with this misconception.

The Process of Implementation

In teaching accountability you need to stress the importance of written agreements and how they are "negotiated". The agreement must be like a contract *(see the delegation chapter)*, specifying very clearly the "when" and "how" of the job in a way that leaves no question as to the understanding by every employee of the commitment they are making.

Remember that this is a contract and as such both parties have a right to discuss its contents and to only agree to what they believe is doable and fair. Listen carefully to "the other side", understand their position and make sure there is mutual agreement for the final version.

You also need to make it culturally acceptable for employees to say "no" when the situation warrants it. Do they believe that the assignment is not realistic? Do they feel they have too much on their plate already and you are trying to add more? Are the conditions right for the assignment? Are the goals SMART? Don't force them to sign on to a contract that they don't accept.

The outcome will be likely a failure to meet the objectives, and a disgruntled work force. Accountability results from a system composed of three elements; clarity of the assignment, commitment by both parties, and consequences for the outcome. If you remove the commitment part from the employees the system breaks down.

Lou Gerstner, former chief of RJR Nabisco and then IBM, once said famously "People do what you inspect, not what you expect." By that he meant that whatever you're emphasizing in your business by measuring it, it is sure to be the area that gets the attention and improves.

This is a no-brainer in some ways, but it can have far-reaching implications. Metrics are important, but sometimes they drive unexpected behaviors. Wrong measurements or measuring the wrong things can have implications in accountability; therefore, it is important to remember to expect what you inspect, and inspect the right things.

When you set expectations, be sure to eliminate any possibility if misunderstanding or leeway that can be interpreted as different things. If you want a report by Friday at 10:00 AM, specify that it is to be a final report, not a draft. If you or the team decides that the goal for the month is seven hundred and fifty thousand dollars, make sure it is understood that it is shipments and not just bookings. By being specific and putting things in writing you will prevent disputes, antagonism among team members, and even disrespect toward you.

Make only promises that you intent to keep; stay away from statements that can be interpreted by some people as promises, but are not. Keep your word; whatever you say is taken as "the word" from the top and it is expected to be true. No one on your team should hold himself or others more accountable than you hold yourself.

Consider that when employees first hear the word accountability, they often wince, thinking it's another name for punishment. By openly holding yourself accountable you are dissipating that belief. Remember and remind everyone that a commitment is much more than "I'll try".

An objective without a plan is just a dream, and dreams are not real commitments or promises at all, just wishes disguised as such. Real objectives are derived from the strategic plan and to make them happen you need a plan. The plan to reach an objective must be real and believed by all. It should provide the opportunity to measure progress and predict the end. Many objectives are never achieved because no one ever planned to achieve them, literally, even if there were good intentions.

Make sure that one team's objectives are not in opposition with objectives of other teams, or where one member's success is guarantee of another member's failure. Have members working with each other and checking for conflicts, and be prepared to confront those who shy away from confronting.

Require team members to take their complaints to each other and not just come complaining to you, and encourage them to complement each other for success. Don't allow them to approve everything you say just because you are the boss; encourage them to challenge you if they believe they have a valid point; you will gain a lot of insight by doing this.

Celebrate triumphs. If the project is finished on time and in the manner originally planned, make sure you take time to celebrate. Let the team know publicly that it did a great job; but make sure you do it fairly and without making others who also may have performed well feel any less successful.

Giving lots of positive attention to this kind of work habit and behavior will help to create a culture of accountability for everyone in the organization. Everyone will start holding each other accountable and you will be well on your way to create or reinforce a culture of accountability.

Coaching suggestion: Never wait until just before a deadline is reached, to check on the progress of a project. If the project is behind schedule it is too late to do anything about it and whatever help you can offer at that time it would not seem sincere. I found that using a tool like Outlook makes the process simpler. Set the dates that you want to check the progress of a project, with reminders that let you know you are supposed to do it, and you can even set messages to be sent to those working on the project, asking for an update. This is a simple way to guarantee that you will not forget and that they will not forget either. (And make sure you remember to offer your help.)

The Difficult Part; How to Correct Lack of Accountability

What can you do as a leader when a staff member's accountability is faltering?

Let's start by recognizing that to have accountability there must be consequences. What are the consequences? Good question. There should be consequences for success and consequences for failure. The grade of consequences for success is easy; for failure are more difficult and would depend on the ranking of the "culprits" and the severity of the fault. It can range from a simple *"that's not acceptable"* to dismissal, but it must be applied fairly and the reason and punishment must be known by all as a consequence of non-accountability. Next you must take measures to make sure the incident won't be repeated.

Consequences for success may include intangibles such as praise, gratitude, recognition, celebrations, increased levels of responsibility and freedom to act, or tangibles such as rewards, promotions, bonuses, raises, etc. Consequences of failure may include emotional components such as team disappointment, letting the team down, tough conversations or "post-mortems" about what happened, erosion of trust, or material penalties such as failure to obtain bonuses, raises or promotions, limited opportunities for desirable assignments, and possibly discipline or termination.

> ***Coaching suggestion:*** *CEO, owners and managers always ask me: "what do you do when people don't meet their goals or don't complete assignments?" That is a hard question to answer because it depends on many factors; i.e., the level of the employee, the severity of the case, the frequency of non-performance issues, etc. One thing that always worked for me is simply to say "that's not acceptable" and mean it. If the message is given the right way, it can have the expected impact. It has to mean "that's not the way we work here and we will not tolerate it".*

Agreeing to do a job or to occupy a position involves a commitment, a promise, and failing to deliver on that promise is equivalent to not keeping one's word. If a team mate fails to keep a commitment it affects the entire team because the team was counting on that promise. Not only has the team the right to expect compliance to the commitment, but it also has the right to expect advanced notice if the commitment won't be made. Your dilemma in this case is do you punish the team or do you punish the individual(s)?

My answer is both, because while the individual's non-performance affected the team, the team failed to hold each member accountable. If you don't act, or worse yet you reward the culprit because after all "he did his job" you can count on the incorrect behavior to be repeated.

But before you consider punishments, consider remedies; what system failed? What part of the training didn't yield the results that it should have? What was your role in the failure? Where the instructions given perfectly clear? Did everyone understand the goals and measurements? Does everyone embrace the team concept? Look into your practices and assess your role. Reemphasize training and education at all levels. Have a meeting to discuss why it happened and get everyone's input as to "why it won't happen again".

In a one-on-one with the employee who did not meet the commitment, let him/her know he/she is not being accountable. Find out why the failure occurred and how he/she plans to make it up and offer your help to implement whatever corrective action is determined to be applied and to coach him/her further in the subject.

Be very clear on what further consequences will be if the incident is repeated for whatever reason. Set up frequent review dates for ongoing projects; help him/her positively reinforce his/her successes and then make the check-in times less and less frequent as the accountability improves.

Learn more about the employee's personality and character to see if there is something there that makes accountability difficult for him/her. Is he/she someone who is unable or unwilling to meet the output or results requirements of the job? Make sure the employee is in the right job and with the right responsibilities; many times employees are asked to perform at a higher level than their capabilities would suggest. Make sure he/she is not suffering from de-motivation due to extraneous circumstances.

Make sure too, the employee has all the right tools and resources. Until those questions are clarified and the shortfalls are pointed out, you will never know whether the person who is falling short is unable or unmotivated, or is simply in need of help. Consider naming a mentor to work with him/her in accountability issues. Help him/her understand that accountability is an opportunity and not a punishment.

When underperformance is discussed openly and straightforwardly but with sensitivity to the feelings involved, underperformers tend to do one of two things; i.e., they either put the effort to improve, or they make the hard decision of leaving the company. No one likes to go to work every day under a cloud of disappointment from the boss or worse yet facing teammates who suffer consequences because of their underperformance.

To design appropriate consequences you have to know your people, what motivates them, what are they capable of doing, what are their limitations, what do they want for their future, etc. Of course you will have many different personalities and you can't have a custom program for each employee, but you should have a plan that fits the general population, and more importantly, the culture that you want in your company.

If we are talking about a team failure, understand too that consequences for employees also have consequences for the leader. The team leader failed to hold his/her members accountable and thus, he/she is at fault too. And if you are the leader of the failing team, you should also have consequences and not show privileges that employees will resent. Remember that accountability starts at the top and you need to set the example.

If you have applied all the solutions that you know how, and performance has not improved, then as the CEO you have the ultimate responsibility to exercise the final option; releasing the non-performer. While this is the most difficult step to take for a manager or even a CEO, by doing it you will gain the respect of those who stay, because they will realize that you are doing what is necessary and fair to the organization.

Conversely, by keeping the non-performer(s) you are sending a message that you don't take accountability seriously. This will permanently damage the organization, its culture, and you as its leader.

Final Thoughts

While establishing and implementing accountability can be seen as the "hard" side of management, the upside is unlimited. It establishes a culture of trust, openness, interdependence, self-confidence, achievement, appreciation, and energetic celebrations.

One of the greatest motivators for workers at any level is an environment where everyone is heard, keeps their word, is constantly coached to grow in competence and confidence, and enjoys the rewards of accomplishing one success after another. A leader who can foster that is one that will engender deep loyalty and extraordinary commitment.

An added benefit of creating a culture where promises are kept is that it eventually encompasses customers who believe that the company stands by its products, services, and promises, creating a valuable competitive advantage.

Finally, few other concepts to remember:

- Give people responsibilities, not jobs. To achieve personal accountability employees must be willing to own a project and personal action must take place to finish the task, and employees must be willing to answer for the results.
- Practice the window and the mirror (from *"Good to Great"* by Jim Collins). When things go right, look out the window and praise others; when things don't go according to expectations, look in the mirror and assess what you did wrong or what you can do to improve the results.
- "What you accept is what you teach" (from the book by Michael Henry Cohen). If you accept people not meeting deadlines or quality standards, or whatever is that you expect from a contract that you created with

someone to deliver, you are teaching your people that is OK not to meet that contract.

- The Pursuit of Mediocrity Is Almost Always Successful. Raise the bar; go for the gold, always aim high. It is better to aim high and miss than to aim low and hit. If you set your goals low enough, you are sure to meet them.

References:

1. Patrick Lencioni, *The Five Dysfunctions of a Team: A Leadership Fable,* (Jossey-Bass; 1st edition, April 11, 2002).
2. John Miller, *QBQ – The Question Behind the Question,* (Putnam Publishing Group; 1st edition, September 9, 2004).

Accountability:
Consequences for ones actions, or lack thereof

From "Accountability; A Little Clarity Please" by Lawrence E. Wharton &
Richard Roi.

Accountability emphasizes liability for something of value either contractually or because of one's position of responsibility. Answer the following questions:

1. **Why do most leaders have great difficulty exercising proper accountability?**

    A. Culture of conflict avoidance
    B. Lack of skills to deal with accountability issues
    C. No rewards from above for dealing well with accountability
    D. All of the above

2. **What is your perception of your accountability practices?**

    - Are you pushing accountability to the lowest possible level? **Y or N**
    - Are you aware of what needs of yours may compromise accountability? **Y or N**
    - Do you know what you are reinforcing and are you effectively dealing with it? **Y or N**

3. **Indicate True (T) or False (F) for the following statements:**

T or F -- Other than holding him/herself answerable to certain agreed-to standards of performance and behavior, the next most desirable level of accountability is from peers, followed next by the supervisor.

T or F -- When an outside force (customer, government, etc.) intrudes on the accountability process a solution is likely to be imposed that may wreak far more havoc than lower levels of accountability would have engendered.

T or F -- As one moves from self-accountability to an outside force, less freedom is available to do what needs to be done.

T or F -- If a leader does what he/she says she/he will do, trust is established but only if the leader also controls his/her behavior.

T or F -- A leader who is a conflict avoider, unreasonable, or abusive to employees probably will not create an environment in which employees feel safe and trust the leader.

T or F -- To remedy an accountability problem, leaders must always start with themselves, and realize that she/he has reinforced the pattern of behavior causing the lack of accountability, and therefore is responsible in some way for what happened.

T or F -- To make accountability most productive, the leader must acknowledge, before addressing the staff member's culpability, that she/he failed to address this issue before, or has not done so adequately.

Chapter XIV – Performance Management

You can't manage what you don't measure

As the CEO of your company, you are taxed with a huge number of things to do and it is almost impossible for you to see all the details of what goes on in the company. You need a system that helps you to "keep an eye" on what's most important; the key measurements that tell you if your business is doing what it must to attain the company vision.

Your team also needs those critical measurements that would tell them if they are achieving what they need to achieve, and to give them a point of reference to let everyone know what's most important. Those measurements that help people perform and monitor their own work in the right context and pull together towards the same overall aims.

Critical Success Factors

You developed the strategic plan that will drive the company to success, but you need the measurements to ensure it. Critical Success Factors (CSF) are those measurements. They are those strategies identified as critical in the success of the strategic plan of the company. They are those factors in which your company must excel for it to succeed and ultimately attain your Company Vision.

John F. Rockart of MIT's Sloan School of Management defines CSF as "The limited number of areas in which results, if they are satisfactory, will ensure successful competitive performance for the organization. They are the few key areas where things must go right for the business to flourish. If results in those areas are not adequate, the organization's efforts for the period will be less than desired".

CSF are intimately related to the strategic goals of the business, focusing on the most important areas and get to the heart of what is to be achieved and how. Therefore, the process to define the CSF start with a review of your Company Vision and your Company SWOT analysis as defined in the strategic plan.

CSF are industry specific and thus your type of business will determine what types of CSF are recommended for it. They should also be tailored for your firm's particular situation, your personal involvement and your team's capabilities.

The CSF that are currently strategically more important than other CSF in bringing about the owner's happiness and the company's future than any other CSF will be denominated your Driving Critical Success Factor (DCSF).

How to Develop Your CSF and DCSF

The first questions you have to ask are:

- What are the critical factors that drive our business?
  - What things we must excel at to be successful?
  - What things if done correctly will make us successful but if not will result in a failed operation?

And then ask the following:

- What new product, service or process must be developed to ensure success?
- What new or continued area of excellence we must ensure?
- What market type or area must be improved or changed?
- What better use of resources will help?
- What improved technology or know-how do we need to employ?
- What improvements are needed in sales and marketing methods, practices or personnel?

Once you have identified the CSF you have to identify the DCSF; the things that drive your business to success. If the DCSF are successful the rest should happen.

Let's look at an example. The following is an example of a process to develop CSF and DCSF for a distribution company. Yours may be entirely different and you may prefer to develop only a couple of DCSF; it depends on a number of conditions, but this should give you an idea of the process.

Critical Success Factors for XYZ Company

We started by looking at the goals developed at the strategic planning process.

Goals from Strategic Plan

Area of excellence
- Expand our reputation for quality and design excellence as well as customer support and value.
- Maintain and promote ISO certification.
- Technical knowledge; financial strength; stable workforce.
- Providing engineered solutions and value added services that resolve customer's issues.

Operations
- Secure low cost international sources for standard and custom product.
- Continually improve our processes so our service levels are the highest in the industry.
- Improve quote follow up and become more consistent with the way we process orders. Add redundancy to the verification process.
- Adjust to the different way business is conducted today and will be in the future.

Staff
- Defined responsibilities and roles.
- Improve or move on with employees that don't perform to our expectations.
- Continually improve quoting and order processing to reduce errors and improve customer service.
- Continue to refine our capabilities and become more efficient every day.

- Grow revenue ten percent over last year's level with current staff.

Technology or know-how
- Embrace technology and adapt to present practices.
- Implement vertical integration.
- Design Portal to streamline order entry in our ERP system.

Sales and Marketing
- Expand growth throughout Eastern Seaboard, preferably through acquisitions.
- Enter into new markets in fields that are growing, to offset the loss of dying business.
- Engineering and Sales departments continuing to work in developing projects with OEM customers.
- "SMART" plan for periodic face-to-face contact customers.
- Ability to expand into other markets utilizing our superior skill sets in sales, engineering and marketing that other distributors don't have.

Critical Success Factors for XYZ Company:

From there we developed the critical factors that will ensure the success of the strategic plan. CFS are those strategies identified as critical in the success of the company and the strategic plan.

Critical Success Factor 1
- Sustainable acquisition strategy to expand to Southern regions.
- Achieve budgeted sales and gross margins.
- Improve communications and accountability within management team.
- Continue to provide engineered solutions and value added services to differentiate from competitors.

Critical Success Factor 2
- Keep effective sales staff, promote low cost supplier of engineering solutions.

- Secure international sources.
- Develop comprehensive succession plan.
- Grow sales through growing areas or disciplines that will be expanding through the next decade; for example wind, solar, other alternative power.

Critical Success Factor 3
- Vertical integration.
- Continue to explore new technologies.
- Strategic Plan that is followed and promoted throughout the company.

Critical Success Factor 4
- Process improvements – internal turnaround times.
- Focus on daily operations; work towards error-free system.

Critical Success Factor 5
- Think strategically to enable us to grow top line revenue.
- Consider acquiring talent that may enable us to provide new services to the customer, possibly including light manufacturing.

Driving Critical Success Factors for XYZ Company

From the CSF, we developed/identified those that are most important and labeled them the Driving Critical Success Factors. The following CSF were determined to be the driving factors.

CSF #1:
- Sustainable acquisitions strategy to expand to Southern regions.
- Achieve annual operating budget.
- Improve communications and accountability throughout.

CSF #2:
- Succession planning for all critical positions.

- Grow sales through growing areas or disciplines that will be expanding through the next decade; for example wind, solar, other alternative power.
- Focus on daily operations; work towards error-free, low cost system.

CSF #3:
- Vertical integration; consider acquiring talent that may enable us to provide new services to the customer, possibly including light manufacturing.
- Continue to explore new technologies.

CSF #4:
- Think strategically to enable us to grow top-line revenue.

Key Performance Indicators (KPI)

Measure your progress toward your company's goals.

Key Performance Indicators (KPI) is an industry term for a type of measure of performance. KPI are used to evaluate the success of activities within the company and of the company as an entity. They reflect the organizational goals.

Success is defined as the achievement of some level of operational goal. Consequently, individual departments will have different KPI based on the goals of each department, but the company as a whole needs KPI that define its success.

What is important to individual departments depends on their charter and goals. For example, the KPI useful to a finance department will be quite different to the KPI for the sales force. Many things are measurable but to "qualify" as KPI they must be key to company's success and must be essential to achieving the organization's goals.

A common method for selecting KPI is to apply a management framework such as the "Balanced Scorecard" *(see explanation below)* which consists of a mixture of financial and non-financial measures each compared to a target value. Indicators identifiable as possible candidates for KPI can be summarized as follows:

- Quantitative indicators represented numerically.
- Practical indicators that relate to company processes.
- Directional indicators showing descriptive progress in performance.
- Financial indicators used in performance measurement as an operating index.

Use KPI as a performance management tool and to measure the performance of individual employees. All KPI should be well known by all employees, regardless of the applicability of the measurements to their individual jobs, and everyone should focus on them.

Publicly (within the company) show the targets and the progress toward the targets; those responsible for meeting the targets will be motivated to reach them and others will contribute to hold those employees accountable. To make it easy for you and everyone else to follow the KPI and the progress toward them, use dashboards that can be placed in the intranet or wherever you choose, and automatically updated.

Without a central location to collect, store, and timely report KPI data, it can be extremely difficult to manage metrics that affect strategies. The data must be accurate, trustworthy, and timely to give the benefits that you expect from KPI. So, having a system that has all the data you need in one central location is important.

Using dashboards with dial gauges, bar graphs or other graphical trends gives easily recognizable visual feedback to groups and individuals on their operational and strategic performance achieved.

Coaching suggestion: Have a recurring periodic (weekly?) meeting where progress towards the KPI targets is reviewed. In the meetings praise good performers and encourage those who are not meeting the targets. Instill team work by having everyone participate in the encouragement, offering their help. If possible have the dashboards in a place visible to all so everybody knows how all targets are progressing.

Focus on what is most important at present. Your strategic planning process should have already identified the key objectives for the next period (12 or 24 months for example). With your team determine a few central goals for the short term, and determine the drivers that you want to focus on. Since the objectives may change over time, their critical numbers may change too and thus your KPI "system" needs to have the flexibility to adjust.

It is typical for each objective to drive critical numbers for different departments. Each department focuses on its drivers, but all drivers together move the company toward the goal.

In the example described above to develop DCSF, one of the goals is to grow the top line revenue (to a fixed number) and this will cascade down to various departments in return on sales, increased profits, and increase in equity, and will also affect manufacturing, purchasing, production control, quality control, HR and perhaps several other departments or functions.

Key Performance Indicators for XYZ Company:

Following are the KPI put in place:

Quality Assurance:
- Supplier delivery performance.
- Customer delivery performance.
- Non-conforming products and services.

Sales:
- Monthly Bookings by salesman and companywide.
- Monthly Shipments by salesman and companywide.
- Monthly gross margins by salesman and companywide.
- Performance to goals for shipped orders, monthly, quarterly and year-to-date.

Engineering:

- Vendor training and R&D, yearly.
- Outside sales calls—three per month.
- Seminar events—ten per year.
- Inside sales staff training—eight times per year.

Accounting:
- Performance to budget for bookings, shipments and margins.
- Monthly charges by territory.
- Monthly statement of income including sales and operating income to budget and to previous year.
- Yearly comparison of financial numbers to industry.

Purchasing:
- Inventory value and turns.
- Supplier on-time delivery.

Information Technology:
- Publicize all items submitted to IT to control ownership and ensure resolutions are prioritized to preserve revenue.
- Identify productivity increasing technological advances to be implemented.

Any business, regardless of size, can be better managed with the help of KPIs; yours too.

> **Coaching suggestion:** *Have each manager develop CSF and KPI for their own section/department and have them present the CSF and KPI for the rest of the team to criticize. This will ensure that once implemented the CSF and KPI will be endorsed by all. Furthermore, in the discussion you (and the team) have the opportunity to make sure that all CSF play in concert toward the goals of the company.*

Balanced Scorecards

One tool used to monitor execution relative to the strategic plan, is the balanced scorecard. The balanced scorecard is a strategic planning and management system used extensively in business and industry to monitor the performance of the organization against strategic goals. It aligns activities of the business to the vision and strategy of the organization while improving internal and external communications.

It is more than a single scorecard; it is a combination of associated scorecards that monitor the successful execution of the strategy. It is designed to help organizations clarify their strategy, communicate it, and then align employees throughout the business to leverage that strategy and create measurable action.

When used properly it translates the strategic plan into an action plan on a daily basis. It not only provides performance measurements, but helps employees identify what should be done and measured. It provides a clear prescription as to what companies should measure in order to "balance" the financial perspective.

It provides feedback around both the internal business processes and external outcomes with the intent to continuously improve strategic performance and results. It takes into account the organization's performance against the strategic objectives within a balanced set of areas that contribute to success.

The balanced scorecard suggests that we view the organization from a business, customer, and financial perspectives, and to develop metrics, collect data and analyze it relative to each of those perspectives. Grouped under each perspective should be the most important organizational goals from the strategic plan.

Balanced Scorecards can provide:

- Focus; ensures an organization is doing the right things.
- Alignment; creates links between and across levels of your organization.
- Accountability; identifies what is strategically important, what performance level is required, and who is responsible.
- Communication; translates your high-level strategy into a message that is understood and meaningful.

To be able to use balanced scorecards you must have information and accounting systems able to capture and report the measurements needed. You also need a descriptive map showing how to implement the strategies. Above all, you need the commitment of management (you) and the committed involvement of all employees.

Automation adds structure and discipline to implementing the Balanced Scorecard system, and helps communicate performance information. There are several software programs available to make the implementation of balanced scorecards easier; one of them is the *"QuickScore Performance Information System*^{TM}*"* [1] developed by Spider Strategies.

References:
1. Balanced Scorecard Institute, *QuickScore Performance Information System*^{TM}, http://www.balancedscorecard.org/Software/QuickScoreB SCSoftware/tabid/395/Default.aspx.

Chapter XV - Systemizing Your Business

Have your company run by systems, not by people.

It is the act or operation of systemizing; the reduction of things to a system or regular method. A system is a set of parts which accomplish something by relating to one other. It is the process of implementing and documenting processes for each task in your business and creating an engine (system) for your business to run automatically.

I am really surprised as to how many owners/CEO of small businesses don't know the value of systems or don't know how to develop them and/or implement them. When I bring up the subject some claim to have systems but upon challenging them I realize they only have simple lists of activities or outlines of tasks for certain operations, or they have systems "in their head".

Very rarely I run into companies that have actually systemized their operations. This is disappointing considering that systemizing yields important benefits, most of which translate into value (and $$$). It is a critical component of business success for the present and of business value for the future.

Dr. Edwards Deming, the statistician credited with revolutionized American business practices, tells us that ninety-seven percent of all failures are due to systems failures and not to employees.

Systemization involves the implementation of optimum processes and the documentation of how to accomplish those processes. It also involves providing a step by step manual so that anyone is able to learn how to use the system. The objectives of Systemization are stability, security, consistency and efficiency.

Your processes—the processes you implement after you prove them—are your way of doing business. Your company won't reach the next level if your processes exist only in the head of those doing the work. Have you documented the way everything must be done in your organization? Does everyone know why they are doing what they are doing, and how it must be done?

A stable business is also a low-risk business which consequently means a higher value business. Investors/buyers are willing to pay more for your business when all of the principles of systemization are applied.

As a business owner you have the opportunity to create the lifestyle of your dreams. You can implement proven strategies that make small businesses work. Systemizing is one of those strategies; it all starts though, with a willingness to change. Are you willing?

What are the benefits of systemizing your business?

- A more organized business that carries lower risk because it does not depend on its staff to work efficiently.
- Reduction in costly errors due to omissions, operations mistakes, and other humanly caused deficiencies.
- Increases reliability in the business by ensuring that all tasks are completed the right way.
- Less time spent fixing problems solved by systemization.
- Consistent and reproducible service to your customers regardless of who does the work (ideally of course).
- Peace of mind for you, the owner, knowing that your business is running smoothly "by systems".
- Increase in the present and future value of your business.

With systemization your focus as a business owner can be on the proactive management of systems, rather than on solving problems or living with erratic results or failures due to lack of systems. Systems give you the ability to look objectively at how your business functions, the things you and your people do, and the relationship between different functions and tasks.

It is essential to have the mechanisms in place to help you manage the daily details so that your business can still operate and get consistent results every time, without you having to get deeply involved in the details.

Effective systems can save you and your team both time and money. There is an expression touted as a basic rule for systemizing: "systemize the routine, humanize the exception." Meaning that anything that can't be systemized needs to be run by people; however, I am convinced that any operation can be systemized and thus, it makes sense to put a system in place rather than adding more people to "humanize the exceptions".

Systemizing your business means creating a disciplined way of operating by which everyone follows processes in place for all activities that are performed on a regular basis. It also means to follow procedures for those activities that are not repetitive and for practically everything that takes place in the running of the business. It means dutifully practicing the concept of "this is the way we do it here".

Systemizing your business is about operating as efficiently as possible by creating the processes and procedures that best fit each operation for optimum execution, and documenting what you do every day for every operation and task. These written procedures produce consistency, reliability and predictability every time a task is performed; they become the mantra for the business as a not-to-be-deviated-from way of doing business.

Systemizing means that no aspect of a business is left to chance, and that your (the owner's) goals are more reachable and his life/work balance is improved because you are not "the driver of all operations".

Systemizing creates value for all stakeholders by establishing and following a discipline of efficiency and quality. In addition to the immediate value created for you, the owner, by the efficiency produced, it creates future value by increasing the worth of the business; a systemized business is worth significantly more than a business without systems.

It also means having checks and balances in place and having every employee well trained in the operations they perform.

Systems and training produce consistent results for the business and for the customers.

Why Aren't all Small Businesses Systemized?

The top excuses I've heard from business owners not to get involved in systemizing:

- We don't have the time to do it.
- It will take too long and will be too much work.
- I don't know how or where to start.
- We do a lot of custom work so systems won't work here.
- My procedures work fine and I don't want to change them.

None of them are valid reasons as:
- Systemizing actual saves time.
- Although it will take time the work is not complicated and the benefits are worth it.
- A good coach can get help you to get it done.
- Systemizing works regardless of the type of work of the business.
- In systemizing your business you don't need to change your procedures, unless you can improve them by making changes.

Many business owners feel there's no need for systems because customers want the personal interaction with them and thus they cannot delegate responsibilities and confide in systems and the action of others. This fallacy prevents them from upgrading the business and creating the value that systems represent.

One of the reasons for companies not implementing systemization is that they don't think they can do it because they do custom work or have many exceptions and special cases in their companies. I'm a believer however, that systemizing the right way will take those special cases into account.

Although the task of systemizing your business can seem daunting, it can help overcome the business' downfall and provide your small business with every chance to succeed.

Systemizing includes creating a system for how you pay your bills, how you manage your people, how you run each operation, how you ship product, how you serve your customers, how you do everything else. It means having a system to do each and all activities of the company; it even includes having a system to create systems.

"Repetition" is the purpose of systems. Repetition creates reproducibility in all aspects of the business and reproducibility of proven systems means the assurance of quality of operation and quality of products or services. Think of it as building a franchise *(The E-Myth)* and providing the operating manual for franchisees to run the franchise stores.

Effective systems are at the heart of successful businesses.

The Process of Systemizing

I like to think of systemizing in terms of the ISO philosophy, **_Do what you say and say what you do._**

You can look at systemization as the tools that run your business that make possible the vision that you want for the business and create your structural framework and provide you with the consistency, predictability, and results to achieve that vision.

> **_From my bag:_** *a number of years ago I helped a manufacturing company become ISO 9000 certified. We completed the process in record time and with a completely "paperless" system, which in those days it was a big feat. In the process of documenting the business to comply with the requirements of ISO, I realized that the same process could be used to systemize any business even if ISO was not a goal. Since then I have helped many companies through systemization using the same concepts, and have seen those companies flourish as a result.*

Firstly, you must understand what is meant by systemizing your business. Simply put, it is implementing and documenting processes for each task in your business and creating an engine (system) for your business to run automatically. By documenting the process required for each task you will have the beginnings of an Operations Manual *(see below)*.

The excuse of no having time to systemize doesn't "hold water" because systemizing your business is probably one of the most rewarding and time-saving things a small business owner can do. Systemization is a cousin of automation and once your business is "automated", the business can "run itself" … to a certain degree of course. Automation is key to consistency, reproducibility and accuracy.

By "automating your business" we mean that you should have a **process** for doing every task in your business, and that this process should be well documented and should be understood by anyone involved in a particular task. In fact, there should be a process for running your entire business, an "Operations Manual" that should be well understood and embraced by all.

The exceptions and special cases present in every small business can make systemizing difficult, but this should not be justification to shy away from doing it. Despite the difficulties, systemizing will result in the right people doing the right things a lot more effectively.

A business system is designed to produce results, so the results expected must be specified in the documentation for each process. The documents also must include instructions and rules about what steps to perform in what order to produce the result. To yield the benefits expected from systemization, the processes must be repeatable and scalable and easy to train others to perform them.

To implement systemization start by drawing a flowchart of your process, then document how it gets done, including as much detail as possible; after the system is confirmed the document can be edited to simplify it (but without deleting important details). Keep the system simple so people won't object to follow it.

> **Coaching suggestion:** *The easiest way to document all operations is to have the person performing the operation to write down every step of it. They can do it in the simplest form, such as in bullets listing, without worrying about grammar or rules, but including every detail of the operation. Then someone else can "clean it up" and make it more formal.*

> *The best way to prove the accuracy of the documentation is to ask an employee who is not the one normally doing the operation, to follow the document to execute it; if it is successful, the document is accurate. If it does not yield the results expected, it should be adjusted and the trial repeated. It is important to keep a consistent format for the documentation; develop a template and use it for all documents and start forming an "operations manual" that will be the "Bible" for the company.*

Follow these steps to systemize your small business:

- Analyze your processes against the goals, strategies and action items developed with the strategic plan.
- Determine which activities are not working to your expectations or you feel can be improved.
- Draw a diagram of the activities for each process, showing results expected, who is responsible for the work, resources needed and timeframe to complete it.
- List all steps of the process including as much detail as possible.
- Prove workability and accuracy of the process *(see Coaching Suggestion)*.
- Rewrite in standard format.
- Obtain necessary approvals.
- Incorporate into Operations Manual.
- Quantify and measure present costs and use it to form the baseline to measure future performance.

If at the end of this process you find that the new system doesn't exceed the performance of the old system, analyze all steps and repeat the process after making changes. Repeat the cycle until you have developed an improved system that you want to implement in your business.

Get everyone involved: The process of systemizing applies to everyone in the company; don't make the mistake of excluding some people because "it doesn't apply to them". It needs to happen throughout the company, from the CEO (you) to the janitors.

Have each employee write the first draft of the process document and get them involved in all rewrites too; after all, if they are doing the work they must be the experts in it. But be sure the written processes are based upon job descriptions for the function and not based upon the person doing the job. This is important because the document should serve to have someone else do the job if the incumbent is not available.

Share the systems company-wide; after the process is documented and confirmed, make it part of the operations manual and make sure everyone is familiar with the manual. Also, have people cross-trained for different jobs so they can fill in if needed.

While the process of creating systems company-wide may seem overwhelming, remember that it is a long-range project, not something you can do in a week. It takes some tedious work at the start before you see the benefits but the benefits are worth the wait. A good business system should include a complete description of the results expected and the measurements to control the process.

Systems run your business and the systems are run by people; as the leader, you control your people, but you also control how systems are implemented and how the systems are run. Your people must know that systems are to be followed and failure to do so will have consequences.

Coaching suggestion: adherence to the documented processes needs to be a strict policy of the company. All employees must be held accountable for religiously following the processes and the procedures inherent in the systemization, including the procedures that apply to documentation, its use and its control.

The Importance of Automating Your Business

Why is it that franchises almost always succeed regardless of who runs them? McDonalds can hire almost anybody to do the work because they have systemized the business to an optimal level. The McDonalds Corporation doesn't sell hamburgers; they sell businesses or business formulas contained in an operations manual that has been constantly updated and upgraded.

Imagine if you were to use this concept, even if you don't intend to open multiple locations, to run your business; by having a well-documented "Operations Manual" for your company you will achieve the benefits of systemizing as those world famous franchises do.

In the process of systemizing your business you can structure jobs in such a way that they can be done by employees other than those who normally do them, by simply following the documented flow.

Once your business is systemized you can feel that you have things is under control and now you can concentrate in doing your job as CEO and grow your company. This feeling is strengthened by knowing that the chances of making costly errors are diminished.

According to Michael Gerber in *"The E-Myth"*, business development occurs through a cycle of innovation, quantification, and orchestration. The starting point of this cycle then is systems innovation and the objective of innovation is improvement.

Innovation is about creating new or improving existing systems, and doing things in a better way. To improve your business you must constantly innovate because the goal of innovation is improvement. Systems innovation is the first step in a cycle aimed at keeping your business healthy and thriving in a consistent basis. Systemizing is part of the innovation.

Developing the Operations Manual

The purpose of the operating manual is to provide consistent value for the business and predictable experiences to customers. It also facilitates many operations to be run by employees with the lowest possible level of skill, without sacrificing quality and efficiency.

Document your system in an operations manual in an easy to access format with all processes documented in a standard form. Implement a formal process of reviews and approvals, with the corresponding signatures.

Before you get started developing your Operations Manual it is important to start with determining the long-term goals for your small business, including the potential number of employees needed to achieve your goals. From there you can create a functional organizational chart for your company as you see it a few years from today *(see Coaching Suggestion below)*.

> *Coaching suggestion: As described in a coaching suggestion in the Organization chapter, develop a functional organization chart as you see the company in two or three years into the future; that is a chart showing all functions in the business, without personal names, in a typical organization chart format. Make sure you cover all functions and the relationship between the functions. Develop job descriptions for each function.*
>
> *Once you are satisfied with it start putting names of present employees into the function boxes, but being careful not to place someone in a position that is not a perfect match (putting a square peg into a round hole). The boxes that are open after you placed all present personnel are the positions to fill as you increase employment. Again, make sure that you hire to match the open positions based on job descriptions for each function.*

Create a detailed job description for each position identified to cover all tasks and responsibilities and begin creating your "Operations Manual" to cover specific job descriptions for each functional piece of your business.

To document each process use a standard template that includes:

- The name of the process.
- Assigned process number and revision number.
- The date that it was created.
- Person or function responsible for performing it.
- Flow of the process including previous steps and steps to follow.
- Detailed steps to complete the process.
- Approval signatures.
- If a revision to a previous process, details of the revision.

The Operations Manual must be used and maintained properly. You must update any changes in policy, processes or procedures immediately in your manual and these changes must be done formally. There must be a procedure to make and implement changes; a form to request changes should be issued and appropriate approval signatures should be required to accept those changes, regardless of their importance.

Document control becomes the heart of the system; it doesn't need to be complicated—the simpler the better—but must be comprehensive and "powerful" (with the power to control all working documents).

Coaching suggestion: it is important to have one person in charge of the Document Control function. This is not necessarily a full-time job (depending on the size of your business) and you can name an employee to fill it on an "as needed" basis, but it is important to have formality in this function. When a new document is incorporated into the operations manual—with all the corresponding approvals—all other versions of the same process should be removed from the manual and from "the floor". All documents must be identified with a code number and always referred to by that number. Nowadays there are a number of reasonably priced software packages available to automate this function.

Revisions to existing documents must be issued and those documents that were revised taken off circulation. There are many versions of document control software available today that can make this task easier.

The organization must continually work on simplifying and refining the Operations Manual to make it as easy as possible to understand. Using visual aids as opposed to lengthy wording can help to make many operations more accessible.

Creating your Operations Manual can be a lengthy process so it is easier to do it when your company is small and grow it as the company grows. Remember that your manual will allow people who you haven't yet met to run all operations of your company; consequently, every procedure must be outlined for every employee and every process must be detailed step-by-step.

Each business is different and has a different operational structure. In your case it might be necessary to only have a few processes included in your Operations Manual at this time, but you should continue to expand and improve your manual as your business continues to grow.

Having procedures written is not the end of the process; you must continually strive to make them better and when you see opportunities to improve them, document the changes and repeat the implementation process.

Just as you need people to have backups, you also need your systems to have backups with plans for day-to-day operations and emergencies.

When a business is thoroughly systematized and it runs by the systems—and not by people—it will have higher probability of success regardless of the business climate, and will have a much easier time of surviving a transition to new ownership.

For these reasons and the reasons enumerated earlier, the business will command a higher price if and when you decide to sell. Furthermore, if you elect to retire or take a lesser role in the management of the business, but prefer not to sell and maintain ownership, the company will be in a much better position to continue its success without your active involvement.

Systems are a business owner's best friend. They'll help keep you on track and running smoothly today, tomorrow and for years to come.

Chapter XVI - Exit Strategy and Succession Planning

When is the right time to exit? What would happen to your business when you do?

You and most entrepreneurs have much of your net worth tied up in your companies. The trick is turning that stock into cash when it's time to retire. However, the BIG question is "when to retire and how?"

Business owners begin thinking about exit planning and succession strategies when they start feeling that they want to do something besides go to work every day. This could be because they would prefer to be doing something else, or they simply no longer get the same kick out of doing what they do. The "fire in their belly" is not burning as it once did.

Another motivator can be the nice feeling of approaching financial independence by selling the business ("cashing in") or at least part of it ("taking money off the table"). When these two thoughts grow in intensity and/or frequency, business owners may start leaning towards exiting the business.

In other cases, exiting can be a goal for which the owner has worked long and hard, rather than just a termination of a cycle. When you develop your exit strategy, you can preserve and control your own entrepreneurial illusion. Whether it is a goal or a final point of a "life-dream", do what is right for you and plan, plan, plan.

When I approach the subject with many small business owners their reaction is "I will never retire", or "I will be here until I die", or "I don't have any plans to retire and I don't know when I would retire". Surprisingly, these are good reasons to plan the exit … voluntary or not.

In fact, your exit from the business can be in your terms (voluntary) or not in your terms (involuntary). Voluntary means that you elect when and how you exit, and involuntary means that you exit because of death or disability. You need to cover both instances in separate plans. In addition, and as a necessary complement, you also need a succession strategy.

This brings up another reluctance from many small business owners. To these people succession only means who will replace them when they retire or become incapacitated; however, succession is much more than that. A succession plan should cover not just your position, but all key positions of the company.

An exit plan must be in place for owners to be able to leave the business maximizing benefits. Exit planning is the tool that would make it possible for you and all owners to leave the business on your terms and schedule.

Sadly, seventy percent of family-owned businesses do not survive to the second generation, according to the Small Business Administration (SBA), and fifty percent of those do not make it past the third generation. You can increase the odds by putting in place a sound exit strategy that includes a thorough succession plan.

Succession Planning

Succession planning is a process that involves several steps, including:

- Definition of the task and evaluating needs.
- Developing criteria for key positions.
- Evaluating multiple candidates.
- Getting outside advice and evaluation.
- Electing the proper candidates.
- Defining the roles for each function.
- Defining metrics to evaluate performance.
- Monitoring the plan to ensure its effectiveness.

We must not confuse succession planning with replacement planning; there are two different things. Replacement Planning is the process to identify backups to fill vacant positions, focusing in past performance and demonstrated skills to fill a particular job.

Succession Planning on the other hand is to identify a talent pool that can be developed in preparation for future responsibilities. It takes in consideration the potential of the individual, not only his/her performance in present or past positions.

Succession planning also considers future needs of the company as the business grows, and prepares the workforce for those needs. It follows then, that succession focuses on the future while replacement focuses in present needs.

A succession plan means being prepared to replace a key person that won the lottery, or the CFO who decided to move to another state, or even that highly trained line employee who is leaving to become a mother, and of course, who would replace you. Succession "planning" means being prepared for those eventualities and not acting out of panic in emergencies.

In your plan, decide what competencies (knowledge, skills, abilities and personal characteristics) people must have to contribute to the progress of the business today and in the foreseeable future. Also, identify the most important positions and their importance to the organization. Is the position critical to the organization's success and how easy will be to fill it? Do you have present employees that may be qualified? Can you "easily" train someone to fill it?

Provide growth opportunities to all employees and charge managers not only to practice self-development, but the development of their reports. In sum, take a proactive approach to succession by creating the environment where people are motivated by the opportunities available to them. Developing and nurturing its human capital needs to be a focus of all companies.

For those jobs you identified as critical and with a need to have potential successors, you should develop specific criteria for requirements and performance, and evaluate potential candidates against those criteria. Do not "force" people into jobs for which they are not qualified or could be top performers. Implement training and mentoring for those qualified to get the performers that you need. For senior management positions, you may want to supplement your own opinion with the observation of outsiders such as members of an Advisory Board.

In the real world, you cannot promote someone unless you have someone trained to take over the position vacated. To implement your succession plan, you need to consider the following:

- The strategic plan of your company; growth, timing, direction.
- Key areas that require the development of employees to qualify.
- Key employees targeted for development and/or promotion.
- Plans to train and develop employees, with emphasis on the most talented ones.

Depending on the situation of your company, you may have to take different approaches. You may need to expedite the development of some employees and expose them to different areas of the business, or you may need to expose them to a lengthier involvement in selected departments. Whatever your needs, make sure that you prioritize their fitting into the culture of the company. Acting out of panic in an emergency may affect the culture that you work so hard to implement.

Succession planning should be a never-ending process with continuous evaluation of present and future needs of the company, but also considering the needs of the employees. Ideally, each employee should have a predetermined path to advancement, with performance targets and his/her own self-development goals. That path should be reviewed when circumstances change, such as position of the company, business environment, personal preferences and progress towards personal development.

The succession planning process can be difficult and if you want it to be right you should take your time in doing it; keep in mind that a bad hire or a bad promotion can have far reaching consequences. Take your time, consider all the factors, get outside advice when appropriate, develop the plan and implement it carefully.

When done properly succession planning can give you peace of mind based on understanding and expectations of its future leadership, and the pride of serving not just the needs of the company but the needs of your people as well.

Coaching suggestion: Typically, business owners think of succession plans as determining who would take over "when the time comes" and when I ask this question I invariably get as an answer "I'm not ready to retire", or "I don't need one because I plan to work for many years". However, succession planning is not just for your position but for all key positions in the company, and it isn't just for when you retire, but in case of the unexpected eventuality.

I get a similar response for questions regarding exit strategy, but you should be thinking about this even if you are five, ten or even fifteen years away from retirement. The key here is that you can start doing now something that will maximize the value of the business when you are ready to retire. Some of my clients say "I will never retire", but you cannot be sure of what life has in store for you, and thus you should be prepared. More on this subject later.

Coaching suggestion: In your "functional organization chart" discussed in Systemization of Your Business, note for each function in the chart who is the incumbent for the job and who is qualified to replace him/her. Put a plan in place to train those qualified to replace incumbents to be the backups for the particular function. This can be the start of your succession plan for key functions or positions.

Succession in a family business is a critical step and a management challenge. Because of the dynamics involved it is a subject that can generate much controversy and can damage the health of the business. I am covering this in the chapter on Family Businesses.

Hiring Your Successor

Obviously this is the most important succession decision; who you chose as your successor can be the determining factor in the success or failure of the business and in the wellbeing of all families tied to the business (your own and all employees and their families).

Unfortunately, many of you do not think about this important issue. Most business owners do not even like to talk about this; it's not in the daily running of the business or even in the regular planning for the business, and thus it isn't a priority. Besides, they are not ready to retire so why waste time in these type of details?

> *From my bag: In a very successful family business, the obvious successor to the CEO was a non-family member. The CEO agreed that this key person was the right successor, but was very reluctant to set target dates for the transition. Because the candidate was growing anxious and there was a risk that he would live the company, I convinced the owner to come up with an alternate plan. He decided to make this person the CEO of a new acquisition, and use that position as training grounds for the ultimate position of running the parent company. The plan was executed successfully and both parties as well as both businesses are doing fine. The CEO candidate is proving his value and the Board of directors of the firm has already approved his candidacy for the parent company, over other employees who are family members but less qualified.*

However, you must realize that you are taking a huge risk in not being prepared. If the right opportunity presents itself in the form of an unsolicited offer to purchase the business, are you prepared for it? The business will be more attractive to potential buyers if you have a plan in place. Yes, I know, you are not thinking of selling, but … don't we all have a price?

Moreover, what about an unplanned exit? An exit forced by becoming disable, or worse yet, if you leave the business being carried out in a horizontal position? I know you don't like to think about this—none of us do—but it is a reality of life (or of death) that at some point we all face.

What would happen to your company if something happens to you? Have you made provisions for this eventuality? Have you named a successor or successors? Have you planned the succession carefully and thoroughly?

Who you identify as your successor or how you go about selecting one depends to a large extent on where you are in your business cycle and in your personal involvement in the daily activities of the company. If you and your company are in the "adolescent" state in which you are deeply involved in all operational activities, you will need a successor capable of performing similarly, but without neglecting the leadership and visionary qualities that a CEO must have.

If you and your business are past that state, you will need a successor who is primarily a leader and a visionary and can take the company to the next level. Yes, of course, he would still need operational knowledge, but I am assuming that by then you will have a capable team that can carry the burden of daily operations.

Regardless of where you are, you need to start the succession process as early as possible. This does not mean to "officially" name someone to the position or even announce it as a "work in process", but you need to identify and start grooming worthwhile candidates. Replacing you is not an easy task and the more time you can dedicate to it the better the chances for your successor to be successful.

Identify—from inside or bring someone in from outside the company—a potential number two; a person who can start to take over some of your responsibilities and be groomed to take over when the right time comes. Again, depending on the state of the company and your exit plans, you may need someone to complement your skills and attributes or someone that mirrors them.

For a number two you may be better off with a complementary type, a manager if you are a leader or a true leader if you tend to be more of a manager; an operations type if you are the sales guru, a more subdue type if you are an energetic driver. As your replacement though, the choice may have to be different; someone more like you with leadership traits to drive the company forward while maintaining the culture that you created.

Otis W. Baskin, a business professor at Pepperdine University advises to avoid the temptation to clone oneself. Two reasons for this advice: a) you will not find the "right clone", and b) a successor, any successor, cannot lead the company exactly like you; personalities are different, styles are different, and goals and plan may be different too. You need a person who will infuse new ideas to drive the company, not one who will make it stale.

> **From my bag:** *A friend and client of mine had a very well planned exit strategy and succession plan for himself. He knew and made it part of the plan, when he would exit, what he would do after he left the business, and who would be his successor. An excellent plan … with one flaw; the named successor was a minority partner in the firm, an excellent person and employee, but not qualified for the top job. My friend had chosen him out of loyalty and friendship, and ignored my suggestions that he was not the right man.*

> *Finally, at a time close to his scheduled exit, he realized the error and scrapped his plan. The end result was that a) he lost a few years and had to postpone his exit; b) he had to completely change his plans for life after the business; and c) it was a huge relief for the "assigned successor" as he also had doubts of his capability to lead, but was very happy in his role as a contributor in the company. Moral of the story: chose your successor wisely.*

Even in a small company, the second in command can balance the workload and the demands on the leader, while helping you diminish your involvement in the day-to-day activities. One of my old time clients always said that his goal was to "work myself out of a job", meaning that he has talented people that can replace him in the various functions of the business. This should be your goal too, to have someone ready to replace you.

Start delegating some of your duties or activities to the number two or those you identified as potential successors. As you see how well they perform, start increasing those functions you delegate and expose them to increasingly different activities of your position. Use discretionary judgment in doing it and accept the fact that there will be mistakes made, but take them as part of the training.

It may be necessary (in fact it may be recommended) for you to change your role at least partially, from leader to coach. As a coach, you should be spending more time asking questions and advising rather than directing and managing.

In discussing a subject of securities, a friend of mine told me about a maxim used in the stock market; it goes like this: "It's a lot different making imaginary investments on paper than putting real money into real stock purchases." The same is true with gaining business experience; there is no substitute for real-life involvement and responsibility.

Once you have identified your successor and have agreed on a process for him/her to be ready, set target dates for the transition; don't just leave it up in the air because your appointed successor may become anxious and may consider leaving the company. In addition, by setting a date it would force you to execute the plan as it was conceived, and would force the successor to expedite his/her development.

> ***Coaching suggestion:*** *If you bring someone from outside the company as your possible successor, do not tell him/her or anybody else about your plan until you see performance that will justify the plan. Of course, here I am assuming that you do not need to promise the opportunity to the candidate in order to hire him/her. Identifying a new hire as your appointed successor can be risky for two reasons: a) you don't really know how the person will perform in the targeted job, and b) you may create resentment among existing employees because they don't know the person and his/her performance. If after a long enough time you are convinced of the capabilities of the person and he/she has demonstrated to the rest of the work force that indeed he/she*

is succession material, you will be in a better position to announce it with confidence.

Hiring Your Successor in a Family Business

One of the most difficult problems you will face when you decide to exit will be whether to transfer the ownership of the business within the family or to sell the business to an arm's length party. Each alternative offers positives and negatives issues. The chances for success increase as the succession plan starts to mirror an arm's length transaction, with the family member having his/her own money at risk by having to buy the business (or a piece of it).

If yours is a family business, succession of the CEO can be a lot more complicated. In most cases, you are not just making positioning changes, but ownership changes as well. So the issues are not just who is the new CEO, but also who owns what or how much. These issues can be even more complex if the family members working in the company are direct family (children or siblings) and others (cousins, nieces, etc.).

Succession in a family business is a significantly complicated affair that deserves more space in this book; therefore, we are expanding on the subject in the next chapter dedicated to family business.

Succession in Partnerships

Succession can also be between partners when one of them decides to retire or otherwise leave the business, or perhaps sell his share to the other partner but stay with the company. In this situation it must be made clear that ownership and authority have been consolidated into the one partner, and that the relinquishing partner no longer has similar authority.

Employees may have loyalty towards the relinquishing partner and may tend to continue to deal with him rather than with the "real CEO", causing dangerous conflicts. It must also be demanded from the relinquishing partner to make sure he directs employees to interface directly with the CEO.

In the case of partnerships, it is a good idea to plan for the dissolution of the partnership at the time the company or the partnership is created. While this seems like a no-brainer, many partners don't do it because either they don't see the need (they will be friends forever) or don't want to create problems right from the get-go. I have seen many "ideal" partnerships go sour without a planned dissolution, creating a nightmare situation for both partners and for the company.

> ***From my bag:*** *Two brothers were co-CEO of a thriving business. They agreed for one of them to buy out the other, but with the seller staying in the business. The expected happened; all employees that previously reported to the selling partner continued to go to him for all business issues, leaving the now sole-CEO uninformed and uninvolved in many situations. Casual talking to the employees did not yield any improvement. Consequently, I instructed both former partners to have a general meeting with all employees to officially announce the change and to set clear instructions as to who was responsible for what. To supplement this action, the selling partner's office was moved to another building, thus making it more difficult for employees to continue to go to him.*

Exit Planning

Please do not confuse succession planning with exit planning, as they are two different but complementary things. Succession focuses on the transfer of leadership and management, while exit planning is the result of a complete analysis of the issues involved in the owner's ability or desire to leave the business.

Succession planning revolves around the business' needs and the survival of the business upon your departure. Exit planning involves the business' needs but also your needs and the factors affecting or being affected by your leaving, including family, financial position and posture, health, goals, plans for the "hereafter" and other personal issues.

"You should be thinking about your exit strategy the day you start your business," says attorney Garrett Sutton, author of

"How to Buy and Sell a Business"[1] part of the *"Rich Dad's Advisors"* series. How and when you exit your business is not a subject to take lightly; much thought and planning must go into it for your happiness sake and the sake of your business.

There are three forms of exiting:
- Transfer the business (by selling it or otherwise changing ownership).
- Keeping ownership and acting in a lesser active role.
- And the above-mentioned "forced" retirement by disability or death.

A good plan should cover all instances and with as many variable as can be foreseen as possibilities.

Many owners do not want to leave the business entirely and they prefer to "retire" but still keep a hand in it. Keeping a hand in it can be as an active owner in a lesser role, or simply as an absentee owner enjoying the fruits of their entrepreneurship via a continuous reaping of the profits generated by the business.

Thus, exiting can be accomplished by:
- Selling the business to outsiders.
- Leaving it to heirs by selling it to them or simply transferring it.
- Transferring full or partial ownership to trusted employees or others.
- Staying involved in a lesser role (as Chairman or advisor for example).
- Being an absentee owner with no daily involvement.

In "planning your plan", you need to answer all of the following:
- Have you decided when you want to retire?
- Do you know the income you need to achieve financial security?
- Do you know how much your business is worth (realistically) and how easy or difficult it would be to sell?

- Do you know what the business's future cash flow is likely to be after you leave it?
- Do you know how to sell your business to a third party in a way that will maximize your cash and minimize your tax liability?
- Do you know how to transfer your business to family members, co-owners or employees while paying the least possible taxes and enjoying maximum financial security?
- Have you implemented all necessary steps to ensure that the business continues if you don't?
- Have you appointed caretakers of the business if you become incapacitated or worse?

I'm assuming that you have already provided for your family's security and continuity if you die or become incapacitated, as this is one of the few things most business owners do proactively through insurance coverage.

Your accountant and attorney must be intimately involved in this process. It may also be a good idea to have your coach participate not just in the actual planning, but also in the "planning of the plan".

> ***Coaching suggestion:*** *Naming a caretaker for the business in case of your inability to function is an excellent preventing measure. A caretaker must be someone who knows the business, who agrees with the way you run it, who has love or respect for you, and—very importantly—who gets along well with your heirs. A caretaker can be a person or a group, as for example an Advisory Board. If you are a member of an Advisory Board group and you know and trust the members without reservations, they as a group can be good candidates to manage your business until your heirs decide what to do with it.*

As I said earlier, many owners do not set exit objectives because they are not interested in retirement and think they will be around forever, or because they cannot separate themselves emotionally from a business they have created and has been the center of their life for many years.

It is difficult, if not impossible, for an owner to engage in the planning process until that owner is emotionally prepared to leave the business. Those who are emotionally ready to face their departure often do not know what to do or where to begin.

The Exit Strategy Questionnaire available in the Appendices section can help you answer some of the many questions related to the comprehensive issue of retirement and exit strategies. Those questions that result in a negative answer should identify work to be done. This questionnaire is not intended to be a very complete list of questions on the subject, and as you go through it, undoubtedly it will bring about other questions that are not listed and are perhaps related to specific personal situations.

Whether you are already thinking about retirement or exiting the business, or this is a subject that doesn't enter your mind at this time, I urge you to start thinking seriously about it. You owe it to yourself, to all stakeholders in the business, and to your loved ones, to do a plan even if you "plan to work forever".

Judy Weintraub of Weintraub Legal Services has put together the following outline of Succession Planning Steps and Workforce Planning. Use it as reference to develop your plans.

Succession Planning Steps

1. Begin by determining your own goals:
    a. When do you want to step away from the day-to-day operations?
    b. What role do you want to play in the business?
    c. What do you want to accomplish in the next 15 years?
    d. How much money will you need?
    e. What would success mean to you in your new endeavor?

2. Think about how you want to transfer the business.
    a. Corporate form allows transfer of stock

b. Review any shareholder agreement, or prepare one to deal with contingencies such as death, disability, retirement

c. Develop a timeline.
   - When do you want to begin transferring ownership?
   - When will you transfer 51% (control)?
   - When will the balance be transferred?
   - When you will retire?

3. Think about your financial strategy: how will your successor pay for your interest
   a. Estate and gift tax issues.
   b. Employee stock option plan.
   c. Insurance (life, disability).
   d. Trusts.
   e. Know the value of your company; get an appraisal.

4. Identify your successor(s)
   a. What are their technical and managerial skills?
   b. What are their strengths and weaknesses?
   c. What needs to be done to enable the person to step into your position?

5. Perform succession management on other key positions
   a. What are your key positions?
   b. Who is currently in these positions?
   c. Do you have candidates for these positions?
   d. What are the skills/competencies required for these positions?
   e. What training is necessary to prepare a move into this position?
   f. Who is a candidate for more than one position?
   g. How are our key players performing?

6. Update your business plan with input from your successors
   a. Any future new products?
   b. Plans for expansion, growth or new investment, and a candid assessment of the company's current environment and competitive positioning.

This joint business plan exercise will give you an opportunity to evaluate your successor's goals and ideas for the firm, while forcing your successor to think through and write down specific plans for running the operation.

Think about an outside board of directors, for continuity. The board can serve as a surrogate parent, guiding the management of the company and acting as mediator, reconciler, cautioner and supporter.

Workforce Planning

We want to make sure that the right people are in the right place at the right time in order to be as prepared as possible for unexpected events. Please fill out the information below and update it annually or as necessary.

1. Who will handle your job responsibilities if you are out of the office? Fill out a table with columns as shown below. In the third column, identify what additional skills you feel are necessary for the people you have designated to be able to handle your responsibilities effectively, and how they should obtain these skills— training, or on-the-job experience.

Job Responsibility   Designee   Skills Needed

2. Do you keep a log of the tasks that you are handling?
   a. If we needed to make sure that your tasks are being taken care of in your absence, what should we do to find out what those tasks are?
   b. Where would we find the names of those individuals whom we should contact?
3. If one or more staff members have to take on your responsibilities, how will their responsibilities be managed? Have you developed a cross-training plan so that other staff members could shoulder some of the load of the person or people handling your responsibilities?

Design another table listing your staff in the first column, and your projects in the first row. For each staff member, place an X in the cell of those projects they are involved in, and a Y in the cells of those projects they have the capability of performing. Put a Z in a cell if you want them to become familiar with the project and develop the skills to become involved in it, for cross-training purposes.

4. Who on your staff has the potential to move into a management role (talent, desire and skill)? Have you discussed with them what they would like to do—career moves, expectations, relocation possibilities, etc.? What training and/or experience do they need to enable them to grow into a management role, and how and when will they obtain that training and/or experience?

5. Keeping in mind your current projects and prospective projects, in what areas is your department weak? For each area decide what you need to improve the functionality of your staff (in leadership/management, business knowledge*, skills/experience<, technical skills, other). How and when should these improvements take place?

   *Knowledge of the company's business, mission and vision, goals, values, key drivers.
   <People skills, maturity, communication skills, presentation skills, team skills, problem-solving skills, recordkeeping skills, etc.

References:

Garrett Sutton and Robert T. Kiyosaki, *How to Buy and Sell a Business: How You Can Win in the Business Quadrant*, (Business Plus, April 1, 2003).

Chapter XVII-Family Business

The leader of a family business has a dual responsibility;
CEO of the business and caretaker of the family.

Wikipedia: A **family business** is a commercial organization in which decision-making is influenced by multiple generations of a family—related by blood or marriage—who are closely identified with the firm through leadership or ownership.

Young eentrepreneurial firms are not considered to be family businesses because they lack the multigenerational dimension and family influence that create the unique dynamics and relationships of family businesses. Only after a second generation joins the firm either in management or ownership (or both) they will be considered to be family businesses.

This is another subject well covered in many books and by many experts, and thus, it is not covered in great detail in this book. I have worked with many family-run businesses in many different industries, and I understand the issues faced by these businesses, but I rather leave the in-depth discussion to experts that specialize in the subject.

Statistics

The survival rate of family businesses is not good (as shown below), and that is because the leaders of these businesses have all the challenges typical of any business, plus the challenges that family relations bring to the scene.

The family business is the world's dominant form of business organization comprising the largest population within the small business community in the United States. Based on figures compiled by the Family Firm Institute (FFI), family firms cover eighty to ninety percent of all businesses in North America.

However, not all family-run businesses are small businesses. In the United States, some thirty-seven percent of Fortune 500 companies are family-owned while sixty percent of publicly-listed companies are family-controlled (Family Firm Institute figures).

Regretfully, the statistics are less than encouraging for them. A recent *Grant Thornton*[2] research study found that about seventy per cent of family businesses never make it to the second generation being in charge. Furthermore, an astonishing ninety per cent of family companies go out of business before a third generation can take over the management of the firm.

One of the issues—perhaps the most challenging issue— family businesses face is the duality or multiplicity of roles for the founder (i.e. as father, husband and president of the company), problems can occur where family members create problems that he/she—the owner—cannot accept. Family conflicts when left unchecked can lead to the collapse of the business.

Despite these challenges, family businesses enjoy opportunities that may not be present in other business organizations. Studies show that family businesses can outperform other companies because family members tend to think long-term. In addition, because the family name is attached to the business, the family members are willing to put more effort, work longer hours and plow back earnings to ensure the success of the venture.

Poor succession planning appears to be another culprit for the dismal statistics of family businesses, according to the study *"Finding the Right Balance"* by Pieter Bottelier and Gail Fosler [3].

However, a number of other issues also affect their survival; for example:

- The founder/owner not spending enough time managing the business, perhaps due to "early retirement", other occupations, or even family disputes.
- The family is more concerned about family issues than about profits of the business.
- Having too many family members on the payroll, creating nepotism and inefficient operations.
- Family members being hired for positions they are not qualified for, creating a culture of resentment.

- Non-family members are unmotivated because of a perceived favoritism among family.
- Personal family battles dominate the workplace creating a hostile environment.
- Lack of planning, including strategic planning and succession planning.
- Succession of the management trusted to family members that are not qualified or not liked by employees, clients and others.
- Inadequate estate planning and failure to properly prepare for the transition to the next generation.

All of these issues can affect the ability to make the business a success. It is, therefore, imperative to address these issues from the start. Successfully addressing these issues can help the balance of emphasis between family and company.

> ***From my bag:*** *I have experienced many unfortunate situations in dealing with family businesses. Most of the bad situations were generated by one or more of the issues listed. One particular example was a manufacturing company that employed in addition to the owner, his four children, his wife, and a nephew. Not all of them were in management roles, but the nepotism was heavily resented by the rest of the employees because, whether it was real or not, the perception was one of favoritism to family members.*
>
> *This situation resulted in the loss of a number of excellent employees, and in a serious difficulty to bring in qualified leaders to strengthen the management team. As a result, the growth of the company stagnated, and it was only after some of the family members left the company that things started to improve.*

More statistics:

- Family businesses comprise eighty to ninety percent of all business enterprises in North America *(Family Business Review, Summer 1996).*

- Family owned businesses account for sixty percent of total U.S. employment, seventy-eight percent of all new jobs, and sixty-five percent of wages paid *(Financial Planning, Nov 1999)*.
- Among the companies listed on the Standard & Poor's 500 Index, thirty-four percent are family businesses. *(Evidence from the S and P 500)*.
- Sixty percent of majority shareholders in the family business are fifty-five years of age or older.
- Thirty percent are sixty-five or older.
- Thirty percent have succession plans in order.
- Less than forty percent have a successor in mind.
- Less than thirty percent have an actually written succession plan.
- Sixty-four percent do not require family members to have qualifications required by non-family businesses, commonly accepted to be successful or not.
- Family-owned businesses generate sixty-four percent of the US gross domestic product.
- By 2050, virtually all closely held and family owned businesses will lose their primary owner to death or retirement. Approximately $10.4 trillion of net worth will be transferred by the year 2040, with $4.8 trillion in the next twenty years [4]
- In five years, approximately forty percent of US family businesses will be passing the reigns to the next generation.
- Of CEOs due to retire within five years, fifty-five percent have not yet chosen their replacement, *Arthur Anderson/Mass Mutual* [5]
- There are 1.2 million husband and wife teams running companies *(NFIB 2003)*
- The number of family businesses run by women have grown thirty-seven percent in the past five years with an average annual revenue was $26.9 million last year *(Boston Business Journal, September 4, 2003)*
- Fifty-two percent of family firms have hired at least one female family member full-time, while ten percent employ two female family members *(Arthur Anderson/Mass Mutual, 2003)*

- Although approximately ninety-five percent of family business respondents advised that they manage their business like any other, far fewer (fifty-six percent) have a written strategic plan, and even less (thirty percent) have a written succession plan. (*Family Business Alliance – Washington DC*).

What you need to do to make your family business successful

The most important issue to ensure success of a family business is easy to explain but extremely difficult to implement. Being able to separate family issues from business issues is a prerequisite to prevent the differences that are unquestionably generated in all family businesses. How those differences are treated and resolved can make or break a business. It is the responsibility of the owner/patriarch to prevent and resolve these issues, but he/she needs the cooperation of all family members who are owners and even—in some cases—family members who are not involved in the business.

The first step to separate family from business is to hire only those family members that are qualified to perform in the business. To do this you must start with good job descriptions that are based on the functional organization as described in the *Organization* chapter. Family members must apply to the job openings based on the descriptions and must meet all requirements of the position.

Measure the performance of family members as you measure non-family employees. Create valid guidelines based on the job description and hold them accountable to established levels of performance that apply to all employees.

Make sure that not all management positions are filled with family members. Strong leadership from non-family members is essential to a culture of fairness. Fairness also applies to within the family; not showing undue preference for some family members over others must be a firm rule.

Put business health and profits over petty family issues. Time spent on dealing with family issues is time robbed from the business. Working hours must be dedicated to the business; any family issue must be treated after working hours. Whenever possible, deal with family issues out of sight of non-family employees.

Understand that the family business system is driven by the values of the family system. Simply put, if you intend to make a strategic plan for the business, a strategic plan should first be developed for the family. (*www.Familybusinessexperts.com*).

All family related issues that concern the business must be discussed, clarified, understood by all and put in writing at the very beginning of the family-business relationship. All rules and understanding must be documented and form part of the operational business plan for the company. No deviations from those rules can be accepted without the clear consent of all parties involved.

Planning is a commonly avoided process in a family environment because there is a many times misinterpreted understanding among family members; however, those "understandings" can be misleading and the cause of serious disputes. The only substitute is good planning and documentation.

Succession planning in a family business is very critical and thus a prime candidate for exhaustive documentation and thorough understanding from all involved. As I said earlier, lack of succession planning or an unfair or incomplete succession plan cab be a major reason for failure of family-run businesses.

When you plan succession you must consider firstly who is ready, willing and able to perform and lead and you must also consider who will be accepted by the rest of the employees. In making the tough decisions related to succession, you must balance what is best for the family with what is best for the business, favoring the business over family. In this evaluation don't neglect to include the feelings of clients and other stakeholders.

A good succession strategy can help business owners plan, preserve and pass on the hard-earned family wealth; both in the form of financial assets and the invaluable business experience of the founding generation.

From my bag: Two examples of badly executed succession in family businesses that I experienced were as follows:

In one case, the father left the business to three sons in equal shares but named the oldest son as the CEO. The personalities of the three sons were different and had clashing styles. As a result, the two younger brothers resented the oldest and did not recognize him as the leader. The business suffered as a consequence and what was a thriving enterprise started to drift downwards.

The second example is similar except that in this case there were four children and the appointed CEO was the youngest. He was selected because he had the most experience in the business as he started to work there as a teenager. The oldest brother was supportive of his youngest sibling, but the other two were not. The situation deteriorated to the point that the CEO had to fire the two non-supportive siblings. But it got worse because the CEO, affected by having to "destroy" the family union, lost his motivation for the business. It took the work of a specialized firm and a lot of business coaching to rekindle the "fire-in-his-belly" for the business.

In both cases, the problems originated because the founder/owner/father made the succession a clean-break; he retired and did not give any guidance to his children. My advice then, is to do a succession in a "phase-out, phase-in" mode, for the founder to provide the necessary guidance during the transition.

Conflicting aims and desires.

Family members participating as managers and/or owners of a business would ideally strengthen the company because they are typically loyal and dedicated to the family enterprise. However, their participation as managers and/or owners can present unique problems because the dynamics of the family system and the dynamics of the business systems are often not in balance and often in competition.

It is commonly assumed that trust and understanding are implicit in a family, and everyone has the same goals in mind. However in most cases, members may have a common goal of high value for the company, but different individual aspirations and wants. These differences can create tension and disputes among family, unavoidably affecting the business environment.

There are various scenarios in which the interests of a family member may not be aligned with the interest of the business. For example, a family member who has the ambition to be president maybe in competition with a non-family member who maybe more qualified for the position. In this case, the personal interest of the family member and the wellbeing of the business may be in conflict.

In another scenario, the interest of one or more family members may conflict with one another regarding the sale of the business. If a family member who is an owner wants to sell the business to "cash-in" or for other reasons, but another family member/owner may want to keep the company for his own reasons, their interest conflict and cause complications in the management of the company.

There can be, of course, many other scenarios of conflicting wants or desires between family members and even of the entire family against what may be best for the business in a particular situation. All these conflicts can cause tension within the management of the company and can affect the wellbeing of the business.

The three functions in play in a family business—family, ownership and management— and the roles imbedded in them, involve different and often conflicting values, goals, and actions. While family members may put a high priority on the family success that unites them through consecutive generations, executives in the business are concerned about strategy and the reputation of their firm in the marketplace. Owners are interested in financial capital—performance in terms of wealth creation—while family members are more interested in the emotional capital of winning as a family.

The picture gets more complicated when the ownership of the business includes family members and outsiders (investors and/or employee-owners). Employees are concerned with emotional capital that represents career opportunities, bonuses and fair performance measures and this can be in conflict with family members' aims.

The most intractable family business issues are not the business problems the organization faces, but the emotional issues that compound them. The challenge faced by family businesses and their stakeholders, is to recognize the issues that they face and understand how to develop strategies to address them.

Achievement obtained through generations can be destroyed by the next generation if the family fails to address the psychological issues they face. Family-run organizations need an understanding and a broader perspective on the human dynamics of family firms from two complementary frameworks, psychodynamic and family interaction.

Succession in a Family Business

Paul Karofsy of *Transition Consulting Group* (www.fortcg.com) says that "a dysfunctional family enterprise is like no other hell on earth, but when such a business works, there are few greater joys." Having worked with many family businesses, I have to agree; succession in a family business ranges from total chaos and infighting to the most pleasant experiences. Unfortunately, the latter are the exceptions.

Family relations in a family business are difficult at best. Jealousy and all other ugly human traits in person-to-person relationships are awake in a work environment where family members coexist. It is a challenge for you the CEO/owner to maintain friendly working relationships and at the same time loving family relationships among your employees who are also family members.

Implementing a succession of ownership to the next generation can be a dream come true or the worst nightmare, depending on the situation and how it is executed. If there is only one child either capable or with the desire to take over the business, the process can be easy, but if there are multiple candidates among the family willing and ready to take over, the process can be excruciating.

Generally, children would be the most logical candidates (particularly the oldest child), but it may be that others are more qualified or better performers, complicating the transition. What you do and how you do it in these types of situations can result in family feuds and business failures.

Should the nomination to be the successor go to the oldest child? To the most capacitated? To the one that most wants it? To all of them as a group to manage the business as a committee? Whatever you do, chances are you will have problems. I have seen many options implemented and almost without exceptions there were unpleasant issues to deal with.

If ownership in the business is transferred—totally or partially—as part of the succession, it can be even more complicated. Do you treat each child equally? Does the appointed CEO get a larger share? How much of the ownership is divided among them? Sadly, whenever there is money involved, there will be issues to contend with regardless of the family relationship.

Family relationships that interfere with the operation of the company can be very harmful and non-productive. Somebody said: "Nepotism can be either positive or negative, depending on the capabilities of the individuals involved. It is rarely neutral." I believe that it is only positive in that family members tend to be more loyal and concerned about the wellbeing of the company, but usually it is a negative force in all other aspects.

It is difficult for an owner/CEO to relinquish authority in a business that he created, but it is even more difficult when the successor is a family member. As a result, typically the founder stays in control (or tries to) longer than it is advisable after a transition, creating stress for the new leader and putting him in a difficult position with respect to how others view his/her role.

In most situations, this is aggravated by the fact that the founder keeps a financial position in the business and thus wants to "safeguard" the investment by influencing how the business is run. This part of the emotional break from the business that an owner suffers when he/she decides to exit, requiring an extensive preparation to overcome that barrier.

In the case of a parent-child situation where the child assumes the leading role, interference from the parent represents to the child a continuation of the natural dominance of the parent, and breaking from it becomes a continuous goal for the child.

> **From my bag:** *The owner/CEO of a very successful business had put together a simple exit strategy by which he would transfer the CEO position to his son-in-law in a gradual form over a period of approximately one year. The son-in-law was a Vice President of the company, pretty well trained in all aspects of the business, and was eager to take that step. Suddenly the owner suffered a heart attack and was disabled for several months, forcing the son-in-law to expedite his "on the job training" and start acting as the formal CEO.*
>
> *He did a commendable job and the company continued in its successful climb. When the owner was able, he came back to work and assumed his CEO role displacing the son-in-law back to the "CEO in training" position. Obviously, this created an uncomfortable situation that was resolved only after I mediated and convinced the owner to trust his successor and allow him to take over permanently. Could this situation have been prevented? You cannot predict a disability, but perhaps there could have been guidelines to cover such an eventuality.*

A surprisingly common case is that of unqualified family members taking over a business only because they are family and the owners want to keep it in the family. This happens when the business exists to serve the family and not the other way around, as ideally it should be. Unfortunately, the probability of success in this situation is practically zero.

During my coaching career, I have seen and worked with a number of bad family business situations resulting in sad outcomes. I have seen fathers suing children and children suing parents; I have seen very ugly court fights among siblings, and I have seen many family destroyed by fighting over business issues.

My advice if you plan to bring children or other family members into the business is to start early, bring them in at low levels and let them earn the promotions. In addition, when you distribute authority and ownership do not do it in equal shares; assign responsibilities according to capabilities and desires, and the share of ownership that go with the positions.

Assuring a smooth transition to the next generation of leadership is a daunting task. Selecting a successor who can continue to grow and move the organization to the next level is even tougher.

> ***Form my bag:*** *I have had the fortunate or unfortunate experience of working with many of the mentioned sad stories in family businesses. One of them involved three brothers that were appointed co-owners by the exiting father. They were also given equal level of responsibilities, with authority over three separate areas of the business. The brothers did not take this split well, resulting in much resentment and infighting. Their relationship was so bad that they hardly spoke to each other. Unfortunately, the business showed the bad karma and was floundering.*
>
> *Reacting to our encouragement all three joined separate peer boards that a colleague and I chaired. We got them involved in a strategic planning process as a way to get them to talk and interface with each other, and we had coaching sessions individually with each of them and as a group. Gradually the relationships improved significantly and it was reflected in the success of the business and in their happiness as individuals and as a family. Had the succession*

taken a different approach, the differences could have been avoided.

An alternative is to hire somebody from outside the firm, but this has its own set of problems. An outsider can't be as knowledgeable and perhaps as comfortable with the culture of the company as somebody that has lived in the environment and even helped establish it. Moreover, if family members and loyal employees are passed over for this opportunity, it may result in a difficult situation for all concerned.

Those differences and antagonisms are particularly true if we are talking about a transition of power; i.e., a change at the top. The best advice is to work hard into separating family from business issues; yes, I know, it is easier said than done, but it is the only sure way to prevent serious effects on the business. Keeping the relationships on a business basis, the criteria for performance are easier to implement and judge.

If the succession plan is for the entire organization (excluding the top position), it must be a carefully planned strategy developed with the input of shareholders, key employees and independent advisers, over a prudent period of time. If it involves key positions occupied or coveted by family members there can be serious disagreements among them, and the CEO has the difficult task of mediating and ultimately making the decisions that may affect family relations.

If the plan includes the promotion of family members over non-family employees, it can also cause disruptions in the organization if not handled properly. A policy of open communication will help to minimize the potential disruptions and even the loss of loyal and talented employees. If family members are promoted to positions of ownership, it may be necessary to consider alternate incentives for non-family employees passed over for promotion.

There are cases in which children agree to join the family business only because they want to make mom and dad happy or because they believe that it is expected of them. Try to avoid this situation at all cost because it is a sure prescription for failure of the business and even of the relationships.

The odds for successful working relationships and succession of family members within an organization, improve when the children grew up working in the business, even on a part time basis. Because of their experience in the company they tend to understand the issues in it and why the owner (dad or whoever) do what he does. They also get to know the rest of the employees and, if they are good performers, have earned their respect. When this happens, the transition into higher positions is easier and faces less resentment from others.

What do family business owners want to happen when they leave the business?

- Forty-six percent want the business to stay in the family.
- Ten percent prefer to sell the company.
- Five percent prefer to sell only parts of it.
- Five percent prefer to take the company public, assuming of course that it is a viable alternative.
- Thirty-four percent was undecided.

From my bag: Among the many situations I experienced with family business, there is one that would be comical if it wasn't so sad. A member of one of the peer advisory boards that I chaired was the owner/CEO of a business that employed several family members, including parents, siblings and others. At one of the board meetings she brought up to the board the following issue: "how does one fire one's own mother?" Needless is to say the board treated the issue with outmost respect and sentimentalism.

Focus on what is important

A family business is still a business and financial trouble in a family business—as in any other business—should be cause for serious alarm. Some of the things you should do to maintain a family focus on a company's economic well-being, are:

Keep solid accounting books. Use the basic financial tools, including balance sheets and income statements prepared regularly and distribute them among family members as you would with a board of directors. Strong financials are an absolutely essential tool for business management. Periodically and regularly analyzing financial data you make your business more predictable, and thus more stable.

Make all family members involved in the business participants of the financial analysis and responsible for understanding what they mean. If no one in the family has sufficient knowledge of financial issues you need to establish a relationship with an outside accountant.

Don't always let family come first. In family businesses often there is a tendency to make decisions that are better or more convenient for the family than for the business. For example, if some relatives want to take a vacation and they want the rest of the family to join them, who will run the business in the absence of the family members? The decision should be based on what is best for the business and if it requires for somebody to sacrifice the trip, then that is what should happen.

Focus on the present, as well as the future. Succession planning is a subject of ongoing communications at intergenerational businesses, and with it jockeying for position in the race to who-would-get-what-and-when discussions. But it is more important to get the generations working productively in the present. The function of the team and the responsibility of the leader are to optimize the operation of the business by utilizing everyone's talents and efforts.

Final thoughts

As I said earlier there is a massive amount of articles and books written on the subject of family businesses, thus there is no need to expand here on the same subject. In addition to the power of articles and books available, there are a number of organizations existing to help family businesses. If you are working in a family business I strongly recommend joining one (or more) of those organizations.

Of course it is also highly recommended to join a peer advisory board as explained in the appendix.

Chapter XVIII - Sale of the Business

Is this your goal?

All successful entrepreneurs share the passion for the businesses they created; but what happens when it's time to move on? Most owners have the mixed emotions of being afraid, being exhilarated, being confused and being joyful.

I know that you, like most business owners, are more preoccupied with the day-to-day operations and growth of the business than with when is the right time to pass the throne to others. However, unless you start planning for it two things can happen: a) you won't know when the right time is; what circumstances and personal state will make it right, and b) when it comes you won't be prepared for it.

Being prepared means not just being ready operationally or financially, but—more importantly—ready emotionally. What happens after the sale is more important than the sale itself. What are your plans for after you sell the business? Do you know what will occupy your time, your drive and your emotions? Do you plan to live a life of leisure, start another business, do voluntary work, get involved in other ventures, become an investor?

For some of you it takes years to adjust at a new life, from being the center of activities, the large fish in a big lake to being just a fish in a pond; from running at one hundred miles per hour every day to having too much time in your hands. Or from being the decision maker to one who follows directions or only participates in the decision making process. Of course it also depends on who you sell to, what are the conditions of the sale; these variables must be part of the planning.

From my bag: One of the very successful business owners I coached for years was suffering from a long downturn in the business do to the economy and as a result, from a psychological down himself to the point of wanting to "get out of the business" and sell the company. Knowing that the down period was temporary (because of the type and success of the business) and of his talent as a businessman, I felt he would be making a terrible mistake.

His wife and partner in the business was supportive of his position, so I decided to talk with her rather than trying to convince him. I asked her what he would do after selling the company. She said that he would likely start another business, to which I replied with another question; I said "tell me, how were the beginnings of this company"? She said: "Oh God, they were very stressful and even painful". So I asked her: "and you want him, and you, to go through all that again?" She looked at me and said" I had not thought about that; that would be the last thing I want for him and for me".

And she proceeded to change her position and convince him to stick it out. He did and today the company is double the size it was then, and extremely successful. Obviously, both of them are very grateful to me for getting them to see the light. The moral of this story is that what happens after the sale is more important than the sale itself.

Being the boss gives a rainbow of emotions too; from ego satisfaction and gratification to the heavy burden of daily stress, but most entrepreneur/owners wouldn't change this for anything. Selling the business—their surrogate child—is an emotional event difficult to face. Can you take the emotions out of it and solely engage in the financial aspects? I'm betting that you can't, but at the very least you must try to keep both aspects on an even level as much as possible.

Can you today say without a doubt where your business ends and you begin? I bet that it may be difficult for you because there may be emotional ties that you are not even aware of. In the business environment you are always dealing with quantifiable objectives, but in an "after business life" you will likely be facing much less quantifiable objectives and a different kind of stress. A successful transition to a new life is what determines the success of the sale.

Because it is so difficult to face most owners put off dealing with planning the sale as long as they can. The exceptions are those who have the exit strategy already in place and look forward to the day when they rid themselves of the daily grind and start a new life.

A CIBC *"Small Business Outlook Poll"*[1] (conducted by Decima Research), indicated that thirty-nine percent of small business owners plan to sell their businesses and fifteen percent plan to have a family member take over. But, two-thirds of the owners polled admitted that they had not yet approached the subject of who will take over the company.

Some questions you should ask yourself when you are thinking about a possible sale:

- Do you need to sell? Do you want to sell? Think about the differences between wanting and having to sell.
- Is there an option to "take money off the table" and stay in business? Do you want to lower your financial risk by cashing in some of your chips?
- Are you pushing the limit of the worth of the company? Are you trying to get too much for it? Does it matter if you get a little less? Is a quick sale more important than squeezing the last nickel out of it?
- Are there other options available? Is getting some cash now versus some potentially higher amount later worth the wait?

The answers to these questions will help you to make some important decisions and come up with a plan that makes sense.

> ***From my bag:*** *A client of mine, CEO of an investment partnership that owned and operated three companies, was faced with a dilemma of selling two of the companies now for X dollars or waiting several years to fetch possible 2X dollars. He was considering waiting to maximize his return, but I proposed the following scenario to him: why not sell now and invest the money in the third company or in other ventures with high potential? The significant factor was that what he really wanted to do was to operate the third company*

and saw ownership of the other two as a burden preventing him from fully dedicating himself to his preferred occupation.

My advice was driven by my belief that it is more important to be able to do what you like to do, than to make a little more money. Another "kicker" here was that the third company had a higher potential than the other two. He did an analysis of both scenarios and decided to follow my advice. Today he is very happy with the decision.

I'm sure that you, like most of your colleagues, keep changing the date you chose to sell and/or exit the business, from soon to never, or you pick an arbitrary date—such as five years from today—that never changes but never arrives.

You and your fellow owners believe that at that time you will be ready and you will have solved the issues that you are fighting today. The truth is that today's issues may be solved by then, but I can assure you that others would have taken their places. The BIG question is when will you be emotionally ready to sell?

Selling the business that you created can be both an expensive and an emotional process. It is difficult for the owner/ founder to embark in the process and the decision usually is delayed beyond an advisable time. The uncertainty and emotional unrest caused by the coming transition tends to slowdown the decision process. As a consequence the business tends to stagnate during this period as the sale process is a distraction for management.

For the owner/founder of a successful business, selling "his creation" is almost in a parallel to selling a child. He/she must be completely sure that selling is the chosen option and must prepare him/her emotionally to do it. I have seen cases where this process involved coaching, advisors and even psychological help. While the initial goal may have been to eventually sell and make a lot of money, as the time approaches the owner realizes that having a company to look back on and be proud of is worth more than the pot of gold in the goal to sell.

Once the decision is made the owner prefers to keep the sale from being public knowledge (for a number of reasons) and treating it as a secret feeds the emotional content of the decision. To do it or not to do it, that is the question. Furthermore, how to do it, when to do it and a million other questions work to generate greater emotions and uncertainty; however, after the decision becomes public and there is no going back, it has the effect of lifting a huge weight of his shoulders. The emotions still continue, but being at a point of no return tends to alleviate doubts.

You have several options to sell:
- Arms-length transaction to strangers.
- Sale to family.
- Sale to employees.
- Sale to partners or other stakeholders.

One of the most difficult problems an owner faces is whether to transfer the ownership of the business within the family or to sell the business to a stranger. Each alternative has its own set of problems.

If you sell your family business to your children, the emotions are less because you may feel like you've never really left. It is highly likely—and emotionally preferred—that your child will reach out to you for advice and direction and you're as if on-call 24/7 for questions about how things work. However, make very sure that you don't give unsolicited advice when it is not sought or wanted; this would be interfering and can motivate your child to evade you and your contributions.

To achieve your goal, the transfer of ownership within the family must be a financial decision, not just a personal/family decision. If you treat it as an arm-length transaction, possibly requiring third party funds to make it effective, it will have better chances of being a successful transaction and will help you reach your goal of a monetary reward for all your hard work. Other goals that you can accomplish in a transaction within the family but with investment by the new owners are:

- Reducing your investment risk by obtaining some liquidity.

- Transferring some control to those who are sharing the monetary risk.
- Opportunity to share part of the reward with other family members not involved in the transaction.
- The new ownership to assume risk together with control.
- The satisfaction to know that the business and its culture will survive and be maintained and that the long-term employees will be dealt with in a fair and equitable manner.

If you sell to someone you don't know the hardest part may come after the sale is final. You may be looking forward to the day you are free from the daily stress, but walking away from long-time employees and clients, and giving up your identity as a small business owner may not be as rewarding or uplifting as you had envisioned.

You need to look inside of you and do an honest evaluation of your goals and desires. Is selling the business what you really want? Is cashing in and getting out your goal? Will you be happy selling and doing something else? Is not having anything more to do with your company what you really want? Or do you feel that you can do a lot more still with your company and will feel bad not reaching those new goals?

These and many others are questions that you must ask yourself and that only you can answer. If you decide that you cannot emotionally part from your "baby", there are other alternatives to get the financial rewards without selling.

Value of Your Business

A key consideration regarding the sale of the business is related to its value and the amount of dollars it could fetch. A significant portion of that amount depends on what value you will be able to add by the time you are ready to sell. This is the main reason why you need to start the exit planning as soon as possible; today is not too soon regardless of when is your target date.

The value of a business is not just its sales volume or net profit margin; other factors go into the (non-mathematical) formula for valuation. Like with everything else in business you need a plan to maximize the value of your business. Some are well known and understood by business owners, as for example the quality of the management team, the quality of client accounts, suppliers, intellectual property, physical property and others.

But other components are not seriously considered by owners as they should be. Systemizing the business, strategic plans, organizational structure and development, and others are not in a priority list of owners when it comes to adding value to the business, but they should be.

Another one of these components is the exit and succession strategies developed by the owner; the better their definition and execution of the plan, the more perceived value they add to a potential buyer. These and other plans can make you "operationally irrelevant" while still being the strategic driver, meaning that you guide the company but don't have to make all the decisions. Having a good succession plan and a well-defined exit plan will give your potential buyers a high degree of confidence that the business can function without you.

A comment about the value of a business: Typically a business is worth less than what the owner thinks and more than what a buyer wants to pay for it. It follows then that the real value must be somewhere between the two.

Final Thoughts

My comments here are very general and assume typical conditions and decisions faced by owners of small businesses, but in reality there are many situations that fall outside what I treat as "typical". Your personal situation, your family, your potential successors, whether you are forced to sell because of a myriad of reasons, your age and health, your industry's present and future, and many other factors can influence your decision to sell or not to sell.

In my many years of working with small business owners I have found another important factor that plays into the decision to sell or not, and that is the differences between an owner that started the business (a founder) and an owner who acquired an existing business. The emotions are generally much stronger in the founder; it's his/her baby, an entity that he created and nurtured for years, and saw it going through infancy to adolescence, and maintained its health against the perils of time, economy, competition and cash flow.

A sale of a business is a complicated matter and I don't pretend to discuss all the details here. These comments are only meant as coaching suggestions, reminders and alerts to small business owners from a business and personal point of view. There are many family, personal, financial (financial planning and taxes) and legal issues to consider and therefore your accountant and attorney must be involved in the planning. If you plan to use a broker to represent you, he should also be part of the initial discussions and planning. And if family is involved, it may be wise to include a family business counselor.

> ***From my bag:*** *In my own experience of selling a business (significantly smaller than yours I'm sure) I set in my plan three conditions to be met: firstly and most importantly, the buyer had to be someone who I could work with and had similar values to mine. Since I would be working with him for a time this was a priority. Secondly, he had to have the drive, personality and desire to grow the business. I really believe in the service we provide and didn't want it to stop for the benefit of my "clients" who had become also my friends.*
>
> *The third clause was materialistic and had to do with him meeting my price. All three conditions were met comfortably and the transition was a success. What wasn't so easy was my adaptation to life-after-business; it took me some time to adjust but it helped that former clients (friends) stayed in contact and kept me "in the loop" of their progress.*

References:

1. Canadian Imperial Bank of Commerce, *Small Business Outlook Poll,* (conducted by Decima Research, http://www.harrisdecima.ca/solutions/market-research).

Chapter XIX - Other Subjects

A number of subjects are not covered in detail in this book, although they are critical to the success of the small business owner and of the business itself. I only included synopsis of them as reminders of their importance, but I did not expand on them because they are specialized subjects that are covered in many books by experts dedicated to those subjects.

Time Management

Wikipedia: Time management is the act or process of exercising conscious control over the amount of time spent on specific activities, especially to increase efficiency or productivity. Time management may be aided by a range of skills, tools, and techniques used to manage time when accomplishing specific tasks, projects and goals.

In reality, time management is somewhat of a misnomer, because time doesn't change; a day always has twenty-four hours, a week always has seven days, and a month always has twenty-eight, thirty, or thirty-one days. All we can actually manage is ourselves and what we do with the time that we have, but the term "time management" is too engraved in the business dictionary to discard it.

We all suffer from time management issues. Time is the one thing that we all have the same amount of, and once we use it, it is gone; it cannot be "recuperated" or "saved" for another time as is often claimed. We can do that with money, but not with time. We can get a loan for money, but we can't get a loan of time. Time management isn't an instinctive skill; it's something you can learn and master with the right tools and strategies.

How we use time is critical and we must learn to manage it. Small business owners tend to mismanage time by doing things that others could do or by not choosing well how we spend it. We also mismanage it by working on "the urgent" rather than working on "the important". To learn to manage time we need to learn to delegate and to distinguish between what is urgent and what is important.

Time management skills are especially important for small business people, who often find themselves performing many different jobs during the course of a single day. As a small business owner you likely spend your day in a frenzy of activity and then wonder why the day is gone and you haven't accomplished much. No matter how organized we are, there are always only twenty-four hours in a day.

Management of time includes not only business activities, but personal activities as well. We can manage time through a wide scope of activities, including planning, allocating resources, setting goals, delegating, monitoring, organizing, scheduling, and prioritizing. All tasks are evaluated using the criteria of what's important or unimportant and urgent or not urgent and treated accordingly.

A method of placing tasks on quadrants using these criteria is attributed to US President Dwight D. Eisenhower, and is outlined in a quote attributed to him: "What is important is seldom urgent and what is urgent is seldom important." He placed tasks in four quadrants ranging from important and urgent to less important and not urgent.

Deciding the difference between urgent and important is critical to achieve time management. Prioritize your to-do list from urgent to unimportant in order to complete the critical tasks first. Work on the important, not on the urgent unless you determine that an urgent issue is also critically important. This is related to the axiom "work ON the business, not IN the businesses."

There are many time management tips suggested in the many books on the subject, to help you increase your productivity and stay organized. Some of them are:

Find your "time bandits". What are the activities that are robbing you of time; your time wasters? You can't change time but you can change your behaviors; eliminate your time wasters. Set time management goals. Decide that for one week you will not surf the net during working hours, or you will not take personal phone calls, and compute the time saved. Use some of the tools available, such as a Day-Timer or software, to plan your time and also to record where your time goes.

By identifying time-wasters, improving communication and minimizing interruptions, you can gain more control over your tasks and over your time, than you ever thought possible. Your time-wasters can include procrastination, socializing during work hours, disorganization, lack of direction, uninvited interruptions, and many others. Say no to unwanted tasks that others lay upon you; be clear in your communications to reject them.

Select the appropriate tools—or create your own—for developing a paper-based time management system that works for you and your work style. Use available technology such as Google Calendar, Rescue Time, Quicksilver, and other applications. Microsoft Outlook for instance, allows you to schedule events (meetings, appointments) and set reminders in advance to help you manage your time.

Using these tools plan your day the day before, using shares of time that don't allow for time wasting. Stick to your schedule as closely as possible and don't allow others to interfere with your schedule.

Don't schedule time for activities that you can delegate. Be aware of "up-delegation" by which employees delegate up to you. This is beautifully explained in *"Who Got The Monkey"* [1]. Accepting delegated tasks from your subordinates is even more dangerous— time robber—than your own weakness in delegating. And of course you need to learn to delegate *(see chapter on delegation)*.

Establish routines and stick to them as much as possible. Following routines can be more productive, assuming they are optimized for efficient outcome. Set time limits for those routines, as for example, limit the time spent writing e-mails, and stick to that time. Make sure your systems are developed for you and your employees to be efficient, and make sure your systems are followed *(see chapter on Systemizing)*.

Be organized, both in your personal things and in your business activities. Have your computer files organized such that it doesn't take you a lot of time to find something. Learn how to set up filing systems, document management and records management so that they are easy to find and to manage.

While most of us consider business record management to be tedious work and tend to give it a low priority, good record management not only makes our working lives easier, but can save us time (for example at tax time). A good document management system implemented at work can save the company many hours of time *(see chapter on systemizing).*

One of the most fundamental principles of productivity and time management is called the "touch it once" principle. We tend to waste time and energy by rereading and reconsidering tasks we have to do. Instead of taking care of the task at hand, we might think "I'll take of this later" and move on to something else. Later on, we will have to re-evaluate what to do with the task and this again eats up time. Over the course of a week, month, or year the time spent could add up to a significant amount. Save time by acting on each task immediately.

Some common examples where you can apply the "touch it once" principle:
- Email correspondence.
- Paying bills.
- Taking the trash out.
- Handling mail.

Try to minimize waiting time. Whether is at clients meetings, your own company meetings, at the doctor's office, or anywhere else, waiting is time wasted. You cannot avoid some of those, but if you are prepared you can use that time in a useful way (reading, writing a report); always carry with you something that you can use to use the time.

Time management, or behavior management, can make you more productive, help you achieve your goals, save you and your business money, and make your life more enjoyable. In addition to the many books available on the subject, there are many competent consultants that can help you with your time management.

> **Coaching suggestion:** *For a set period (two weeks for example) write down everything you do and how much time you spent doing it. At the end of the period add up all times spent on same or similar activities (talking on the phone, staff meetings, etc.). Analyze all "categories" and see what you can do to reduce some of the time spent on them. It takes discipline to do this exercise, but if you stick to it and are meticulous about it you will see the benefits.*

> **Coaching suggestion:** *In the Delegation chapter I suggested the following exercise that can also be appropriate for this section. Make a chart with four columns; in the first column list all the things that you do, and in the second column list the time it takes you to do them. In the third column list all the things that you can delegate now, and in the in the fourth column list that you could delegate if you had the right people. Analyze the chart and decide to delegate those tasks that you can delegate now. Then, set goals to be in a position to get the right people so you could delegate other tasks. Add all the times that you could save and smile.*

Balancing Work with Family

As a business owner, you are in charge of your most precious resource, your time, even if it doesn't feel that way to you on a daily basis. Because you are the owner, you believe you should be able to take some time of and leave work early for dinner at home or with friends. You have more control over your time, but you also could easily allow the demands of work to come at the expense of your personal life. Don't do it.

You are the owner and the overall expert, and you think you can do it all, but if you want your business to succeed and you want to have a balanced life, you must learn to delegate, to balance your business-family world, and take care of yourself and your personal development.

Think about the time you spent at work; do you work long hours because the business requires it? Or is it because you don't delegate enough? Or is it because you want to set an example to your employees? Or is it because you allow others to take shares of your time? Or is it because you are not a good manager of time or work inefficiently?

If you can free yourself from some time-sapping duties, you could dedicate that time to family life or to improve your personal life. Set some rules for you to limit the hours at work or dedicated to the business; for example not to be out of town more than two nights a month and see most clients on day trips. These simple-to-set and difficult-to-act rules can become the foundation for your dually focused life.

If you are caught up in the all-consuming details of building a company, think of the effect it has on your family. You may not realize it, but your work is having a serious impact on their happiness. Learn to separate the "two lives" and to focus on each at the appropriate time. When you are on the job, be on the job, and when you are at home, be at home, not just in a physical presence but both in body and mind.

From my bag: This relates to my own experience. At one of the start-ups that I helped found, I was working very long hours and enjoying every minute of it, but I was isolated from my family by the job. One day my wife asked me if I realized what I was doing to the family (her and our four children), and reminded me that I had missed several soccer games of the children, which I had never done before. This conversation had a revealing action on me because until that time I was blind to the effect that my dedication to the new company had on our personal life.

Immediately I made the decision to limit my hours to reasonable amounts and I made sure never to miss another soccer game. On game days (afternoons) I would live work, attend the game and return to work satisfied that I had done my fatherly duties. I realized too, that I enjoyed work more and had more stamina to dedicate to the job, as I had found a balance in my dual life. My children are grown now but

they proudly tell their friends that I almost always attended
their games, regardless of how busy I was. When I hear that,
I feel truly rewarded.

I'm a believer that in life you have to have priorities. As the hard driving entrepreneur that you are, you probably don't agree with this, but sacrificing yourself for everything work related will not give you family happiness. You need to keep your professional goals ***and*** your personal goals on the same plane and share time for both proportionally.

It helps for you to understand why you are in business. Is it to have the freedom of being your own boss? Is it to accomplish some goals of yours? Is it for financial independence? Is it because you are driven by an altruistic goal? Whatever the reason, remind yourself that you are much more than your job. What is personal success to you? Reflect on this and give priority to your personal success ... that should include family.

Whenever a conflict arises between a commitment to the business and a need at home, evaluate the impact that your decision will have on both fronts. If it is a client meeting for example, don't hesitate to ask the client to postpone it. Yes, I know, this can be risky, but what makes the difference is the way you communicate your need to the client. Be truthful and let him know that you are doing it for your family; my guess is that he will understand and he may even respect you more.

You are committed to your business one hundred percent; nearly all your waking (and some of your sleeping) hours are devoted to it. Your business depends on you, and you view time away from your business as "lost time." Even a small amount of extra activity may seem impossible to fit into your day, and the business takes priority over everything else. You are driven, intense and demanding of yourself. This attitude may be great for your company's bottom line, but it might not be so great for your personal life.

Growing a business and creating wealth for you and your family is very exciting, but be aware of the challenges that come when you get distracted by the unlimited number of options that wealth can offer. Money can expand opportunities to make life simpler and more enjoyable if you manage it right, but it can also complicate life by the opportunities it offers.

Simplifying your business is also a matter of knowing your priorities. When you're clear about your goals, you can focus on those rather than be distracted by non-important things. If you stay focused on your goals, it's easier to make the important business decisions you need to make.

Never lose sight of the fact that you are the one in control. You can get caught up thinking that you have to work a great number of hours to get the job done, but when you do that, it's because you haven't analyzed what is doing to your family life. Do the right thing and delegate the duties you don't personally need to do, and dedicate yourself only to those that couldn't be handled by anyone else *(see chapter on Delegation)*.

The Home Effect

If both you and your spouse are in business you need to work out an agreement to deal with the dual obligations of work and family for both of you. However, no two family plans are identical. Different types of entrepreneurial couples face different challenges—and they should plan accordingly. If you and your spouse are active in the same business you need to clarify how business decisions will be made, what roles and responsibilities you'll take in the business and at home, and how to keep the romance alive when you're together 24 hours a day.

From my bag: One of my coaching clients was a successful husband/wife team that dedicated massive number of hours to the business. Both worked practically every evening until late, and in addition, being the "rain-maker", he traveled much of the time, both within the US and internationally. In the relatively few hours they spent at home together, they used the business as a common subject of conversation. Fortunately, they had no children at home. Having suffered through some difficult economic times, they were reluctant to hire some key people that would have reduced their work load significantly.

Their routine started to take a toll in the marital relations until it reached a point that resulted in a "wake-up" call to their senses, helped by coaching and advice from their Peer Advisory Board. They proceeded to hire the people so badly needed and were able to delegate sufficient functions to reduce their work to reasonable levels. Following coaching suggestions they began taking trips together, spending weekends in recreational spots, and limiting the business conversation at home to only the necessary. As a result their personal life improved, their relationship rekindled, and the business continued to grow without their almost permanent presence.

I'm sure you have a strategic plan for your business, but you must also have a strategic plan for your life, and you must be the principal character of that play. Knowing your goals and having a plan will help you take care of your family, your business, and yourself. Smart entrepreneurs need to plan not just for their business but also for the impact it will have on their family life.

Do an inventory of what you want in life and what is most important, and align yourself behind this assessment. Develop a life plan and review it with your spouse and children, and set a well-defined course for you and your family. Focus on what is most important both at work and at home, and if one overrides the other, find ways to balance them and don't allow work to have an overwhelming share of your time.

As the driving entrepreneur that you are, your business may dominate your life, but remember what I said in a previous chapter: the business should be *a part* of your life *apart* of your life, and it should not be your entire life. At times it may seem impossible to you to blend both parts of your life, but focusing on your life goals will help you do it. Treat the business as the tool to help you achieve what you want out of life.

Just as you did for the strategic planning of your business, ask yourself: where am I? Where do I want to go? How will I get there? If you can answer these three questions clearly, focusing on your core values, you should be able to delineate the road to your future. Realize that you may have to make sacrifices to get there, and include them in your planning.

Protect Your Health Too

Your life is stressful because of the range of activities you must do on a daily basis as the CEO of your company. Adding your family duties to that can overflow your cup creating even more stress. You must release some of that stress, and to do that may require some other activity, like exercising. So, now you say; another activity when I hardly have time for the others? The answer is yes, if you want to also take care of your health.

Many times, home life can be the stress release that you need, but even so, you need physical activities to stay healthy. You are surely exceptionally motivated and driven when it comes to your company, but when it comes to your own health that motivation is gone. What good is to have a healthy company when your health is not what it should be?

Using lack of time as an excuse is not acceptable. You can commit to an hour at the gym three or four times a week without neglecting your business. You can take a few easy steps to improve your overall fitness without investing a lot of time in it.

If you are the all-or-nothing type of person, realize that "nothing" in this case can mean risking health problems, so it doesn't have to be the "all" either; a happy medium with a few hours a week dedicated to your fitness can yield huge returns.

Also, work and exercise need not be mutually exclusive; you can combine the two at times, for example by reading a report while you are on the treadmill. There is no need to feel guilty since you are not trading work time for play time; the time invested in physical activity will increase your productivity and benefit your business.

Finally, to be in control and have a good balance between your business world and your family and personal world, you must learn to delegate, to focus on what is important, and take care of your health. With control, you can create a workplace that is flexible giving you the opportunity of a good dual life. You will ensure that all conflicting ties in your life— work, spouse, children, and friends—will be taken care of, connecting with one-another.

Financial Management

This is another subject that will not be covered in detail in this book despite being *the* most critical element in managing a business. The reason, as with other subjects not covered here, is that it is a specialized subject covered extensively elsewhere, and by plenty of experts in it. My comments are only general ideas that fit into the coaching style of this book.

What is financial management?

Financial Management can be defined as the management of the finances of a business in order to achieve financial objectives. It includes the planning, directing, monitoring, organizing, and controlling of the monetary resources. It also includes accounting and financial reporting, budgeting, collecting accounts receivable, risk management, and insurance for a business. It is a system to finance and manage the money in the business.

The key objectives of financial management are to create wealth for the business, generate cash, and provide an adequate return on investment considering the risks that the business is taking and the resources it invests.

An expanding business offers excitement to the owner and the potential for numerous growth opportunities. It also presents challenges in managing this growth, requiring some skills in the managing of its financial resources. As a small business owner, managing the financial affairs of your business can seem like a daunting task, but one that you need to learn as a critical element of your job.

Financial management involves all the activities to maximize the income potential of the business, including obtaining capital for growth and the efficiently allocation of resources. It requires a comprehensive financial management plan encompassing the assets, debts and current and future profit potential of your business. It also includes a comprehensive monitoring of financial and operational results obtained through well designed accounting documents.

There are three key elements to the process of financial management:

- Financial planning to ensure that enough funds are available at the right time to meet the needs of the business for the short term as well as for the long term.
- Financial control to help ensure that the business is meeting its objectives.
- Financial decision-making using the information gathered from a good management system, to allocate resources and manage funds.

How and Who

How proficient are you in this subject? The answer to this question should determine how you set up your financial management system. Would you do it yourself or would you trust it to outsiders? What software would you use? The alternatives are to do it yourself, to hire an employee to do it, or to use outside sources. And in outside sources you also have several choices: part-time bookkeeper, bookkeeping services, an accountant to keep the books or to review them monthly or quarterly, or a "CFO for hire" service.

Much depend on the size of your business and where you are in the business development cycle. Outside bookkeeping services are acceptable for very small or embryonic businesses, but once you reach a certain level you want to have this in-house. As the business grows a Controller is needed to add certain systems and controls and to provide management with valuable reports to help you make the right decisions in the operation of the business.

As the enterprise reaches a higher level (for most business types, somewhere around the twenty million dollars mark in revenues), a Chief Financial Officer (CFO) is highly recommended. A CFO can do much more than just manage cash; he/she can manage investments, regulate cash flow, deal with bankers and other outside stakeholders, and apply the controls and reporting that will make your job not just easier, but more effective.

Similarly, applicable financial software must be upgraded as the business growth demands it. While a new or small enterprise can manage perfectly well with—for example—QuickBooks, as the business grows you will need a more sophisticated package. Enterprise Management Systems (EMS) that incorporates all financial and operational factors provides an easier and more effective tool for you to manage the business.

Even if you outsource the accounting functions, you need them to provide some type of recordkeeping systems to allow you to manage the day-to-day operations of your business. You also need your accounting system to provide financial statements, and you need to become knowledgeable in how to "read" them and use them and analyze them to really understand the financial condition of the business. Financial analysis shows the "reality" of the situation of a business.

Budgets

You need a financial plan and a budget to make certain you know where you are headed in your business finances. Without a plan and a budget you would be operating in the dark when it comes to cash flow … and survival of the business.

Some business owners tell me "I know how much money is in the bank" as their control of finances; others operate on a "cash as needed" basis, and it surprises me how many business owners don't believe in budgets or don't know how to develop one.

Financial planning interacts with and it is deduced from the strategic plan to identify what financial resources are needed to achieve the goals in the plan. From it you develop very relevant and realistic budgets to manage cash. A budget depicts what the revenues and expenses will be over a time period. Budgets are used for planning your finances and tracking if you're operating according to plan. The overall format of a budget is a record of planned income and planned expenses for a fixed period of time.

Although many businesses operate with a "fixed" plan for the entire year, I'm of the opinion that budgets—like strategic plans—can and should be adjusted for changing conditions during the period of the budget. For example, if an unexpected event occurs that significantly changes the financial posture of the company, either for the positive or negative, you should adjust the budget for the remainder of the period to reflect that change. Not doing it can result in severe money losses or in the loss of opportunities.

Budgets should also be used for projecting how much money you'll need for a major initiative, as for example, hiring new employees, purchasing needed equipment, etc.

Financial Analysis

In addition to budgets your financial system should give you the facility to do—and use—other analysis to help you manage your business. These include:

- Income statement, or P&L statement, showing all income and expenses and the resulting profit or loss for a given period.
- Balance sheet showing assets and liabilities, giving a true picture of the financial health of the company.
- Break-even analysis. Using information from the income statement and cash flow statements to compute how much sales much be accomplished in order to pay for all of your fixed and variable expenses.
- Cash flow analysis to manage the use of cash, regulating it in accordance to expenses, accounts payable and accounts receivable.
- Ratios that can be used to help determine the current and future condition of a business. The ratios are produced from numbers on the financial statements.
- Risk analysis intended to minimize the risk exposure of the business. Insurance coverage validity is part of this analysis.

Regardless of your proficiency in the subject you should set aside at least a few hours every month to do financial analysis and to learn more about it and how it can help you and your business. How you carry out the analysis depends on the nature of your business and your needs as well as the needs of your business.

Financial Balance

If your business is in a growth mode—and as the competent CEO that you are, you must be—you must balance the operational aspects of growth. This means that the financial capacity to sustain growth cannot exceed the financial capacity to operate the business at its present rate of business. A balance must be maintained between asset and liability items that are on the balance sheet and operating items that are on the expense and income reports.

To ensure this balance, growth should only be attempted for businesses that are already profitable. As the company grows, profits will be negatively affected at least until a breakeven point is exceeded in the growth. Also, the existing debt position must be balanced with equity; if not, additional equity must be secured to balance future debt.

Final Thoughts

Unfortunately, the business world is full of examples of businesses that achieved good growth but were unable to sustain their new position because the owners/CEO did not pay enough attention to managing the finances that support the growth. Managing your finances accurately will enhance the growth potential of the business. For this, financial planning should be viewed not as an obstacle but as a means of ensuring your success.

> ***Coaching suggestion:*** *Get your team involved in managing the financial aspects of the business by coaching them to manage budgets for each of their groups or departments. Instruct them to develop budgets and to run their "individual businesses" within the budget. Yes, they will make mistakes at first, but eventually they will learn to do it. Assign rewards for staying within budget. You will help them develop into better "business people" and make them feel*

more a part of the business. The business will benefit because it will run within boundaries, and it will save you money.

Financial management clearly is a crucial element of your job as CEO and of your business health. Therefore, you must take time to set the financial systems right. It will surely make a significant difference in your stress levels and in the bottom line for your business.

> ***Coaching suggestion:*** *It is useful to benchmark your financial posture against other companies in the same or similar field and of the same or similar size. This exercise can tell you if your profits, for example, are in line or if your expenses need to be addressed. Whenever possible, compare balance sheets too to compare the financial health of your business with that of your peer companies.*

I have included a nice exercise to see the effect that small increases in certain revenue and expense items can have on profits. It is called *"The Power Of One"* and it was published by the National Association of Wholesale Distributors, Washington, DC. You can find it in the Appendices section. It should be interesting for you to use it injecting your real numbers and see how you can increase your bottom line.

References:
1. William Oncken Jr., Donald L. Wass, Stephen R. Covey, Management Time: *Who's Got the Monkey?*, 9 pages. Publication date: Nov 01, 1999. Prod. #: 99609-PDF-ENG
2. Grant Thorton (www.grantthorton.com).
3. Pieter Bottelier and Gail Fosler, *Finding the Right Balance*, Jan. 17, 2008, TIME Magazine Business, http://www.time.com/time/magazine/article/0,9171,1704402,00.html
4. Robert Aver, Cornell University, *The Ten Trillion Dollar Question: A Philanthropic Gameplan*, http://www.amserv.com/familystatistics.html.
5. Joseph H. Astrachan and Kathy Lund Dean Arthur Andersen/Mass Mutual American Family Business Survey 1995 and 1997, Social Science Research Network,

http://papers.ssrn.com/sol3/papers.cfm?abstract_id=1511
481.

Appendices

Appendix I - Business Owner's Personal Roadmap^{SM}

Adapted from the plan developed by Robert Diefenbacher of Denbrook Systems Associates.

Introduction

Most business owners understandably give too much of themselves to their business life and take too little time for themselves and their families. Very few owners of small and medium sized businesses recognize the value of creating a documented *vision for themselves* to help them gain better balance in their lives, even though they may have a vision for their organization in a written strategic plan. Yet creating your own private vision is vital for long-term personal fulfillment.

This private vision is a **Personal Roadmap** that supplements a business strategic plan. It takes into account the private plans and aspirations that *really matter* to the business owner. Your **Personal Roadmap** is like an individual GPS system to tell you where you are, where you want to go, and what roads will take you there. It is a customized guidance system for today's hard-working business leaders.

Completing this workbook, in conjunction with the guidance from your executive coach, will help you restore balance to your life and add meaning to why you work so hard every day. It will help you determine a personal strategy for living...a **Personal Roadmap** to your future.

You have a choice: You can create your future. Or, you can let the future create you. Which is better? The answer is obvious, yet most CEOs seem to live a life of re-action rather than one of pro-action. They run from one crisis to the next...from business predicaments to family problems, feeling like they are at the mercy of events instead of in the driver's seat of their lives. They are moving through life without a GPS System...without a **Personal Roadmap** to their future! And that's not an enjoyable way to live, is it?

Need more reasons to develop your *Personal Roadmap?* Consider what four thousand retired executives said when asked: "If you could live your life over, what would you have done differently?"

They said they would have:

- Carved out life goals.
- Taken their health more seriously.
- Managed money more effectively.
- Worked on quality family goals.
- Spent more time on personal development.
- Had more fun in life.
- Planned their career better.
- Lived in oneness with God and given back to the community.

Here's your chance to benefit from the wisdom of these seniors! Invest the brief time necessary to create the Personal Roadmap to your future. Then enjoy the luxury so few of your peers have—a life balanced between working at what you enjoy and relaxing with people you treasure.

Business Owner's Personal Roadmap

The GPS System For Your Life

Self-Assessment

How well is your current life measuring up to the ideal in your mind?

Very Dissatisfied   **Neutral**   **Very Satisfied**

Establishing life goals
1---------------2------------------3-----------------4------------5
Taking my health seriously
1---------------2------------------3-----------------4------------5
Managing my money effectively
1---------------2------------------3-----------------4------------5
Created quality family goals
1---------------2------------------3-----------------4------------5
Investing time in personal development
1---------------2------------------3-----------------4------------5
Enjoying my life
1---------------2------------------3-----------------4------------5
Planning my career
1---------------2------------------3-----------------4------------5
Giving of myself to the community
1---------------2------------------3-----------------4------------5

What conclusions can you make from reviewing your responses to this assessment?

1.

_____

2.

_____

3.

_____

4.

_____

Developing your Personal Vision

Where do you want your GPS System to take you?

Carefully consider each question and jot down your responses.

Why do you own a business?
1.

_____

2.

_____

3.

_____

What do you like most about your work?
1.

_____

2.

_____

3.

_____

What gives you the greatest difficulty in your work?
1.

_____

2.

_____

3.

_____

If you won the lottery for $20 million tomorrow, how would your life change thereafter?

1.

_____

2.

_____

3.

_____

If an employee is able to run your business as well as you can, what changes, if any would there be in your life?

1.

_____

2.

_____

3.

_____

What are three things in your personal life with which you are satisfied today?

1.

_____

2.

_____

3.

_____

What are three things you would have done differently in your life?

1.

_____

2.

_____

3.

_____

What are three things you have yet to accomplish in your life?

1.

_____

2.

_____

3.

_____

What are three core values/beliefs you hold?

1. .

_____

2.

_____

3.

_____

What are three words others would use to describe you?

1.

_____

2.

_____

3.

_____

What are three words others would never use to describe you?

1.

_____

2.

_____

3.

_____

What do you want to be remembered for?

1.

_____

2.

_____

3.

_____

Record Your Strengths, Weaknesses, Opportunities, and Threats

What are the unique factors your GPS System needs to know about you?

Think about yourself honestly and then complete these four categories.

What are your greatest strengths/aptitudes?

1.

_____

2.

_____

3.

_____

What are your greatest weaknesses?

1.

_____

2.

_____

3.

_____

What personal opportunities do you see for your future?

1.

_____

2.

_____

3.

_____

What threats may disrupt your life in the future?

1.

_____

2.

_____

3.

_____

Personal Vision

Where do you want your GPS System to take you? Where does your Personal Roadmap lead?

Review the answers to the previous sections and draft the personal vision for your life.

Within the next _____ years, achieve

_____

by

_____

with

_____

to

_____

for

_____

Reworded Personal Vision

After thinking your first attempt over a bit, reword it to be sure it reflects the aspects of your business and your life that excite and satisfy you most strongly.

_____

_____

_____

_____

_____

_____

_____

Twelve-Month Path

How must you program your GPS System for the next year?

Review your previous answers. Then identify up to five milestones you can achieve in the next twelve months to move along your Personal Roadmap towards your personal vision.

A milestone is a spot you pass as you travel along your Personal Roadmap. State the milestone in specific terms with a date by which it will have been passed.

In thinking about the kinds of steps you might develop, consider the following:

- Health issues
- Time management
- Stress management
- Company role long-term and short-term
- Net worth
- Annual income
- Hobby or other outside interests
- Time spent at work
- Vacation time
- Personal character
- Management style

- Family leadership
- Responsibilities to your children
- Happiness
- Self-accountability
- Difficult relationships
- Unnecessary worry
- Handling problems at work or home
- Succession plans or exit strategy from business
- Sandwich generation issues
- Family involvement in business
- Retirement financing
- Personal financial liabilities
- Outside friends
- Activities you enjoy

1.

2.

3.

4.

5.

Longer-term Path

Program your personal GPS System to guide you beyond the next year.

Identify several key milestones you can look to achieve within the next two to five years that will move you significantly along your Personal Roadmap. Review the list of areas to consider, as well as your previous answers and your personal vision to identify the important longer-term milestones.

A milestone is a spot you pass as your travel along your Personal Roadmap. State the milestone in specific terms with a date by which it will have been passed.

1.

_____

2.

_____

3.

_____

4.

_____

5.

_____

Comparing Personal Vision to Company Vision

Contrast your personal vision to your company vision and note your conclusions below.

Company Vision:

_____

_____

_____

_____

_____

While your personal vision need not support your company vision completely, when there are significant conflicts between the two visions, they should be resolved to avoid increasing personal frustration and potentially more serious issues that can through you off your Personal Roadmap.

In what ways do both visions support each other?

1.

_____

2.

_____

3.

_____

4.

_____

In what ways do the visions conflict?

Strategies for Following Your Personal Roadmap

How do I move towards my personal vision?

Strategies are overriding principles or guidelines to assist in selecting appropriate paths and directions that will guide you towards your personal vision. They are the things that will keep you on the road and out of the ditch.

Identify three strategies that are important to reaching your personal vision:

1.

_____

2.

_____

3.

_____

Actions and Decisions

What must you do to follow your GPS System guidance?

Actions and decisions are specific steps you take to reach a milestone on your Personal Roadmap. Each action or decision must be specifically stated and include a date by which it must by completed.

State the most important actions to reach each milestone on your twelve-month path towards your personal vision.

Milestone One:

_____
1.
_____
2.
_____
3.
_____

Milestone Two:

_____
1.
_____
2.
_____
3.
_____

Milestone Three:

_____
1.
_____

2.

_____

3.

_____

Milestone Four:

_____

1.

_____

2.

_____

3.

_____

Milestone Five:

_____

1.

_____

2.

_____

3.

_____

Final Thoughts

With whom will you share your Personal Roadmap?

What commitment will you make to ensure that you are following your GPS System guidance?

How will you know when you have passed all the milestones on your Personal Roadmap?

What will you do if you get lost on your way?

Add any other thoughts now that you have created your Personal Roadmap.

Appendix II - Exit Planning Questionnaire

Answer the following questions with "Yes" or "No". If the answer is No, you need to work on that issue. If the issue doesn't apply, ignore the question or label it "NA".

I. General Requirements for Exiting

- Do you have an exit strategy?
- Do you have a written exit plan?
- Have you decided on a time frame to exit?
- Do you know what continuing role—if any—do you envision for yourself?
- Have you decided if your withdrawal will be partial or complete and what your time frame will be?
- Have you prepared yourself emotionally to separate yourself from the business?
- Can you imagine life without thinking about the business?
- Is the business saleable?
- Have you performed an evaluation of the business?
- Is competent management in place with duties and responsibilities clearly defined?
- Do you have a current written statement of strengths and weaknesses of the business?
- Do you have a current business plan that represents how you are currently doing?
- Do you have a written strategic plan?
- Do you have a current written marketing and sales plan?
- Are you concentrating your efforts in the business areas where returns will be highest?
- Are all your policies, procedures and systems documented and updated?
- Have you identified the key areas which require continuity and development of the people resources within your company?

- Are you maximizing the tax-planning opportunities available to you?
- Do you have a savings plan in place anticipating future expenses (for example children education, property purchases, etc.)?

II. Retirement Exit Strategy

- Are you committed to selling your business/partnership?
- Have you taken estate-planning steps to manage the proceeds of the sale?
- Do you know what income you need to achieve financial security?
- Will proceeds from the sale finance your retirement?
- Do you know how to maximize your cash and minimize your tax liability from the sale?
- Do you have a business partner?
- Have you discussed your exit plan with your partner?
- Is there someone currently in the business who is capable and willing to purchase it?
- Is there an opportunity for an employee buyout?
- Do you know what you need to do to maximize the value of the business at retirement?
- As currently configured, will your business survive (stay profitable) without you?
- If not, do you know what you have to do to have it survive without you?
- Do you maintain accurate financial and corporate records suitable for a potential buyer's review?
- Do you know how you will get the liquidity or proceeds that you need to live comfortably during retirement or to meet your estate-planning objectives?

III. Succession Planning for Exiting

- Does the concept of succession planning fit into your strategies?

- Do you have a succession plan for all your critical positions?
- Can the business function without the physical presence of the owner?
- Do you know who the key people are that you want to develop and nurture for the future?
- Do you know what career paths your most talent people should be following?
  - Is each path customized to fit the abilities and talent of the people involved?
- Have you done contingency planning in case of the loss of a key employee?
- If the business is to stay in the family, do you know which family member(s) would you select to control it?
  - Are they truly committed to the long-term business objectives of the company?
- Is there a need for transition management involving key non-family employees?
- If you choose to transfer the business as a gift (or at a price below fair market value), can you be fair to non-active children and protect the business from their demands?

IV. Succession of Partnerships

- Do you have a buy-sell agreement between partners in place?
- Have you decided what happens in case of disability or death of one or more partners?
- Could you work effectively with the spouse or family of a decease or disable co-owner?
- Would you be concerned with him or her continuing to have a voice as co-owner in the way the business is run?
- Do spouses and heirs continue to be paid even though they are not contributing?
- Have you decided when payment starts?
- Have you decided for how long payment will continue?
- Have you decided who takes over as managing partner?
- Have you decided how partners would sell the company?
  - Have the other partner(s) have right of first refusal?

- Have you decided what the rights are for partners to buy each other out?
- Have you decided how the partners would evaluate the worth of the company?
- Do you have the funds to buy the co-owners' share/interest from the family members when there is no pre-agreed price in a written agreement?

V. Succession for Family Owned Business

- Is there a written succession plan for family members?
- Are your heirs interested in running the business?
- Are family members qualified to run the business?
- If you sell the business to your children or other family members (or even to your employees) do you have the means to finance the sale?
- Will the succession plan be fair to family members (usually children) not involved in the business?
- Can family members work harmoniously in the business?
- Is there sufficient capital to keep ownership of the business in the family?
- Has a plan for management continuity been prepared and reviewed with family members and key employees?
- Have compensation and ownership goals been clearly defined and reviewed with family members?
- Has a plan been developed to deal with personal guarantees of business obligations?
- Has a plan been developed for the lifetime transmission of family business ownership to the next generation?
- Are there any special family circumstances with the transition of the business?
- Is there a mechanism in place for resolving internal conflicts pertaining to the management of the family business?

VI. Business Continuation if You Become Disable or Die

- Do you have a plan in place in case you become disabled or if you die?
- Do you want the business to continue after you die?
- Do you have key employee insurance for yourself and other key personnel?
- Are the financial needs of your family and your state met in case of your disability or death?
- Do you have a estate plan in place that ensures that your assets go to your intended beneficiaries and minimizes taxes?
- As currently configured, would your business survive (stay profitable) without you?
  - If not, do you know what you have to do to have it survive without you?
- Do you know who would take over the day-to-day operations if you're disabled or no longer here?
- Does your spouse or children have the ability to take an active role in the management of the business?
- Do they even want to be involved in the business?
- Do you want to keep the business in your family?
- Do you know which heirs come into the business?
- Have you decided who has the authority to continue its operation?
- Have you decided if the business will be sold, liquidated or continued?
- Do you know who the potential buyers are and do they have the cash to purchase it in a timely fashion?
- Do you know who will manage the business?
- Are any of your heirs ready to take control, even if temporarily?
- Have you assigned a caretaker manager until your heirs make a final decision regarding continuity?
- Have you documented who will assume control and under what conditions?
- Have you "legalized" and recorded the above documents?
- Have you obtained the agreement of the caretaker or successor, and have you and they agreed to the conditions?
- Have estate planning documents providing for ownership succession been prepared and signed?

- Are business agreements such as for employment and death benefits and leases in place?
- Have Federal Estate and State Inheritance Tax liabilities been calculated?
- Is there sufficient cash available to cover the Estate Tax and Inheritance Tax?
- Is adequate life insurance in place?

Appendix III – Advisory Boards and Coaching.

Improve yourself as you improve your business

Your development as CEO is critical to the success of your business, but perhaps an even more critical benefit is the feeling of self-worth and your self confidence that you gain. I urge you to work on your personal development with the same energy and enthusiasm that you invest in the development of your company.

There are many ways that you can go about your development, but for most people the utilization of outside resources is the right approach. Outside resources can be courses at colleges or universities, seminars, training classes in various subjects, participation in round tables and peer groups, use of a personal coach, and having a board of directors or a board of advisors.

All are valuable and all offer benefits; what you chose to use is a matter of preference (and sometimes of money, time, involvement, etc.). Because of my experience in coaching and with advisory boards I favor these as perhaps among the most valuable resources for a small or midsize business owner and/or CEO.

Board of advisors take the place of formal board of directors, while a coach can guide you in a very personal way along the route that you most need. The constant interaction with a coach will represent for you a crutch to help you walk the sometimes difficult road of the business world, while also offering a shoulder to lean on in difficult times.

Importance of a Board of Directors

Boards of Directors are common among high-tech start-ups and fast growing companies, and are mandatory for public companies. They are, typically, key contributors to the success of those companies. Most boards of directors are composed of experienced businesspersons, investors and others who can provide expertise in the direction of the venture.

They yield sufficient power to replace the management team if they consider the performance to be less than acceptable. Commonly, they receive monetary compensation and in many cases, equity participation as well. Being responsible for the business, board members are exposed to personal liability, thus forcing the company to provide costly Directors and Officers Liability Insurance coverage.

Boards of directors exist to hold management accountable for achieving the business plan, creating shareholder value and assisting the owner/CEO in growing the enterprise. They also provide advice and counsel, but their primary function is to ensure accountability. A strong board can also help a young company build credibility in the outside world.

Most small businesses don't have a board of directors because they cannot afford one and because their owners don't think they need one. In fact, the perception of most small business owners is that "a board of directors is only for big business." This cannot be further from the truth though, as most entrepreneurs desperately need a source of advice and support, and the accountability of having to report to someone.

Accountability is a key to the success of entrepreneurial ventures. Business owners love the fact that they report to no one; as owners they have the "God-given right to procrastinate" and consciously or unconsciously, this is one of the major driving factors for many people becoming business owners. The flip side, however, is a lack of accountability that too often leads them to complacency and failure.

As entrepreneurs, they get too involved in the day-to-day running of the business, in firefighting, in doing the things that they like or they feel comfortable doing, while neglecting the leadership activities, and eventually they lose sight of their driving vision. The end result is that the business doesn't evolve, and owners eventually find running the company increasingly unpleasant or beyond their capabilities.

For private companies, putting together a board with outside directors is optional, but there are undisputable reasons to have one. Assembling a team of diverse, active directors sets a course for long-term stability of the company and having that external source of accountability is key for keeping companies, and particularly privately owned businesses, moving forward.

The reality is however, that most small business cannot afford a costly board of directors, and thus, they must find other effective ways to get the accountability and help they need.

Advisory Boards

An advisory board is a viable alternative. "Companies can get tremendous benefit from thinking outside the box; this may mean approaching business executives in very different industries, or someone who sees the world of business from a very different perspective," advises *Jeff Simmons*, a partner at *Raphael and Raphael*, a Boston accounting firm. Setting up a team of advisers can provide the entrepreneurs with valuable outside guidance.

The entrepreneur who starts a business on a great idea but has no managerial experience, can be "lost" in the hard world of business. Seasoned entrepreneurial executives who have been through it all before can guide them and help them avoid pitfalls.

It is a fact that very few entrepreneurs have all skills needed in running a business. It's rare for someone to understand administration, operations, finance, sales and marketing, and human resources, and to be a great leader as well. So it makes sense to find board members who can complement the skills of the entrepreneur.

For many start up companies, the "board" ends up being the founders of the company and perhaps the accountant, attorney, family and friends. However, there is huge value in expanding the board to include outside directors—those who do not work for the company, are not family or friends, but offer their time and advice to help shape and guide the company. There is a price to pay for these benefits, as the founders give up some control when they put outsiders on the board.

A board of peers relieves the feeling of "it's lonely at the top" that most owners and leaders of small enterprises have. Entrepreneurs need a forum where they can openly express their ideas, concerns and plans. In every company there are many issues that the CEO cannot openly discuss with employees; i.e., plans that affect those inside the company, but an outside board gives him a valuable sounding board where he can openly and candidly talk about them.

Selecting Members

Once the purpose of the board is clearly defined, the CEO must dedicate the effort to recruit the right board members. They must be the best people available who fit the purpose; they must have the expertise to help in the management of the company and a shared understanding of what the mission and needs of the company are. An effective board is composed of outsiders who have been through the entrepreneurial process and understand the operating issues that a growth-oriented company typically faces.

If the advisory boards are composed of CPAs, attorneys and other professionals who work for the company in their profession, the board may fail. It is difficult for them to give disinterested opinions because they are paid by the business and they don't want to lose it as a client.

Similarly, family and friends may be interested in the wellbeing of the company but they do not necessarily make good Directors. Friends may not want to go against the wishes of the CEO, and family members may be more interested in getting personal benefits or knowing "where they are going on vacation this year" than in discussing some of the key issues of the business.

Also, having a group of "yes-men or women" in a board may be good for the ego of the owner/CEO but they will not contribute with innovative ideas or harsh criticism sometimes needed.

It is important to recruit board members that have similar values to those of the CEO so that the board would not be a mismatch with the culture created by the owner/CEO. He/she must be clear about the expectations and must make sure the potential board members agree with them. Personal chemistry does matter; it makes sense to take the time to find qualified outsiders who have a good rapport with the company's leadership and an informed interest in its industry's challenges.

It is clear that having a board of directors or advisers can be very useful to the entrepreneurial CEO; however, it is not a question of forming or joining a board and expect results automatically. The CEO must be willing and able to be completely open and truthful with it and to dedicate effort and time to the board and its directives or advice.

Communication with the board must be frequent, candid, and complete about all aspects of the business, good or bad. The board cannot help the CEO develop strategies or solve problems if it doesn't know what's going on.

What Type of Board?

What is the right type of board for a small company? Can the company afford a highly paid board of outside experts? Is the CEO/entrepreneur ready to report to a body of outsiders? Can he/she interface openly and humbly with them? Can he/she accept that a group of outsiders who previously had no role in the company, will "tell him/her what to do?" After all, he/she is the one who put all the sweat and tears in forming, growing and managing the company. Is an advisory board or a managing board best suited for the situation?

These are choices that the CEO must make to select the best alternative for the business. The decision on whether to have a board with outside directors should be based on an understanding of the value expected from the board, the needs of the company and the needs of the CEO/entrepreneur. A board of directors that is formed without well-defined purposes or with the wrong expectations is doomed to fail.

The most common type of boards is paid boards with outside directors who meet to monitor the progress of the company. If everything is going well, they tend not to have much to say. If there are problems or issues, they are often critical of the CEO and the management team and can take action of some sort. A board can also meet more frequently and offer significant ongoing support and help the owner or management team in the strategic decisions affecting the company.

The working board brings the CEO into regular contact with knowledgeable people whose wide experience can prove enormously helpful. The working board also helps the CEO fight the isolation that comes with leadership no matter what the size of the company. Since management must report to the board regarding all aspects of the business, the working board brings a helpful discipline to the operations of a closely held firm.

The board can also help resolve family issues surrounding the small or midsize firm, particularly when management must deal with disgruntled family members. Another tangible advantage is that a board gives the firm visibility in the outside world, connecting it with financing sources, acquisition targets, strategic partnership opportunities, and with the community in general.

Nevertheless, paid boards also have significant disadvantages. In addition to the high cost and the issues already discussed, some entrepreneurs don't want to spend time recruiting members, planning agendas, and luring advisers to meetings. Not every CEO of privately held corporations is fond of independent boards of directors because, by definition, the working board strips the CEO of his or her autonomy, and for many CEOs that's a good reason not to have one.

Many privately held companies are opting instead for informal advisory boards. As elected members, directors have a fiduciary duty to the shareholders and to the corporation and are potential targets of lawsuit; consequently, they must be insured by the corporation with D&O liability insurance. Advisers don't face the same risks; as a result, a very viable alternative that is becoming very popular is for busy entrepreneurs to turn to peer advisory groups, in which local businesspeople meet regularly with a facilitator and help one another solve problems.

Alternative Peer Advisory Boards

In their best form these alternative boards are formed and facilitated by specialized organizations that have developed systems proven in the multiplicity of boards formed within them, and improved with the experience generated in the large number of boards managed. The system relies on the combined experience of the members in their various fields, bringing to the table a wide range of expertise.

They offer small and mid-size business owners independent views that are based on a variety of approaches to the solution of problems. They also act as sounding boards and infuse each member with valuable new ideas. Key advantages of these alternative boards over the paid boards are their much lower cost and the absence of liability of the members.

There are several companies offering membership in advisory boards, with the best known being Vistage based in San Diego, CA *(www.vistage.com)* and The Alternative Board TAB based in Denver, CO, (*www.TheAlternativeBoard.com*). Both have similar programs but differ in some aspects, offering alternatives to the preferences of business owners.

Two elements that make the system work are the commitment of members and the use of experienced, trained facilitators as chairs of the boards. *(Vistage calls them "Chairs" and TAB calls them "Facilitators")*. Membership is by invitation only based on each candidate's qualifications. The facilitator (or Chair) confers with each member prior to the monthly group meetings, and identifies issues to be placed on the agenda for timely discussion. These standards result in compatible and committed groups; members typically stay in the system for several years.

The Facilitators or Chairs also serve as personal coaches for the members. They have private coaching sessions with each member every month and they are "on call" if they are needed by a member. As coaches, they challenge members to improve and provide exercises in leadership and management to help them. The coaches and the Board hold members accountable to do what they commit to do.

The boards are composed of owners and leaders of non-competing businesses of similar size. They meet monthly (TAB Boards for four hours and Vistage boards typically for eight hours) to discuss problems and opportunities in a relaxed and confidential atmosphere. Members are matched according to business size, type and complexity of the businesses, experience, and even personalities. Each board usually has members operating businesses in different industries.

This diversity of backgrounds provides a cross-fertilization of ideas that are not locked-in the thinking of anyone industry. Perspective may be one of the most important business assets money can't buy but the approach of these alternative boards provides fresh ideas and vision from different perspectives.

By adding the dimension of the monthly meeting, and a coach/facilitator who they meet with every month in private sessions, the system adds continuity and consistency in the reporting and exchange of ideas. Surveys also show that members improve their personal income and company results, and also enjoy their leadership role more.

At the meetings, owners discuss issues of common interest and problems, concerns and opportunities of each member. The meetings are chaired by a facilitator trained in the system, who himself is a business expert with many years of management experience. In fact, between members and facilitator, a typical peer advisory board has between two hundred and three hundred years of combined management experience.

At the board meetings business owners receive advice and support but also the accountability so badly needed. The accountability and advice are more valuable because they come from fellow successful business owners who most likely have faced or will face similar problems or issues. The dynamics of the meeting keeps the participants moving in the right direction, because all the business owners in the group understand each other's formulas for success and what the individual and collective needs are.

From my bag: "It is my business and management psychiatry board" says NI, President and CEO of a manufacturing company in Norristown, PA referring to his TAB Board. "Is the place where I can take my guard down and openly discuss my issues, knowing that I will get honest and candid inputs", he explains. He is a member of a TAB Board with six other CEOs of completely different businesses and he likes the out-of-the-box ideas not locked-in his industry's way of thinking.

One of the keys is that each member shares their company strategy and action plan, as well as their personal visions and missions. It is the strategic vision that is so difficult to maintain when you're spending all your energy making the business work from one day to the next. Consequently, one of the priorities of these boards is the guidance provided by the coach to develop the vision, mission and strategic planning of each of the member companies. The plans are reviewed by the boards and followed throughout the implementation of the strategies and tactics.

From my bag: SS, President of a manufacturing company in Kenneth Square, PA says, I know that I need to work on strategic planning but it seems that I always have some fires to put out that are more urgent than the planning," "But the peer pressure of my Board and the guidance of the Facilitator help me to get off-center and work on much needed strategies."

He continues, "In a recent meeting we reviewed our budgets for the year, comparing them to benchmarks for our businesses. We all learned from the process and we feel better about our ability to plan and budget." He is referring to his Board of Advisors, a TAB Board in which he participates with five other leaders of non-competing businesses.

Even companies that have their own board of directors find having access to a group of peers is invaluable, says Charles Boisseau in *"Peer Pressure For Entrepreneurs"*[1]. He quotes JE, CEO and founder of a Sterling, Va.-based company, who said the four outside directors on her board are helpful in providing contacts in the industry, such as venture capitalists, but they can't help with sticky day-to-day issues of running her company.

She joined a Peer Advisory Board that has several women among its members. She said that this board provides her support and insight from other women business owners she cannot receive from her formal board. Just as important, she said, is that the group provides her a regular outlet to think longer term about her business. "They remind me to keep my role as the visionary of the company," she said.

The key to success is the willingness of the participating business owners to expose the details of their businesses to the group, under the protection of confidentiality. Since only non-competing businesses are allowed in the same group, members talk about touchy business issues, such as selling a business or firing an employee that they may not be able to discuss with their employees. "It's a no holds bar environment".

From my bag: As JC, President of a distributor in Norristown, PA says "I am a member of TAB because I like having my own "kitchen cabinet" that will tell me what they think rather than what I want to hear. It's the only group I can answer honestly when I'm asked, "How's business?" If I do something that is not the "right way", they let me know in no uncertain terms, he says.

Both organizations mentioned also offer peer boards for non-owners. These are intended for employees at the executive level and for second-in-command kind. They use a very similar program of monthly meetings and coaching, maintaining the discussions at the appropriate level. TAB also includes "teaching" sessions at every monthly meeting, covering all subjects that members face on a daily basis at their jobs.

The dramatic growth of Peer Advisory Boards, underscores the effectiveness of the system, which The Wall Street Journal described as *"the affordable alternative to a high-pay board of directors."*

Coaching suggestion: In my eleven years involvement with peer advisory boards I have lived through many success stories of companies and business owners "growing" to a point of excellence. In fact, what made it rewarding for me was to see the improvement in practically all participating members and their businesses.

Many of the **From my bag** *anecdotes that I relay in this book were generated from that experience. Our members stretched their membership for many years because of the value they obtained by participating. I strongly recommend to all owners and CEO of small and midsize businesses to join a Peer Advisory Board program; you'll be glad you did.*

Investigate the organization and program that best suites your needs, then make sure you are placed with members that will be able to provide the assistance that you want. Do not ask to be matched with other members from the same industry, as the variety of types of businesses in a board, and the corresponding different perspectives they bring, is one of the many values of the program.

A key for you will be the coach assigned to your board; he or she will be the piece closest to you and the main cog of the system. Learn to work with him or her, confide and make him/her your closest advisor.

References:
1. Charles Boisseau, *Peer Pressure for Entrepreneurs,* www.LocalBusiness.com

Appendix IV - The Power of One

Improve your bottom line by improving each line by one percent

An exercise published by the National Association of Wholesale Distributors, Washington, DC.

A change of one percent in the typical lines of financial statements may not seem like much, but implementing this small change in a cumulative form can yield significant improvement in your bottom line profits.

The following exercise illustrates this. Start by calculating the effect of a one percent change in each of the following parameters:

- Selling Price
- Sales Volume
- Cost of Goods Sold (COGS)
- Expenses

Then complete the exercise by combining all improvements into one statement.

A typical simplified statement (for the XYZ Company) is shown as a guideline. Complete each statement by using the figures from your company (or approximate values representing your operating statements) and computing the effect of each change in the bottom line profit margin.

Combine all improvements in the last exercise. You will see a significant increase in the net profit margin.

Don't think that you cannot apply this to your business; the reasons that you can list for not doing it are just excuses. If you try hard enough you can find ways to implement these changes. Yes, it is true that some of these parameters do not apply to some businesses; e.g., in the insurance business you cannot increase the sale price of widgets. Nevertheless, every business can apply at least some of these improvements.

Obviously, you don't have to apply them all at once; start with the simplest to execute and follow them with others as the opportunity presents itself. The reward will be a significant improvement in your profits.

The sooner you start the sooner you'll enjoy your reward.

Simplified Operating Statement from XYZ Company

List the actual or approximated values for your company.

LINE	XYZ Company	Your Company
Sales (100,000 widgets at $10 each)	$1,000,000	
Less Cost of Goods Sold ($7.50 per widget)	$750,000	
Gross Margin	$250,000	
Less Expenses	$200,000	
Net Profit Before Taxes	$50,000	

1. Effect of Increasing Selling Price by 1%

Increase sales price by one percent keeping other parameters constant

LINE	XYZ Company	Your Company
Sales (100,000 widgets at $10.10 each)	$1,010,000	
Less Cost of Goods Sold ($7.50 per widget)	$750,000	
Gross Margin	$260,000	
Less Expenses	$200,000	
Net Profit Before Taxes	$60,000	
Change in Net Profit Before Taxes	+20%	

2. Effect of Increasing Sales Volume By 1%

Increase sales volume by one percent keeping other parameters constant

LINE	XYZ Company	Your Company
Sales (101,000 widgets at $10 each)	$1,010,000	
Less Cost of Goods Sold ($7.50 per widget)	$757,500	
Gross Margin	$252,500	
Less Expenses	$200,000	
Net Profit Before Taxes	$52,500	
Change in Net Profit Before Taxes	+5%	

3. Effect of Lowering Cost of Goods by 1%

Lower the COGS by one percent keeping other parameters constant.

LINE	XYZ Company	Your Company
Sales (100,000 widgets at $10 each)	$1,000,000	
Less Cost of Goods Sold ($7.425 per widget)	$742,500	
Gross Margin	$257,500	
Less Expenses	$200,000	
Net Profit Before Taxes	$57,500	
Change in Net Profit Before Taxes	+15%	

4. Effect of Reducing Expenses by 1%

Reduce expenses by one percent keeping other parameters constant.

LINE	XYZ Company	Your Company
Sales (100,000 widgets at $10 each)	$1,000,000	
Less Cost of Goods Sold ($7.50 per widget)	$750,000	
Gross Margin	$250,000	
Less Expenses	$198,000	
Net Profit Before Taxes	$52,000	
Change in Net Profit Before Taxes	+4%	

5. Effect of Combining Improvement of 1% in Sales Price, Sales Volume, Cost of Goods Sold and Expenses.

Combine all previous improvements.

LINE	XYZ Company	Your Company
Sales (101,000 widgets at $10.10 each)	$1,020,100	
Less Cost of Goods Sold ($7.425 per widget)	$749,925	
Gross Margin	$270,175	
Less Expenses	$198,000	
Net Profit Before Taxes	$72,175	
Change in Net Profit Before Taxes	+69.27%	

Appendix V – The CEO Secret Handbook

From Bill Swanson's original notes, as interpreted by Oswald Viva

Several decades ago Bill Swanson, Raytheon's CEO, wrote some notes intended only for using them in training his managers. Later he converted them into a Power Point presentation, but always intending to use them only internally for the purpose of training, and not for publication. Eventually, Warren Buffett received a copy of the presentation and he liked it so much that he requested many additional copies to give to his friends, other CEOs and family. Similarly, Jack Welch showed a keen interested in the notes and said that Swanson's management style makes the "little book" of notes a worthwhile read for any CEO.

Other well-known leaders have lauded the Rules outlined by Swanson; Bruce Whitman, President of Flight Safety International has compared the book with a Bible to use every day in the business world. Daniel Goleman, author of Emotional Intelligence likes the humor in the Rules and said, "the art of leadership is getting work done well through other people, and laughing together is one of the best ways to do that."

The publication *"Business 2.0"* in its July 2005 issue presented an excerpt of the book of notes. I have taken parts of that excerpt and added my own interpretation of some of Swanson's Rules.

Rule #1; *You can't polish a sneaker.*

Regardless of how much you try to polish a sneaker, it will remain a sneaker. You can say this in reference to a plan, a strategy or even a manager. If you don't have the "right" material to start with, it doesn't matter how much you polish it; likely it will never be the bright shiny star that you would like it to be. According to Swanson, trying to polish a sneaker can actually be dangerous because it may inadvertently convince others that the sneaker has a value that it doesn't really possess. This can lead organizations down unproductive dead ends. As CEO you must make sure that you have the right human material to work with.

Rule #2; *Look for what is missing. Many know how to improve what's there; few can see what isn't there.*

It's human nature to focus on what's in a presentation. But sometimes what isn't there is more important. Same in people; it is easy to see outward values and performance, but not as easy to see potential and limits of growth. Is the person leadership material? Has he/she the vital strategic thinking qualities of a true leader? As CEO you must recognize those strengths and weaknesses of your people.

Rule #3; *If you are not criticized, you may not be doing much.*

It is common for insecure people in positions of responsibility to avoid making difficult decisions, and the risk of criticism. But avoiding decisions only creates different risks. Unlike wine and cheese, problems don't get better with time; the sooner they are confronted and resolved, the better. There is a saying in skiing circles that "if you don't fall once in a while, you are not pushing yourself to do your best". Avoid the risk of being criticized for not making those difficult decisions; take your best shot and the chance to win.

Rule #4; *When facing issues or problems that are becoming drawn-out, short them to the ground.*

This engineering metaphor means finding the quickest path from problem to solution. If you sense that your organization is spending more time on the bureaucracy of problem solving than on actually solving problems, it's time to simplify the process. The solution to the problem is much more important than the process.

Rule #5; *A person who is nice to you but rude to others is not a nice person.*

Watch out for those with situational value systems – people who turn the charm on and off depending on the status of the person with whom they are interacting. Those people may be good actors but they don't become good leaders. Leadership requires a consistency that's greater than mere situational awareness. Values of a leader must be consistent. Consistency assures the leader the respect of the organization and peers, and the success of strategic decisions.

Rule #6; *You remember 1/3 of what you read, ½ of what people tell you, but 100% of what you feel.*

If a parent tells a young child not to touch a light bulb, the child generally won't remember, but after he touches a hot light bulb, he'll never forget it. A leader needs to communicate in a way that makes people feel what they need to do. Voicing an order or a directive to a subordinate may get action but it won't get the buyout and understanding that "selling" and idea and creating a "feeling" would get.

Rule #7; *Learn to say "I don't know." If used when appropriate, it will be used often.*

How many times have you seen those who need to be heard, even if they don't know what they are talking about? Many people feel compelled to contribute in meetings, even though they don't have anything valuable to contribute. In those circumstances silence is golden. As a CEO you know that everyone wants to impress you, but confident people know their strengths and weaknesses and won't risk giving you wrong information just to impress you. When he became CEO of GE, Jack Welch used to get "cheat sheets" before going to a Board meeting, in order to "prepare him with the right answers". He quickly discarded that practice because he didn't want to pretend to be what he was not or to know what he didn't. There is much value in saying "I don't know."

Rule #8; *Treat the name of your company as it were your own.*

A company's reputation is built on the actions of each employee. A CEO must spend a lot of time emphasizing ethics and integrity, but he/she must humanize those issues by asking people to treat the name of the company the same way they treat their family name. Anyone who would bring embarrassment to the name of the company should not be part of the company.

Rule #9; *When faced with decisions, instruct your people to look at them as if they were one level up in the organization.*

By looking at the issues from a higher level, their perspective will change quickly. This is analogous to how much smarter your parents suddenly seemed after your teenage years and into your twenties. At lower positions you can have your arms around the whole job, but at higher levels you need the perspective of the higher perch. Making the leap to leadership means learning to delegate; you receive inputs and you make decisions with the total perspective of the higher level.

And… Rule #10; *Have fun at what you do; it will be reflected in your work.*

We all spend many hours at work; it is much more pleasant to spend those hours with people who have a bounce on their step and a smile on their face, than with those who mistakenly associate professionalism with a dour disposition. The best managers give of themselves by having fun at what they do – and you should look for that in those around you.

We can add to this list a few others from "Good to Great" by Jim Collins:

1. **Practice the window and the mirror.** Point out the window to credit others when things go well, but point in the mirror to accept responsibility when things go wrong.
2. **A "stop doing" list is more important than a "to do" list.**
3. **Skills can be learned; core values cannot.**
4. **People are not your most important asset; the right people are.**
5. **Give people responsibilities, not jobs.**
6. **Do not confuse celebrity with leadership.**

And a final one also from Jim Collins:

7. **Do not reject wisdom just because it comes late.**

Conclusion

You read this book because you want to have a company that is well run and financially successful, but you also want to improve your leadership qualities and become the CEO that your company deserves. I hope that I gave you, if nothing else, things to think about and clues as to how you can improve.

You have already achieved a significant amount of success and have shown entrepreneurial savvy by starting (and hopefully growing) a business. This accomplishment sets you apart from the mainstream and places you in a select group. However, as your business continues to grow you will be faced with new and more demanding challenges. How you react to those challenges will determine your true value as a CEO.

This book is not a flavor-of-the-month or idea-of the-week recipe; it is intended to be a practical guideline based on real-world experiences gained over many years of being in positions similar to yours or coaching your peers. The advice given here is simple but not simplistic. I don't pretend to tell you what to do; I give you advice and suggestions and prefer to let you pick the road that you choose to reach your destination.

My message is that you are not—should not be—your business. Your business is an entity that you created and nurtured and will continue to nurture for as long as you keep it, but it is not you. You have a life outside the business and you should not neglect it in favor of the business. You must create the environment, the systems, the culture and the organization for the business to run without you. Your contributions are the vision and the leadership to make it happen.

In the over fourteen thousand hours that I invested in coaching your peers, I learned that you, as the owner of a small or midsize business, have the talent and the drive to reach the pinnacle of your class. My passion for all that time has been and continues to be to help you succeed. My purpose is to work with you to ensure you accomplish what you set out to accomplish.

Now that you read this book, use the coaching in it to continue your journey to excellence. If you got some value from the previous pages and you put that value to work for you in your journey, I will consider my modest contribution to your success a gift to myself. Develop a plan to improve yourself and put it in practice every day; you will need consistency and the discipline to maintain it, but you will be greatly rewarded.

Take your company and yourself to the next level and, as *Jim Collins* said, ***"don't reject wisdom just because it comes late"***.

About the Author

Oswald R. Viva is the founder and President of V&A Management, LLC; a consulting company he founded in 1985, now dedicated to helping small and midsize businesses. He has over 20 years of top corporate management in large and small companies, including multiple CEO and other "C" Level positions, 15 years as consultant in high-tech and manufacturing industries worldwide, and 13 years as CEO and executive coach for small and midsize businesses.

Oswald participated in eight startups either as a Principal and Founder or as a consultant in an acting leadership position. He was also the owner of one of the most successful franchises of The Alternative Board (TAB), a business of peer advisory boards. He has served in the Board of Directors of eight entrepreneurial companies in various fields.

He is the author of several books and e-books, including "Its Lonely at the Top"; "A Practical Guide to Becoming a Better Leader of Your Small Company" published by iUniverse, September 2011, and others listed in the introduction. He is an occasional speaker in subjects related to business ownership and management and has been a guest at a number of radio programs.

His education includes degrees in Mechanical Engineering and extensive training in Business Administration, Finance and Management. He is a Certified Management Consultant, Coach and Facilitator, a member of the National Federation of Independent Businesses, and a member of the Fortune Business Leaders council. He is the inventor of record in several patents and has received several awards in the management and entrepreneurial field.

Born in Argentina, he migrated to the US as a young man driven by his hunger to learn. He has been married to the love of his life for fifty-seven years and resides in Acworth, GA. He is the father of four and grandfather of twelve.

Printed in Great Britain
by Amazon

48422483R00233